MW00579031

# French Foreign Policy since 1945

# FRENCH FOREIGN POLICY SINCE 1945

## An Introduction

FRÉDÉRIC BOZO

Translated by Jonathan Hensher

**berghahn**

NEW YORK · OXFORD

www.berghahnbooks.com

Published in 2016 by
**Berghahn Books**
www.berghahnbooks.com

English-language edition
© 2016 Frédéric Bozo

French-language edition
©2012 Flammarion, Paris

Originally published in French in 2012 as *La politique étrangère de la France depuis 1945*

All rights reserved.
Except for the quotation of short passages
for the purposes of criticism and review, no part of this book
may be reproduced in any form or by any means, electronic or
mechanical, including photocopying, recording, or any information
storage and retrieval system now known or to be invented,
without written permission of the publisher.

**Library of Congress Cataloging-in-Publication Data**

Names: Bozo, Frederic, author.
Title: French foreign policy since 1945 : an introduction / Frederic Bozo ; translated by
Jonathan Hensher.
Other titles: Politique etrangere de la France depuis 1945. English
Description: English-language edition. | New York : Berghahn Books, 2016. | "Originally
published in French in 2012 as La politique etrangere de la France depuis 1945"--Title
page verso. | Includes bibliographical references and index.
Identifiers: LCCN 2016021776 | ISBN 9781785332760 (hardback) | ISBN
9781785333064 (paperback) | ISBN 9781785332777 (ebook)
Subjects: LCSH: France--Foreign relations--1945- | France--Foreign relations administra-
tion. | Cold War--Influence. | France--Politics and government--1958-
Classification: LCC DC404 .B6613 2016 | DDC 327.44--dc23
LC record available at https://lccn.loc.gov/2016021776

**British Library Cataloguing in Publication Data**

A catalogue record for this book is available from the British Library.

ISBN: 9781785332760 hardback
ISBN: 9781785333064 paperback
ISBN: 9781785332777 ebook

# Contents

# TABLES

# ACKNOWLEDGEMENTS

This is the translation of a book that first appeared in French in 1997 with Editions La Découverte. I am grateful to Jean-Paul Piriou and Christophe Prochasson for convincing me some twenty years ago to produce a brief synthesis on a large topic. The book was published again in 2012 by Flammarion with important revisions and updates. Thanks are due to Hélène Fiamma, Pauline Kipfer and Cédric Weis for their assistance with this project. I am also grateful to Marie-Pierre Rey and Jean-Frédéric Schaub for their help and advice.

The present volume is a translation of the 2012 book; the only update appears in the epilogue, covering France's foreign policy since 2011. I have also added some recent bibliographical references. Thanks are due to Jonathan Hensher for his precise and elegant translation from the French. As ever, I am grateful to Marion Berghahn for her interest in making my work known to an English-speaking readership. At Berghahn Books, I am indebted to Chris Chappell and Jessica Murphy for their assistance.

The translation was made possible by a grant from the Centre National du Livre (CNL) and funding from the Agence Nationale de la Recherche (ANR).

Finally, I am indebted to both my students and colleagues for making possible the ongoing conversation on the ever-intriguing topic of France and its (desired or effective) role in the world.

# INTRODUCTION

Many people in France and elsewhere still remember the concluding lines of the speech delivered on 14 February 2003 to the United Nations Security Council by the French foreign minister, Dominique de Villepin, during the run-up to the US-led military intervention against Saddam Hussein's Iraq:

> In this temple of the United Nations, we are the guardians of an ideal, the guardians of a conscience. The onerous responsibility and the immense honor that fall to us must lead us to give priority to disarmament in peace. And it is an old country, France, from an old continent like mine, Europe, which tells you this today. . . . It believes in our ability to construct, together, a better world.

The speech – something almost unheard of in this usually solemn chamber – elicited spontaneous applause from those present. According to some, it was lyrical; for others, it was over the top; yet it is hard for commentators not to see in it an echo – albeit a rather muffled one – of the epic struggles of the Gaullist era: the last time France had faced up to an all-powerful United States so squarely was the speech given by President Charles de Gaulle in Phnom Penh in September 1966, in which the General denounced the error of the United States in waging war in Vietnam. The recent Iraq episode thus resonates with the long history of French foreign policy, and in so doing highlights one of its recurrent themes: the ambition – some would say the pretension – shown by France, despite having lost its status as a great power, in seeking to hold onto a certain 'rank' on the world stage.

Ambition, or pretension? The man who rallied the Free French on 18 June 1940 not only embodied these two terms, but he also theorized them: 'It is because we are no longer a great power that we need a grand policy, because if we do not have a grand policy, given that we are no longer a great power, we will no longer be anything at all.'[1] This brutally honest appraisal, given by de Gaulle towards the end of his life, sums up the problem faced by French foreign policy for more than half a century: that of balancing the country's aspirations to a major role on the international stage against a realistic assessment of its actual capabilities.

This reality and this ambition are not necessarily doomed to contradiction: the aim of a country's foreign policy – which is both a discourse on and the actual conduct of foreign affairs – aims precisely to reconcile them. This book, which can only claim to be a brief introduction to the subject, seeks merely to sketch a broad outline of the history of French foreign policy, to locate its guiding principles and reveal its inherent logic. It also aims to uncover its principal constants: not only the quest for 'rank' but also, inextricably linked to this, the pursuit of the European project and the search for a world order, which are the two other perennial themes in French foreign policy – the former because the extra leverage afforded by Europe has long provided France's only hope of continuing to carry any weight on the world stage, and the latter because only a stable and balanced international system can guarantee the interests of France and of Europe. Yet this book also seeks to tease out the still unresolved dilemmas and contradictions of French foreign policy, torn as it is between the competing needs of France's national project, its European ambitions, its place in the Western world and its universalist ideals.

The historian's task, however, is not to freeze reality within timeless, unchanging paradigms. What follows is therefore above all the narrative of a shifting dialectic – sometimes favourable, sometimes less so – between France's ambitions and the reality of the means at its disposal. While de Gaulle, having started with absolutely nothing on 18 June 1940, achieved the almost miraculous feat of carving out a place for his country alongside the victors of 1945 and making France a great power once again, he had in reality re-established a status that existed only on paper. After de Gaulle left power in 1946, the Fourth Republic believed it truly possessed this great power status, and so France was able to put off the redefinition of its international role until the country was forced to do so by the eventual realization of its powerlessness – which resulted, most obviously but not exclusively, from decolonization. After returning to power in 1958 de Gaulle would effectuate this redefinition of France's international role and succeed in creating, together with the foundation of the Fifth Republic, not merely a policy of 'grandeur', but a truly grand policy whose ambition was no less than the reconsideration of the superpower bloc system and the creation of a new alternative to the order of 'Yalta'.

In an international context long characterized by the persistence of the East-West status quo, de Gaulle's successors, from Georges Pompidou (1969–1974) to Valéry Giscard d'Estaing (1974–1981) and to François Mitterrand (1981–1995), strove to perpetuate his legacy. Wasn't this defence of a long-term vision that changing realities seemed increasingly to contradict, but which nonetheless allowed France to retain a national policy in the face of the resilience of the established order, the best option open to them? Be that as it may, while holding for more than two decades the dismantling of the bipolar bloc system as its declared objective, French foreign policy progressively adapted to the East-West status quo. Did France and its leaders thus fail in their proclaimed ambition to exit from the Cold War in 1989–1991? Was France reluctant vis-à-vis the central and eastern European revolutions, German reunification and the splintering of the Soviet Union? This was, in fact, far less the case, as we shall see, than is commonly thought.

Still, the end of 'Yalta' has dealt a whole new set of cards: the era of the blocs has been replaced by globalization, for better or worse. From Jacques Chirac (1995–2007) to Nicolas Sarkozy (2007–2012) and to François Hollande (since 2012), maintaining continuity with the foreign policy legacy handed down by the founder of the Fifth Republic has appeared, as it had in the past, to be a tempting lifeline in the face of an international system that has become increasingly unwieldy and unpredictable. But are the guiding principles of Gaullist foreign policy and its modes of action still valid in this new world and its new realities of power? Can France, in a multipolar system in which, alone at least, the country carries less and less weight, still deploy a foreign policy it can really call its own?

## Note

1. Philippe de Saint-Robert, *Le Secret des jours. Une chronique sous la Ve République*, Paris: Lattès, 1995, p. 131.

# Part I

# THE ERA OF FRUSTRATION
## (1945–1958)

# Chapter 1

# FRANCE'S DIFFICULT ENTRY INTO THE COLD WAR (1945–1950)

According to the classical definition of 'power', France at the end of the Second World War could no longer really be called one. Its economy had shrunk by half compared to prewar levels; its infrastructure was devastated; its population had been sapped by the human cost of the conflict; the country was cut off from the resources of its colonies; its armed forces were only just beginning to rebuild. What was France compared to the formidable economic and military power of the United States, the demographic mass and powerful war machine of the Soviet Union or the (admittedly declining) grandeur of the British Empire?

Above all, France's power in 1944–1945 was overshadowed by the events of May–June 1940 when it had been dramatically defeated by Germany. At the end of the war, France's early collapse remained the major determining factor with respect to the country's role in the world, as shown by the reluctance of the Big Three (the United States, the Soviet Union and the United Kingdom) to grant France the place on the world stage to which it aspired. Reversing this situation, placing France among the victors and restoring its right to stand alongside the other great powers, had been what de Gaulle had sought to achieve from his Appeal of 18 June 1940 onwards. For the next four years, he had seen politics as the continuation of war by other means.

Was de Gaulle's vision of a restored France one of vain pretension – or one of vital ambition, necessary both for the country and for the world? Be that as it may, the task General de Gaulle had set himself four years earlier did not end with the liberation of France's national territory from spring–summer 1944 onwards (with the Allied landings in Normandy in June, and in Provence in August) or even with Germany's surrender in May

1945. It was quite clear that the restoration of France's 'rank' was going to be a long-term project. Postwar French foreign policy was thus in many ways a continuation of the country's wartime diplomacy.

## De Gaulle's Policy

In order to be a power once more, France would have to conduct a policy of power: this was the line taken by de Gaulle when he came back to Paris at the end of August 1944 following the liberation of the capital as head of the Provisional Government of the French Republic (Gouvernement Provisoire de la République française, GPRF). De Gaulle held the main levers of foreign policy, namely the diplomatic service, which had been progressively rebuilt from London and later Algiers and was led by the Christian-Democrat Georges Bidault (whom de Gaulle had made foreign minister for the reason that, in the eyes of the wartime Allies, he represented the internal French Resistance) and the armed forces, now rising from the ashes to help seal France's status as a victorious power alongside the Big Three.

Indeed, the first great battle fought by the provisional government was a diplomatic one: the GPRF needed to gain international recognition from the Allies. On 23 October 1944 this was achieved, the United States, the United Kingdom and the USSR having finally overcome their reticence regarding a power whose legitimacy they only grudgingly accepted, as shown by de Gaulle's difficult relations with Franklin D. Roosevelt and Winston Churchill over the previous years: 'The government', de Gaulle famously (and ironically) commented, 'is most satisfied to be called by its rightful name.' The struggle for 'rank' did not stop there, however: recognized at last as an international player by the Big Three, de Gaulle's France wanted above all to be considered as their fourth member. This was what was at stake in the big international conferences of 1945, which would finally see this status conferred upon France even though, paradoxically, the country was not represented at these same meetings. At Yalta (4–11 February 1945), the Big Three assigned France a zone of occupation (ZO) in Germany and a permanent seat on the Security Council of the future United Nations (to a large extent the result of Churchill's keenness to see France standing alongside the United Kingdom as a counterweight to the growing power of the USSR); and, at Potsdam (17 July–1 August 1945), France was given a seat on the Allied Control Council (ACC), which had authority over German affairs, and on the Council of Foreign Ministers (CFM), which oversaw the drafting of peace treaties with the former Reich and its ex-allies.

In 1945, then, Germany constituted the highest priority in French foreign policy, the 'central problem of the universe', as de Gaulle put it. The goal was clear: Germany must be left incapable of launching a new act of aggression, and its resources must contribute to repairing the damage done to the victims of the Reich, starting with France. As well as demilitarization, France sought – at least to some extent – Germany's economic dismemberment and political fragmentation. There could be no question of a return to any form of centralized Reich: Germany could only be reborn as a highly decentralized federation, and three of its territories would be detached, namely the Saar (which would be economically attached to France), the Ruhr (to be internationalized) and the Rhineland (to be occupied for the foreseeable future). With regard to Germany, de Gaulle's France, in other words, sought to pursue a classic policy of coercion, or at least of 'reinsurance', which carried clear echoes of the aftermath of the First World War. And yet, as early as 1945, French policy-makers, under the cover of this policy of intransigence, were privately quite conscious of the limits of the hard-line approach that they adopted in public when it came to the German question, regarding which they would reveal themselves over the months and years that followed to be quite capable of compromise when needed.[1]

Acting alone, France would obviously be unable to impose its views regarding the fate of the former Reich. Faced with the prevailing uncertainty around this question, the possibility – in the long term, at any rate – of a resurgent German threat therefore remained a central preoccupation of French foreign and defence policy in the immediate aftermath of the war. Sceptical with regard to a possible long-term involvement of the United States on the old continent following the end of hostilities, yet ruling out a formal alliance with the United Kingdom because of the serious Franco-British disagreements that persisted in the Near East (in particular over Syria and Lebanon), de Gaulle opted for a classic *alliance de revers* with Moscow, which was concluded on 10 December 1944 during his trip to the USSR. Parallel to this alliance, he believed that France, at the head of a sort of 'grouping' of western European states (Belgium, The Netherlands, Luxembourg and the German territories west of the Rhine) and acting in concert with the USSR, would be able to control a defeated Germany. Such a west European consortium would also allow France to act as a counterweight to the Soviet presence in the east of the continent, while maintaining the balance between the USSR and the 'Anglo-Saxons'. This, in broad terms, was the geopolitical vision that lay behind French diplomacy in 1944–1945.

When de Gaulle stepped down from government in January 1946, the results of his foreign policy were mixed. It was true that, as an occupying power of the now-defeated Germany alongside the United States, the United Kingdom and the USSR, and a permanent member of the United Nations Security Council, France had managed to establish its status as the fourth 'Big' power, a scarcely believable result given the country's real situation at the end of the conflict. For the moment, however, this status existed only on paper, a fact made clear by France's exclusion from all the major diplomatic conferences of 1945, from Yalta to Potsdam. Above all, while de Gaulle may have managed to reaffirm his country's 'rank' and independence, he was largely unable to impose his foreign-policy vision, in particular with regard to the German question, on which France's demands left the country isolated. Meanwhile, the background of the nascent Cold War meant that international relations were now increasingly governed by the Soviet-American standoff, from which even the United Kingdom, despite its unquestioned status as a victor, in effect found itself sidelined. De Gaulle's intransigence, which was in stark contrast to how little power his country actually possessed, could only increase France's isolation in the context of the progressive disintegration of the 'grand alliance' between the Western powers and the Soviets – an alliance that it was naturally in France's interest to maintain. De Gaulle's January 1946 decision to step down from power was certainly not unconnected to this: as well as denouncing the return to the discredited party 'system' in French domestic politics, de Gaulle was also beginning to feel the limits placed on his freedom of action on the international stage, at a time when the country, after the trials it had just come through, wanted more than anything to concentrate on its own reconstruction.

## After de Gaulle

With de Gaulle's departure, Bidault gained full control over foreign policy, which he would run for the next two and a half years almost without interruption. A complex character, always in awe of, and sometimes humiliated by, the General, a strident defender of national independence, Bidault wanted above all to continue de Gaulle's policy of maintaining a balance between East and West and to pursue his declared objectives with respect to the fate of Germany. Yet the domestic and international context was increasingly unfavourable. While the succession of 'tripartite' governments that followed de Gaulle's departure (composed of the MRP, the SFIO and the PCF, i.e. the Christian Democrats, the socialists and the communists) stated in public that they sought to prioritize continuity in France's foreign policy, in reality the various coalition parties differed increasingly with regard to its principal aspects, namely the question of Germany and relations with the USSR and the 'Anglo-Saxons' respectively. Even more portentously, while the intensification of the Soviet-American confrontation strengthened the desire of the French to maintain an equidistant position between the two emerging superpowers, it also made this objective all the more difficult to achieve. Despite this stated emphasis on continuity, then, French foreign policy was bound to change once de Gaulle had left power. Even if the major shifts would not occur immediately, by 1946 it had become obvious to France's leaders that these were inevitable in the longer term.

This was especially true of the policy towards Germany. In the face of the steadily deepening rivalry between the Western powers and the Soviets over Germany from 1946 onwards, France's policy seemed less and less sustainable. By this time the United States, followed by the United Kingdom, were moving towards a policy of rapid reconstruction of the western half of Germany, as heralded by the speech given in Stuttgart on 6 September 1946 by US Secretary of State James Byrnes and the creation of an Anglo-American economic 'Bizone' on 2 December of the same year. While the French still maintained their hard-line approach in public, they were aware by now that the sort of dismemberment of Germany that they had been calling for since the end of the war was no longer realistic: in the climate of the gathering Cold War, a form of partitioning of the country between East and West seemed to be a far more likely outcome. Among France's demands with regard to Germany, only the economic attachment of the Saar to France seemed acceptable to Washington and London in 1946, provided that Paris abandon its projects regarding the Rhineland and, even more importantly, the Ruhr – the internationalization of which would have given the USSR a say in the running of Germany's industrial heartland. Although for the time being France's domestic political situation prevented Bidault from making a clean break with past German policy (not least because the communists were in favour of maintaining the alliance with Moscow at any price), a move towards the position of the United States and the United Kingdom, called for increasingly openly by many French politicians, was now on the cards.

In any case, such a shift seemed inevitable from an economic point of view. The exhausted country was dependent on a stream of US aid that was still by no means guaranteed. Admittedly, the Blum-Byrnes accords, signed on 28 May 1946 in Washington between the former leader of the *Front populaire*, Léon Blum, and US Secretary of State James Byrnes, providing new credits to France and writing off a part of its debt, did promise some breathing space. Yet the result of these long and difficult negotiations in Washington (carried out by a French team headed by the ageing socialist leader and by the commissioner-general of the National Planning Board, Jean Monnet) fell well short of what was needed. Nor, or not yet at any rate, did the Blum-Byrnes accords result in a realignment with US policy, a move Bidault continued to oppose. (The communists nevertheless loudly denounced the accords as a capitulation in the face of US imperialism, not least because they ended the quotas placed on US films shown in France.)

It was with the UK Labour government, then, that it was possible in 1946 to see the beginnings of a rapprochement. This was to a large extent the result of the eagerness of the French socialists (who were also showing themselves ready to be more accommodating over the German question) to balance the power of the USSR with a Franco-British counterweight. The rapprochement was confirmed by Blum during his short-lived government (December 1946–January 1947); had it not been for the subsequent divergences between the two countries on European integration, it could have led to the construction of a Franco-British Europe, desired by many at the time. For the time being, the improved relations between London and Paris resulted in the signing on 4 March 1947 of the Franco-British Treaty of Dunkirk, which was ostensibly designed to prevent any resurgence of the German threat; this bilateral military alliance indeed completed a diplomatic triangle between Paris, London and Moscow, which appeared to fulfil the Gaullist policy of 'reinsurance' with regard to Germany and of equidistance between the 'Anglo-Saxons' and the Soviets. Yet the time for such schemas, premised on maintaining a 'grand alliance' between the powers that had defeated the Reich, had passed; 1946 had seen the confirmation of the growing confrontation between East and West, and thus by the beginning of 1947, France's policy of independence from either camp had clearly become a dead end.

## France Moves Over to the West

It would be something of a caricature to define spring 1947 as the moment at which France 'chose' its camp in the East-West conflict. France was, by nature, a Western power: in this sense, there was no French 'choice' in favour of the West. Moreover, France's entry into the Cold War was not the result of a sudden decision. As early as 1945–1946, there had been a realization among de Gaulle's entourage and certain key military figures, such as General Pierre Billotte (the Army's deputy chief of staff and then the head of France's military mission to the UN), that the looming Soviet threat was a more pressing danger than any hypothetical German resurgence. Yet it was only in the spring of 1947 that French foreign policy really began to take this fact on board – and the path it took was anything but straightforward. The institutional system of the Fourth Republic (whose constitution was approved by a referendum in October 1946) indeed established a very diffuse decision-making process: while the main responsibility for foreign policy resided with the foreign minister at the Quai d'Orsay and with the president of the Council of Ministers (i.e. the prime minister), the president of the Republic could exercise a degree of influence over it, and parliamentary wrangling defined its general orientation. The very nature of this system, in other words, left little scope for abrupt changes of direction.[2]

The events of spring 1947 would nevertheless precipitate tendencies that had been gathering momentum for months, finally leading to a decisive shift in France's posture in the East-West confrontation. The announcement by President Harry S. Truman on 12 March of the doctrine (that would hence-forth bear his name) of US assistance to countries menaced by communism confirmed that the logic of the Cold War was now firmly established. In this context, the French delegation at the Conference of Foreign Ministers in Moscow (10 March–24 April 1947) could be under no misapprehension as to the deterioration of East-West relations and its consequences for France. Bidault was particularly shaken by the failure of the Moscow conference and now realized the impossibility of reaching any agreement with the USSR over the German question and the lack of any Soviet support for French demands, especially with regard to the Saar. It was now clear that any agreement over the future of Germany would have to be made with the United States and the United Kingdom – in exchange, of course, for French concessions. The German question had become more central than ever to the future development of Europe and, from now on, it would be both the indicator of and the catalyst for the inevitable alignment of French policy with the positions of the United States and the United Kingdom.

At the same time, this shift could only exacerbate the contradictions of French diplomacy and the domestic tensions underlying it. The expulsion of the communist ministers from the government by the socialist president of the Council of Ministers, Paul Ramadier, on 4 May 1947 was thus a sign not just of growing differences on economic and social issues – crucial as these were to his decision – but also of increasingly intractable disagree-ments over German policy, East-West relations and Indochina. While this decision was not taken under direct pressure from the United States, it was obviously a most welcome one for Washington, for it could but con-firm France's realignment with the United States.[3] It was clear that foreign policy was more than ever before being governed by domestic politics, and that the latter, in turn, were to a great extent being determined by the international context. With tripartitism irrevocably abandoned in the wake of Ramadier's decision, the subsequent *troisième force* governments (gath-ering the SFIO, MRP, UDSR, Radicals and Moderates) found themselves confronted not only with communist dissidence – which, during the violent strikes of 1947 and 1948, was beginning to look like a serious domestic threat – but also with a major Gaullist offensive. For the creation of the *Rassemblement du peuple français* (RPF) in spring 1947, de Gaulle combined anti-communist and anti-Soviet rhetoric with a questioning of France's whole political regime, whose institutions and party system the General mercilessly berated. France was settling into the Cold War, and the Cold War was settling over France.

## The Repercussions of the Marshall Plan

More than any other single factor, however, the US assistance plan for Europe, announced by Secretary of State George Marshall on 5 June 1947 at Harvard University, would profoundly alter the make-up of French foreign policy. Given the uncertainty surrounding the long-term involvement of the United States in Europe, the adoption by Washington of a more forceful response to Stalin's aggressive policies – which could in turn only lead to a further hardening of the Soviet position – had up to this point been considered a dangerous prospect by the French: western Europe risked being exposed to an increased Soviet threat without having the guarantee of US protection. However, the announcement of the Marshall plan – which came a few weeks after that of the Truman doctrine and was part of the new US strategy of 'containment' – confirmed that the United States was ready to make a long-term commitment to Europe, at least in economic and political terms. This explains the enthusiastic welcome given to the Marshall plan by the French government, who, following its announcement, quickly took the lead with the United Kingdom in preparing the European response to the United States' offer at the Paris conference of 12–16 July 1947.

Concerned to ensure that the Marshall plan should not result in too brutal a split between East and West, France's leaders at the beginning of the summer of 1947 were nonetheless unnerved by the USSR's rejection of the plan – however predictable this rejection may have been – and above all by the Soviet ban imposed in July, which prevented the countries of central and eastern Europe from benefitting from the US assistance program. The French now had to stand by powerlessly as they watched the counterstroke to the Marshall plan, i.e. the rapid formation of a communist bloc under Soviet rule in central and eastern Europe, confirmed by the creation of the Kominform at the conference in Szklarska-Poreba (Poland) in September 1947. With the division of Europe now appearing inevitable, France could no longer claim to serve as a bridge between East and West. Rather than being a Western 'choice', then, the evolution of French policy – both domestic and foreign – over the course of 1947 reflects France's realization of the growing inexorability of the confrontation between the blocs, and the impossibility of escaping this new geopolitical reality.[4]

Following the meeting of the four foreign ministers in London, which confirmed the split with the Soviets (25 November–15 December 1947), France now had to look westwards for the solutions to its problems. This realization would, from 1948 onwards, force the French to make some painful policy changes: accepting the Marshall plan amounted effectively to accepting the economic and hence political dependence of France, whose reconstruction – although organized according to the choices set out in the National Plan under Monnet's guidance – relied primarily on US aid. This dependence, while undoubtedly consensual and negotiated, led to an inevitable degree of US control over national decision-making while at the same time moulding the remarkable transformation, over the following decades, not just of the economy, but also of French society and even, to a certain extent, France's culture. Was this Americanization, or simply modernization? Putting aside the political arguments and historical debates, US influence, although it did in fact have its limits, was undoubtedly a new and fundamental factor from 1947 onwards. Most of the general tendencies and decisions, along with most of the contradictions and frustrations of foreign policy under the Fourth Republic, would derive from it.[5]

| 1945–1947 | January 1948 –June 1948 | July 1948 –June 1949 | July 1949 –June 1950 | July 1950 –June 1951 | Total |
|---|---|---|---|---|---|
| 1947.3 | 646.4 | 978.4 | 687.9 | 443.6 | 4703.6 |

**Table 1.1.** US aid to France, 1945–June 1951 (in millions of dollars)[6]

The transformation of France's foreign policy was, in the first instance, perceptible with regard to the German question. With the Marshall plan, from which the French, US and UK zones of occupation were meant to benefit, the revival of (western) Germany was now a certainty. France had to abandon for good the vision of a permanently subdued and fragmented former Reich; France's objectives would now be better served by attempting to exert its influence over the creation of a West German political and economic entity, and ultimately a West German state, which would be the predictable outcome of this process. During the Franco-Anglo-American discussions in London (February–March and April–June 1948), the Western powers indeed considered the future of West Germany; they resolved that a constituent assembly would be formed, that the three western zones would be merged, and that the Ruhr would not be detached – although its steel and coal production would be overseen by the Western powers through an International Authority for the Ruhr (IAR). Very little remained of France's initial formal demands – with the exception of the Saar question, which would be resolved among the Western Allies.

Although by now inevitable, the prospect of a future West German state was nevertheless difficult to swallow for the French political classes, at least initially. During the debate in the *Assemblée nationale* (11–17 June 1948), the decisions taken in London were only narrowly approved: the Communist Party on the one hand, and the traditional Right and the Gaullists on the other, were staunchly opposed to the abandonment of the German policy of 1944–1947. Some senior officials at the Quai d'Orsay, such as Director for Political Affairs Maurice Couve de Murville, a Gaullist, openly opposed Bidault. The latter, while fully acknowledging the failure of the previous policy and now advocating the new approach, paid a price: Robert Schuman's cabinet fell on 19 July 1948, and Bidault had to leave the Quai d'Orsay.

## A New European Geopolitics

From 1948 onwards, France would thus have to take its place within a new European geopolitical order, moulded by the United States and premised above all on the inclusion of a nascent West Germany within the Western economic and political fold. As part of this new geopolitics, and likewise driven by the United States, the beginnings of what would soon become a central tenet of French foreign policy could also be seen: the decision to move towards European unification. The latter was indeed the condition placed by the United States upon their commitment to the rebuilding of western Europe, leading to the founding in April 1948, in Paris, of the Organisation for European Economic Co-operation (OEEC), tasked with supervising the distribution of aid from the Marshall plan (this would become the OECD in 1961). France played an important role in this initial phase of European construction, as shown by the large number of French delegates present at the European Hague Congress (7–10 May 1948) and, more generally, by the interest aroused within large sections of France's political classes and wider public opinion by these new developments. It was therefore no surprise that Paris, in the summer of 1948, took the initiative in calling for the creation of a European Assembly, a proposal that would lead to the creation on 5 May 1949 of the Council of Europe. It was a relatively modest result given that its powers would remain limited (though the protection of human rights rapidly became one of its foremost concerns) and its operations were firmly restricted to the intergovernmental level, but nevertheless one that reflected the realization that the building of Europe was vital, both as a means of strengthening French influence and as an economic and political framework in which a renascent Germany would remain embedded.

| | |
|---|---|
| United Kingdom | 32.9 |
| France | 21 |
| West Germany | 11.7 |
| Italy | 10.5 |
| Benelux | 8 |

**Table 1.2.** Distribution of US aid in western Europe, 1945–1953 (by percentage)[7]

Yet France's main priority in 1948–1949, against a backdrop of worsening East-West relations, was to obtain a firm commitment from the United States to the security of western Europe, which was seen as the logical corollary of the US decisions of spring 1947. While some French officials had sought to obtain such a commitment as early as 1945, it was only at the end of 1947 that the United Kingdom and France took any official steps in this direction. In line with Marshall's recommendations, the first stage consisted in setting up, at a European level, a military alliance that would demonstrate these nations' willingness to organize their own defence – which was the condition placed by the United States upon their support. This alliance was established with the Brussels Treaty, signed on 17 March 1948 between France, the United Kingdom and the three Benelux countries, following rapid negotiations carried out amid anxiety in the wake of the communist takeover in Czechoslovakia (the 'Prague coup' of February 1948). Although the danger posed by Germany was vaguely mentioned in the Brussels Treaty, it was, in contrast to the Treaty of Dunkirk just one year earlier, no longer its principal *raison d'être*: the Soviet threat was now clearly the primary focus of French concerns.

With the Brussels Treaty signed, Bidault and his UK counterpart, Ernest Bevin, began calling for a formal military alliance between Europe and the United States. Unthinkable in the context of the United States' earlier iso-lationist doctrine, such an alliance had now become a possibility. The first major East-West crisis, the Berlin blockade (24 June 1948–12 May 1949), which was imposed by the USSR in the (vain) hope of halting the creation of the West German state, formed the backdrop to this decisive shift in US policy. The process set in motion in spring 1947 with the Truman doctrine and the Marshall plan had thus come to fruition: on 4 April 1949, the North Atlantic Treaty was signed in Washington between the United States, Canada, the five signatories of the Treaty of Brussels, Italy, Portugal, Norway, Denmark and Iceland. Having been so ardently sought by Paris, the creation of the Atlantic Alliance was greeted with relief by the French government. Robert Schuman, foreign minister in the government of Henri Queuille, saw it as 'what we hoped for in vain between the two wars: the United States now recognize that there can be neither peace nor security for America if Europe is in danger'.

However, the negotiations leading up to the Washington treaty, which had begun in July 1948, had not been without their difficulties, and their outcome, from France's point of view, was only partially satisfactory. Indeed, the rather vague US guarantee given in the North Atlantic Treaty (with article 5 not automatically committing members to act in the case of aggres-sion against another member) was not accompanied by any effective military measures for the defence of Europe on the part of the United States, at least not for the time being; moreover, the strategic identity of western Europe, now the key theme of French policy, had been subsumed within a US-dominated Atlantic Alliance. Last but not least, France's claim to the status of the third 'Great' Western power was by no means guaranteed within the Alliance, where the United Kingdom's so called 'special relationship' with the United States threatened to exclude the French from any major strategic responsibilities, all of which were held by the 'Anglo-Saxons'. In the final analysis, the signing of the North Atlantic Treaty, actively sought by the French, was a major step, insofar as it brought the reassurance of an alliance with the United States and confirmed France's membership in the Western bloc. Yet it also marked the beginning of a period of frustration: while the alliance afforded France a certain degree of security, by the same token it formalized the country's dependence with respect to the United States.[8]

## From Ambition to Submission

In the immediate aftermath of the creation of the Atlantic Alliance, and after four years of a largely reactive French policy, the time had now come for Paris to take the initiative. Up until this point, France had participated somewhat reluctantly in the creation of the Western system, fearing not only an unnecessarily brutal split with the USSR, but also an uncertain US commitment to Europe and an overly rapid German resurgence. The realization that the Cold War was here to stay changed this picture: with the completion of the Soviet *cordon sanitaire* in eastern Europe, the East-West split became an unquestionable, if not irreversible, reality; the United States' commitment to Europe at last seemed guaranteed in the long term; and Germany looked set to remain divided for some time. With the creation of the Federal Republic in May 1949, France faced an important choice: should it continue its policy of suspicion with regard to Germany, or seek to lay down the bases of a new Franco-German relationship that would fit into the wider context of the construction of western Europe? Since the second half of 1948, the second option had been gaining ground within the state apparatus, the elites and the political classes in France. Several factors drove this: fears regarding a revival of German national sentiment and the concomitant realization of the long-term possibilities of Franco-German reconciliation; the United States' insistence that West Germany should take its place among the other Western nations; and, finally, the prospect of making the Franco-German relationship the driving-force of European construction.

The idea that France could at last take a leading role among Western nations through a major Franco-German and European initiative was, in 1949–1950, very much in the air in Paris, Bonn and Washington. Two men with very different profiles would contribute more to it than anyone else: Schuman and Monnet, the statesman and his 'inspirer' (in de Gaulle's characterization). As early as 1943, when he was a member of the French

Committee for National Liberation (*Comité français de libération nationale*, CFLN) in Algiers, Monnet had been considering the question of integrating Germany within a Western grouping. His one key idea, which came out of an almost obsessive idealism combined with a solid pragmatism, was the need to transcend the nation-state, both out of economic necessity and as a political condition for European unification and Franco-German cooperation. Schuman, a native of the east of France whose personal existence had up until that point been shaped by Franco-German antagonism, was not immediately taken with the idea. When he took over from Bidault at the Quai d'Orsay in July 1948, after the difficult negotiations leading up to the ratification of the London Accords, he was still in favour of a firm policy with respect to Germany. Gradually, however, he came to be convinced, owing partly to the influence of some in his entourage, of the need for a new approach to the German problem. With the Rheinland Catholic Konrad Adenauer as his partner in dialogue, this Christian-Democrat from Alsace-Lorraine soon became a missionary for Franco-German reconciliation.

## From the Schuman Plan to the Pleven Plan

Events would see to the rest. In September 1949, Dean Acheson, Marshall's successor as US secretary of state, told Schuman that the United States was expecting some concrete proposals by the following spring with respect to the firm incorporation of the young Federal Republic within a west European grouping. From then on, the French were in search of a way to bring the Federal Republic into the Western fold on an equal footing (at least in the medium to long term) with the other member-states while at the same time ensuring that Germany would not once again become an unfettered economic, and therefore also political and perhaps even military power. The solution, which had been under discussion in vague terms for several months, was hammered into shape by Monnet and his entourage in April 1950: this was the project for a European Coal and Steel Community (ECSC), which was intended as a supranational European response to the German problem. By placing France and Germany's coal and steel production under a shared High Authority, it aimed to make it impossible for heavy industry ever again to be used for the ends of German nationalism or militarism. The proposal was, for the moment, limited to this strategic industrial sector; but, in addition to its primary objective of creating a coal and steel 'pool', it also aimed, by creating 'de facto solidarities', to lay the long-term foundations of a fully fledged European federation (beyond the Federal Republic, the proposal was meant to be extended to other European countries as well).

The announcement of the proposal, which had been drawn up in absolute secrecy, was made by Schuman on 9 May 1950:

World peace cannot be safeguarded without the making of creative efforts proportionate to the dangers which threaten it.

The contribution which an organized and living Europe can bring to civilization is indispensable to the maintenance of peaceful relations. In taking upon herself for more than 20 years the role of champion of a united Europe, France has always had as her essential aim the service of peace. A united Europe was not achieved and we had war.

Europe will not be made all at once, or according to a single plan. It will be built through concrete achievements which first create a de facto solidarity. The coming together of the nations of Europe requires the elimination of the age-old opposition of France and Germany. Any action taken must in the first place concern these two countries.

With this aim in view, the French Government proposes that action be taken immediately on one limited but decisive point.

It proposes that Franco-German production of coal and steel as a whole be placed under a common High Authority, within the framework of an organization open to the participation of the other countries of Europe. . . .

The solidarity in production thus established will make it plain that any war between France and Germany becomes not merely unthinkable, but materially impossible. The setting up of this powerful productive unit, open to all countries willing to take part and bound ultimately to provide all the member countries with the basic elements of industrial production on the same terms, will lay a true foundation for their economic unification. . . .

By pooling basic production and by instituting a new High Authority, whose decisions will bind France, Germany and other member countries, this proposal will lead to the realization of the first concrete foundation of a European federation indispensable to the preservation of peace.[9]

This time, the institutional system of the Fourth Republic had, rather unusually, allowed France truly to take the initiative on the international stage: Bidault, the president of the Council of Ministers, took little interest in it, while Schuman, conscious of the opposition it was likely to encounter, made no mention of it in the Council of Ministers until 3 May – and even then referred to it only in vague terms (even the Quai d'Orsay, where some officials disapproved of the new German policy that was taking shape, was kept in the dark by its own chief). Five years after the German surrender, France's initiative was greeted by the major capitals, starting with Washington and even more so in Bonn, as a historic turning-point: for Franco-German relations in the first instance, which were now clearly moving towards reconciliation and cooperation; and also for European unification, which had thus been set on the path of integration within a true European community rather than simply through cooperation between European states, as was the case with the OEEC, the Treaty of Brussels and even the Council of Europe.

The Schuman Declaration was rapidly translated into concrete action. Opened in Paris by Monnet on 20 June 1950, the European negotiations that resulted from it were all but concluded by the end of the year. Admittedly, closing the negotiations proved difficult: conscious of the inevitability of the integration of the Federal Republic within the Western bloc given the backdrop of the worsening East-West conflict, the Bonn government sought to minimize the restrictions placed on their national industries, while the French, for their part, remained wary of German national ambitions. Nevertheless, on 18 April 1951, the ECSC Treaty was signed at the Quai d'Orsay by France, the Federal Republic, Italy and the Benelux countries. It would come into force the following year, with Monnet becoming the first president of the High Authority. With the Schuman Declaration, French foreign policy had been able to bask in a brief moment of glory; instead of suffering impositions, it was at last blazing a new trail and taking the lead in European construction.

Yet by the summer of 1950, the Cold War was already beginning to catch up with France's policy. The outbreak of the Korean War, on 25 June, radically changed the political landscape. The atmosphere in Europe, as had been the case following the Prague coup two years earlier, was one of paranoia: was the communist attack in Asia a prelude to potential Soviet aggression in Europe? Was West Germany in danger of sharing South Korea's fate? In the United States, the Korean War accelerated the militarization of the policy of containment, which had already been in the pipeline for several months following the recommendations of NSC 68, an April 1950 top secret policy paper issued by the National Security Council; it could now be 'sold' by the Truman administration to Congress and public opinion. As a result, the question of an effective US military commitment to the defence of western Europe going beyond the strict terms of the Washington Treaty – a move called for by the west Europeans – had become sharply relevant. The United States, however, placed a preliminary condition on such a commitment: in September 1950, Washington demanded a West German military contribution to the defence of Europe. Yet with this demand, broaching as it did the hitherto more or less taboo issue of German rearmament, the deterioration in East-West relations of the summer of 1950 suddenly brought into question the very fundamentals of the European project as Monnet and Schuman had conceived it just a few weeks earlier.

France's leaders, and foremost among them Schuman, were caught off guard by a demand that they had been unable, or unwilling, to anticipate. Of course, in this context of deteriorating East-West relations, they realized that some sort of West German military contribution to the defence of Europe would at some point become inevitable given the magnitude of the Soviet threat and the insistence of US demands. Yet, for the majority of the French public, and most of France's political classes, such a prospect, just five years after the end of the war, remained difficult to stomach. The Schuman plan, as already mentioned, aimed to avoid the remilitarization of Germany by preventing the country, on a national level, from controlling the industrial base necessary for any potential rearmament; in fact, the plan implied that the military question would be put off virtually indefinitely, until the final stage of a process of European integration that was thought of as gradual. In addition, opening up the issue of West German rearmament prematurely could make the Federal Republic keenly aware of its importance within the scheme of Western defence and, as a result, make it a more difficult and demanding partner in the still unresolved negotiations over the ECSC. Last but not least, the French had concerns regarding the possible reaction of the Soviet Union, which was implacably opposed to the rearmament of the Federal Republic; as a result, it was more advisable in their view to wait until a robust system of defence had been established through the Atlantic Alliance before considering such a step. For all of these reasons, France's leaders in autumn 1950 would no doubt have preferred to adopt more of a wait-and-see approach when it came to West German rearmament.[10]

Under pressure from events, however, they had no other choice but to attempt to formulate a response to US demands while at the same time seeking to preserve the nascent process of European integration. Hence, on 24 October 1950, the president of the Council, René Pleven, once again at Monnet's instigation, proposed a European solution to the problem of German rearmament. While it had been thought up by Monnet with rather less verve than the Schuman plan (which the new plan to some extent simply transposed from the area of steel production to that of defence), the Pleven Plan indeed sought to allow, as the United States demanded, a West German military contribution to the defence of western Europe while preventing the reconstitution of a German national army; hence the contingents supplied by the Federal Republic would be integrated at battalion level within a 'European army', which would effectively be under French control. France was attempting to make a virtue out of necessity: through this project of a European army the French were hoping to achieve various objectives that had hitherto seemed contradictory, namely, gaining a US military guarantee while keeping Germany under control, and fostering the emergence of a European identity while defending France's own status as a great power. At first, though, it was hard for the French to get their partners to accept the solution that they had only reluctantly formulated: the Germans saw it as blatant discrimination and the United States as a stalling tactic. To be sure, the United States would finally give their active support to this project in summer 1951 after Monnet managed to convince general Dwight D. Eisenhower, NATO's newly appointed supreme allied commander Europe (SACEUR), of its merits. Yet it would, for three years, become the focus of all the contradictions of the Fourth Republic and its foreign policy, eventually leading to one of its most serious crises.

## Notes

1. For an overview of this question, see Geneviève Maelstaf, *Que faire de l'Allemagne? Les responsables français, le statut international de l'Allemagne et le problème de l'unité allemande (1945–1955)*, Paris: ministère des Affaires étrangères, Direction des archives, coll. 'Diplomatie et histoire', 1999; and Michael Creswell and Marc Trachtenberg, 'France and the German Question (1945–1955)', *Journal of Cold War Studies* 5:3 (summer 2003), pp. 5–28.

2. See Georges-Henri Soutou, 'Les dirigeants français et l'entrée en guerre froide: un processus de décision hésitant', *Le Trimestre du monde* 3 (1993), pp. 135–149.

3. See Irwin Wall, *L'Influence américaine sur la politique française (1945–1954)*, Paris: Balland, 1989, p. 94 ff.

4. See Serge Berstein and Pierre Milza (eds), *L'Année 1947*, Paris: Presses de Sciences-po, 2000.

5. For an overview, see Gérard Bossuat, *La France, l'aide américaine et la construction européenne (1944–1954)*, Paris: Comité pour l'histoire économique et financière de la France, 1992, 2 vols; Richard Kuisel, *Seducing the French: The Dilemma of Americanization*, Berkeley: University of California Press, 1993; and Irwin Wall, *L'Influence américaine sur la politique française (1945–1954)*, op. cit.

6. Source: Gérard Bossuat, *La France, l'aide américaine et la construction européenne (1944–1954)*, op. cit., p. 860.

7. Source: Robert Frank, René Girault and Jacques Thobie, *La Loi des géants (1941–1964)*, Paris: Masson, 1993, p. 177.

8. See Frédéric Bozo, *La France et l'OTAN. De la guerre froide au nouvel ordre européen*, Paris: Masson, 1991; and Jenny Raflik, 'La France et la genèse institutionnelle de l'Alliance atlantique (1949–1952)', *Relations internationales*, 2008/2, no. 134, pp. 55–68.

9. Translation from EU website: http://europa.eu/about-eu/basic-information/symbols/europe-day/schuman-declaration/index_en.htm.

10. See Creswell and Trachtenberg, 'France and the German Question (1945–1955)'.

# Chapter 2

# FRENCH POWERLESSNESS (1951–1958)

The parliamentary elections of June 1951 confirmed the overall dominance of the political parties that supported the regime and the general direction of its foreign policy. Yet this result, made possible by an electoral system that sought to cut the extremes of the political spectrum out of the electoral equation (the so-called *apparentements*), was far from being an accurate reflection of the real political situation in France. Almost half of the votes polled went either to the Gaullist RPF or to the French Communist Party, which both, albeit from opposite points of view, opposed the regime and its foreign policy. The governing parties, meanwhile, were themselves divided on two key issues: European construction, which was at that time going through its first major crisis with the European Defence Community (EDC); and the future of the colonial empire, under pressure first with the war in Indochina (1946–1954) and then, from 1954, with the conflict in Algeria.

Against the backdrop of the increasing East-West conflict in Europe and throughout the world – and largely determined by this conflict – these two issues would henceforth weigh heavily upon French foreign policy. Both issues indeed challenged its core principle, namely national sovereignty, which was simultaneously threatened by the European project and by the decolonization movement. Would France be able to face what was perceived as a dual challenge to its power status – both in Europe and overseas – and even to its existence as a nation? Could it accept one of these two processes and refuse the other? Could it refuse both? These two issues, with the Cold War in the background, were in fact becoming more and more closely intertwined, feeding a growing sense of powerlessness on the international stage. This was particularly true of decolonization: while the Fourth Republic, in spite of all the problems and crises it encountered, would in the end prove able to carry forward the European project during a period of economic growth and modernization, it was the Algerian War that would place the heaviest burden on France's foreign policy, and eventually lead to the collapse of the country's political system.

## Caught between the EDC and Indochina

At the beginning of the 1950s, France was getting back on its feet; reconstruction and modernization were underway. Nevertheless, the country remained dependent on outside assistance, and its foreign policy was thus subject to external influences. The Marshall plan ended in 1951; it had certainly borne fruit, but another form of US aid was now taking its place. For the war in Korea had not only led to the militarization of the strategy of containment, but also to the militarization of US aid to western Europe, whose rearmament the United States was now to a large extent taking charge of through the Mutual Security Act. Yet US military assistance came with still more strings attached than Marshall plan aid; against the dual background of the organization of the defence of Europe within the NATO framework and of the intensification of the war in Indochina, the United States sought to influence the choices of European nations regarding weaponry and strategy. And given the international economic context created by the war in Korea and the still fragile state of France's economy, US aid remained vital.

| 1951–1952 | 1952–1953 | 1953–1954 | 1954–1955 | Total |
|-----------|-----------|-----------|-----------|-------|
| 500 | 615 | 897 | 125.3 | 2137.3 |

**Table 2.1.** US aid provided to France after the Marshall plan, July 1951–June 1955 (in millions of dollars)[1]

This situation was hard to stomach for France's leaders; it would give rise to some notable incidents, such as when, in October 1952, the president of the Council, Antoine Pinay, voiced a forthright reaction to what he considered to be US interference in France's defence budget, and in so doing received an immediate boost in popularity among an electorate who felt humiliated by France's dependence on the increasingly dominant superpower. This frustration was made all the more difficult to bear by the general feeling among the French that the worst was now behind them, and that France no longer had any need for outside help, the country having now recovered its status as a great power. Yet this feeling was illusory. France's status on the world stage was now being decided in the war in Indochina, where US assistance was becoming more and more crucial in the fight against the Viet Minh and its armies. As for France's European policy, it too was under increasing pressure from the United States, as the EDC affair would show from 1951 onwards. In both cases, US influence on French policy was decisive.

Let us first consider Indochina. Since 1950, the conflict had ceased to be a solely French affair. Between 1946 and 1950, the French had had some difficulty in convincing the United States of the legitimacy of their fight to keep Vietnam within the French Union; Washington had begun to tone down its anti-colonialist stance starting in 1947, but this was above all in order not to add to the difficulties of France's leaders, faced as they were with the threat of internal destabilization in a context of growing Cold War tensions in Europe. Yet the dramatic events that occurred at the end of the decade in East Asia (Mao Zedong's victory and proclamation of the People's Republic of China in October 1949, the outbreak of the Korean War in June 1950) transformed Southeast Asia into the major testing ground of the US strategy of containment, fundamentally changing the terms of the Indochinese conflict and of the United States' involvement in it.[2]

At the beginning of 1950, the French had requested and obtained military aid from the United States in support of the military campaign in Indochina through the Mutual Defence Assistance Program. As a result, the war in Indochina was becoming the business of the United States as well. Yet by the same token this turned the conflict into a point of contention, and soon of friction between France, fighting primarily to retain its protectorate, and the United States, concerned above all with keeping Indochina in the Western camp against the backdrop of the worsening situation in Asia. These objectives were distinct, if not contradictory: the French resented US interference in the conduct of the war and the growing influence of the United States in Vietnam; as for the United States, their policy led them to encourage Vietnamese nationalism and to oppose the perpetuation of the colonial status quo that France still clung to behind the façade of sovereignty granted to Vietnam. These contradictions could only deepen as US assistance increased, accounting by the end of 1952 for almost 40 per cent of the cost of the French military effort in Indochina.

| Year | Cost of the war (in billions of French francs, 1953 value) | US share (by percentage) |
|---|---|---|
| 1949 | 209 | 0 |
| 1950 | 313 | 17.5 |
| 1951 | 383 | 14.3 |
| 1952 | 568 | 30.8 |
| 1953 | 598 | 43.4 |

**Table 2.2.** Cost of the war in Indochina and US contribution[3]

By 1953, the friction between France and the United States over Indo-china was being further exacerbated by the deterioration of the situation on the ground. Although they clearly would have been unable to wage war without US assistance, the French were increasingly angered by what they perceived as interference by the United States in the Indochina conflict. At the same time, their determination to carry on fighting was dwindling as the war's initial objective – maintaining control over Indochina – now looked increasingly untenable; the French felt more and more that they were simply fighting on behalf of the United States, for goals that were not really their own. The United States, meanwhile, was becoming impatient with what they saw as French political inertia with regard to the question of Indochina, coupled with military ineffectiveness on the ground. Yet they were still not prepared to consider direct intervention in the conflict – however vital it might be in their eyes to the security of the West.

### The Moment of Truth Draws Near

The moment of truth, as a result, was now approaching inexorably. First of all on the political front: the Panmunjom armistice, which brought hostilities in Korea to an end on 27 July 1953, prompted the French to begin looking for a negotiated outcome in Indochina – a prospect which the Americans opposed as a dangerous retreat by the West in the face of communism. The president of the Council, Joseph Laniel, faced both with the unpopularity of the war and with a worsening military situation, nevertheless accepted the principle of such a move at the Four-Power conference in Berlin (25 January–18 February 1954); it was agreed that the question would be added to the agenda of the Geneva conference, scheduled for the end of April, which was meant to discuss the question of Korea. However, the moment of truth was also approaching on the military front: the United States had now made increased aid conditional on a more effective conduct of the war by the French. The result was the plan drawn up by General Henri Navarre, commander-in-chief of the French forces in Indochina, which was approved by Washington and put into action in autumn 1953. Yet after a few short-lived successes, the situation deteriorated once more; the French base at Diên Biên Phu was encircled and, on 13 March 1954, General Vo Nguyen Giap launched what would be the final offensive by the Viet Minh armed forces.

From the outset, a link had existed between the war in Indochina and the situation in Europe. In the context of the US strategy of containment, France was a key player both in the Far East and on the old continent. However, on its own the country could not simultaneously maintain its war effort in Southeast Asia and also make a significant contribution to the defence of Europe within the NATO framework; for France to participate fully in the latter, US assistance was needed in Indochina. In fact, the support of the United States was all the more vital in this respect because the condition placed by the United States on their own military commitment to Europe – the rearmament of Germany – hinged on the outcome of France's military operations overseas: it was indeed clear that a defeat in Indochina might shake French self-confidence so much that public opinion and the political classes alike would find it hard to accept German rearmament, even if strictly integrated within a European framework.

From the summer of 1951, the original concept of a European army had given way to the idea of a European Defence Community. The change had been driven to a large extent by friends of Monnet, including the diplomat Hervé Alphand, who were anxious to place German rearmament within a larger plan for European integration. This changed title reflected a shift away from the original project as formulated by Pleven in October 1950 and subsequently negotiated among the Six from February 1951: the establishment of German divisions (rather than just battalions) was now envisaged, and the principle of equal rights, as demanded by the Germans, was central. Furthermore, the project now formed part of the framework of a new organization with full community status, the EDC, which would come into being in parallel with the ECSC. As such, the project now enjoyed the full support of the United States, who had initially given the Pleven Plan a cool reception.

Negotiations over the EDC were long and arduous, but finally resulted in the signing by the six governments of the Treaty of Paris on 28 May 1952. Yet the text of this document was lengthy and impenetrable. Above all, it was controversial: as recently as February 1952, a debate in the *Assemblée nationale* had shown just how difficult it would be to convince the French political classes, still lukewarm towards the idea of German rearmament, to accept the EDC. This argument would in fact rage on for a further two years, during which time it would become increasingly clear to successive governments that they would be unable to get the country's parliament to ratify a treaty that had been called for in the first place by the French themselves – even with the modifications and amendments that they had requested from their European partners between 1952 and 1954 in the hope of making the project acceptable in the eyes of the political classes and wider public opinion. There were a number of reasons for this failure. Some were domestic: while France's leaders, by making the fundamental choice in 1950 to pursue Franco-German reconciliation and European integration, had no doubt accepted German rearmament as inevitable, the wider public had misgivings about a project originally conceived as a way of placing limits on this very process and guaranteeing France's military superiority over Federal

Germany. Many feared that it would eventually lead to the loss of France's sovereignty and the establishment of German domination over Europe. The political classes were also divided: aside from the entrenched opposition of the Gaullists and communists to the EDC, the dividing line between the *cédistes* (the supporters of the *Communauté Européenne de Défense*, or CED) and the *anticédistes* cut across the governing parties and the political and military establishment alike. The international situation also created significant difficulties. The death of Stalin, in March 1953, heralded a drop in East-West tensions, reducing the perceived urgency of German rearmament and thus undermining the rationale for the EDC. More importantly, the attitude of the United States would misfire spectacularly: with the arrival of Dwight D. Eisenhower in the White House in January 1953, US policy began to look more and more like a crusade for the EDC; but Washington's growing pressure merely fuelled the doubts of the French political classes, who were beginning to question the extent to which the project really served the national interest. This became particularly clear when, in December 1953, US Secretary of State John Foster Dulles clumsily brandished the threat of an 'agonizing reappraisal' of US policy in Europe should the EDC fail. So, just as the war in Indochina was turning into a quagmire, a national psychodrama over the EDC was simultaneously being played out, once more throwing into sharp focus the contradictions of a foreign policy that now placed France in a dual European and colonial impasse.

### The Choices Made by Pierre Mendès France

'The fundamental cause of the ills besetting our country is the sheer number and weight of the tasks that it seeks to undertake at one and the same time.' This diagnosis, formulated by Pierre Mendès France in June 1953, during his first attempt to form a government, was confirmed one year later when he was sworn in by the *Assemblée nationale*. His accession to power in June 1954 would thus, more than anything else, mark the end of four years of procrastination and indecision: as far as the incoming president of the Council was concerned, France could not – or at any rate could no longer – afford the luxury of having no real policy. The country's finances, Indochina, the EDC: these problems were all linked and, as he saw it, demanded a coherent response that would involve at last striking a balance between means available and ends sought. Mendès France's policy can in this sense be seen as an attempt to redefine French power. It was no longer possible, he judged, to maintain the mirage of a France that had remained a great power; the time had come to accept the fact that the country was now no more than a middleweight power. The new president of the Council (who simultaneously held the Quai d'Orsay, from which he worked after being sworn in, a sign of the pressing international situation that shaped his policy) marked a clear break from his predecessors in terms of personality and background alike. Mendès France was neither a defender of France's colonial heritage nor a campaigner for European supranational integration. In short, he did not belong to the 'system' that was endlessly decried by the Gaullists.

As a result, the orientation of his actions on the international stage did not follow on seamlessly from what had, over the years, come to constitute the Fourth Republic's foreign policy: it would in fact, in many ways, point to the policy direction followed by de Gaulle from 1958 onwards. Following the fall of Diên Biên Phu, which came on 7 May 1954 after nearly two months of siege, negotiating an end to the war directly with the Viet Minh became inescapable. Once any remaining illusions regarding the possibility of direct US intervention saving the situation had been dispelled, the only realistic option was to try to save whatever could be saved through the negotiations that had started after the fall of the base. Yet when Mendès France took power on 17 June, the Geneva conference talks were locked in stalemate: Bidault and Laniel, whose government fell on 12 June, had followed no clear line in the negotiations, while on the ground the Viet Minh forces were advancing. In this context, Franco-American relations were becoming increasingly strained: the United States accused the French of wanting to compromise Western positions in Indochina, while the French suspected the United States of wanting to bring about the failure of the Geneva conference without being prepared to make any military commitments. Nor were there any signs that relations between Paris and Washington would improve with the arrival of the new president of the Council, whom US officials suspected of being too favourably inclined towards the USSR and China. Mendès France therefore realized that his only hope lay in boldness, so he duly laid down an ultimatum during his swearing-in ceremony on 17 June: if a negotiated settlement had not been reached by 20 July, he announced, he would request that French army conscripts be sent to Indochina, after which his government would resign. But the principal actors involved were keen to avoid such a scenario: the Viet Minh, with whom Paris was now in negotiations, were militarily weakened in spite of Diên Biên Phu; the USSR wanted to avoid any escalation that might involve US intervention; China, which also feared such an eventuality, wanted to set itself up as an honest broker (Mendès France had met with Premier Zhou Enlai on 23 June in Bern); and the United States did not want to run the risk of losing Indochina outright.

Hence a last-minute agreement was reached in Geneva on 21 July, following the terms of a compromise proposed by the Soviet foreign minister, Vyacheslav Molotov: a demarcation line between North and South Vietnam would be drawn along the seventeenth parallel; French troops would all be moved to the South and those of the Viet Minh to the North; and nation-wide free elections would be held within two years. The Geneva accords (which also recognized the independence of Cambodia and Laos) were an official recognition of France's defeat and marked the end of the former colonial power's presence in the country, with French troops all being with-drawn in 1956. While the French initially thought that they would be able nevertheless to maintain a certain degree of influence in Indochina, such hopes did not last long. It quickly became clear that the Geneva accords would not be thoroughly implemented (the nationwide elections, in particu-lar, were never held) and that the United States – who never formally signed them – had decided to take the lead alone in Southeast Asia by turning the South Vietnamese regime into a forward outpost of Western power. To this end, Washington would set up the Southeast Asian Treaty Organization (SEATO), which was founded in Manila in September 1954 (France became a member for reasons of political realism and transatlantic solidarity in spite of its growing divergence with US policy). The United States thus in effect took over in Indochina, leaving France in a marginalized role. Given the situation that Mendès France had inherited, however, the overall result of his actions by no means constituted a failure. By obtaining in Indochina an outcome that did not amount to French surrender, he had managed to put an end to a conflict that his predecessors had been unable to stop in spite of mounting opposition to the war. In so doing, he had unshackled France from a burden that for years had been hindering its economic recovery and hampering its foreign policy.

### The EDC Crisis

Having resolved the question of Indochina, Mendès France intended to keep up the momentum and deal once and for all with the problem of the EDC, which was weighing just as heavily on the country's foreign policy. He held no strong position on the subject, but he did have his doubts. While by no means hostile to European unification, he was committed to preserving France's sovereignty; as an anglophile, leaning towards cooperation with London rather than with Bonn, he also wanted the United Kingdom to be part of the project; his closest associates, for their part, were divided on the issue. In these difficult circumstances, Mendès France wanted to achieve a Franco-French consensus before approaching his European partners to demand a review of the treaty; without this, its ratification by the French parliament, as he saw it, would be impossible. Yet a compromise, which he asked two ministers with opposing opinions on the matter, the Gaullist Pierre Koenig (defence) and the pro-European radical Maurice Bourgès-Maunoury (industry) to deliver, proved unattainable. The ensuing governmental crisis led to the departure, in mid-August 1954, of three Gaullist ministers from the government, including Koenig and Jacques Chaban-Delmas; as for the pro-EDC ministers, they expressed reservations regarding the positions that Mendès France wanted to take as he prepared for a fresh round of negotiation with France's five European partners.

As a result, it was from a position of weakness that the French head of government came to the talks discussing French demands among the Six, which opened on 19 August 1954 in Brussels. These demands, predictably, aimed to weaken the supranational content of the May 1952 treaty while at the same time strengthening the mechanisms through which German rearmament would be controlled. Mendès France's European partners, however, encouraged as they were by the French supporters of the EDC (including Schuman), were set very much against him. The Five believed that the treaty could be ratified in its present form; some, foremost among them Adenauer, believed that Mendès France (suspected of nurturing neutralist tendencies by Bonn and Washington alike) in fact wanted to sabotage the EDC in order to come to an arrangement with the Soviet Union and prevent German rearmament. Mendès France was suspected, in essence, of having negotiated with the Soviets to obtain a favourable exit from war in Indochina in exchange for the non-ratification of the EDC by Paris. The (unfounded) rumour of such a 'global deal' had been circulating in Western capitals since July, aided and abetted by a segment of the French Right. In addition, the United States was exerting extreme pressure on France's European partners during the Brussels conference (the United Kingdom, though, showed a moderate attitude).

Mendès France came up against a united front. On 22 August 1954, the Brussels conference, which had been especially bruising for the French premier, ended in failure. The events that followed were, arguably, inevitable. On 30 August, the *Assemblée nationale*, having taken a perfunctory procedural vote, refused even to discuss the ratification of the treaty; this move amounted to burying the EDC for good. In so doing, France triggered an unprecedented crisis for the West. This rejection of the European solution to the problem of German rearmament, a solution that the French themselves had proposed almost four years earlier, indeed looked likely to compromise further moves towards the construction of a European community, the EDC having taken over from the ECSC as the scheme's key project. It also delivered a heavy blow to the transatlantic alliance, the credibility of which depended on the rearmament of the Federal Republic, demanded by the United States as its condition for a long-term commitment to the defence of Europe. In short, France's Euro-Atlantic influence was compromised, the Franco-German relationship was severely tested and Franco-American relations were at their lowest ebb.

Paradoxically, though, the crisis would not last long. Mendès France very quickly restarted a dialogue with Adenauer in order to clear the misunderstandings that had built up in Franco-German relations: marking a fresh start, Paris and Bonn set off on a new path of politico-strategic cooperation.[4] At the same time, the French premier began working towards restoring a relationship of trust with Washington. Convinced that the Atlantic Alliance must be preserved at all costs to avoid the rearmament of the Federal Republic being negotiated bilaterally between Bonn and Washington, he played a decisive role, in close concert with UK Foreign Secretary Anthony Eden, in devising the alternative approach that would be officially adopted by the conferences held in London (28–30 September) and Paris (20–23 October 1954). The result – enshrined in the Paris accords of 23 October 1954 – constituted a major step forward: the Federal Republic (along with Italy) was allowed to join the Brussels Treaty of 1948 (which, in modified form, gave rise to the Western European Union, or WEU) and, even more vitally, to become part of the Atlantic Alliance.

After four years of prevarication, the Western security and defence framework was fixed in lasting form, following terms very similar to those initially rejected by the French. Paris had finally agreed to give NATO – meaning the United States – the task of overseeing future German military power: US security guarantees and the existing Atlantic framework, in essence, were preferred over a European defence system that for the moment remained purely notional and mired in uncertainty. By opting in respect of the latter for the purely intergovernmental WEU – in contrast to the supranational character of the defunct EDC – France, in addition, elected to preserve its national sovereignty in the military sphere, a topic that had become all the more sensitive following the government's decision, in the wake of the EDC crisis, to turn its efforts towards the building of a French atomic bomb (the decision was made formally during a meeting of 26 December 1954, chaired by Mendès France). Overall, the outcome of the crisis was thus broadly favourable: the solution adopted in the autumn of 1954 signalled the completion of the sort of Euro-Atlantic security system long desired by the French, and France – in spite of the drawn-out psychodrama of the EDC – remained a central element within it.[5]

Although his government was short-lived (it fell on 6 February 1955, a little more than seven months after its inauguration), Mendès France would leave his mark on French foreign policy. To be sure, for the most part he had been settling old scores; however, by cutting his losses both in Indochina and with the EDC, he had laid the foundations for a new foreign policy, namely that of a middleweight power that accepted its status as such. Once the question of Indochina had been settled, decolonization gathered pace; the process set in motion with Mendès France's speech in Carthage on 31 July

1954 resulted in the granting of independence to Morocco and Tunisia in 1956. On the European front, meanwhile, supranationalism, synonymous with the loss of sovereignty, no longer appeared as the inevitable corollary of Franco-German reconciliation and European construction, though both remained key objectives of France's policy. Furthermore, by advocating dialogue with the East and the USSR over European security and disarmament in his speech at the UN on 22 November 1954, Mendès France offered a vision that went beyond East-West confrontation, something de Gaulle would later pursue. As for US influence on French policy, Mendès France's actions showed that it could be contained so long as France's policy was coherent with respect to its objectives and the means at its disposal. In time, all of these policy directions would become firmly established: the Mendès France interlude, an anomalous (and successful) passage within the foreign policy of the Fourth Republic, in many respects paved the way for that of the Fifth.

## The Algerian Deadlock and the Relaunching of the European Project

For the moment, however, the Mendesist interlude was well and truly over. Faced with the beginning of the Algerian insurrection in November 1954, the Mendès France government fell following a debate over its policy in North Africa. With the war in Indochina barely over, along came the Algerian conflict to drain the country's military and economic power, imposing new limits on the room France had to manoeuvre on the international and European stage. Whereas previous French governments had been able to persuade others that the war in Indochina was a 'Western' fight, they would never manage to convince their US and European allies of the legitimacy of the Algerian conflict despite its being portrayed by Paris as part of the global struggle between the free world and Soviet expansionism. The climate of peaceful coexistence was not propitious to such justifications, especially given that Algerian nationalism was in truth neither a product nor an instrument of Soviet policy or international communism; with the Third World bursting onto the international stage, it appeared on the contrary to be a legitimate incarnation of the peoples' struggle for self-determination. In spite of the legal arguments put forward by the French – Algerian territory was an integral part of French national territory and hence in theory covered by the North Atlantic Treaty – the internationalization of the Algerian question, quite naturally sought by the Front de Libération Nationale (FLN), very quickly looked inevitable. As early as September 1955, the Afro-Asian States were demanding that it be debated by the General Assembly of the UN, and French diplomacy, led by Foreign Minister Antoine Pinay, was unable to prevent this. An Algerian obsession would from then on dominate French foreign policy, and it would remain central until 1962.

It was in these unfavourable circumstances that one of the most important developments of the period would be played out, namely the relaunching of the European project that, contrary to all expectations, took shape less than a year after the failure of the EDC. France was now admittedly less of a driving force than in 1950: in the wake of the vote of 30 August 1954, an official initiative coming from Paris with respect to the European community was hardly conceivable. The leading roles in that crucial period thus went to others, in particular the Benelux countries, while successive French governments remained on the sidelines; Jean Monnet nevertheless again played a key personal role, in particular by compelling Belgian Foreign Minister Paul-Henri Spaak to take the initiative. After giving up the presidency of the ECSC in February 1955 in order to devote his efforts to this European relaunch, Monnet created the Action Committee for the United States of Europe (ACUSE) in October. He thus found himself at the meeting point of all the influences that, following the conference of the Six in Messina (1–2 June 1955), were converging on the idea of restarting the European community project. Since the fate of the EDC ruled out any European relaunch in the political arena and, even more unequivocally, that of defence, European leaders sought to give the project a more 'technical' character. The relaunch would therefore centre on two areas: atomic energy, following French wishes, and the wider question of a general-purpose common market, preferred by the Germans.

Preoccupied with events in North Africa, the French government initially was only marginally involved in this fresh European initiative, instead giving free rein to its experts, such as Louis Armand, the president of the French railways (SNCF) and a staunch proponent of a European atomic energy community. Edgar Faure (president of the Council from February to December 1955) was not particularly pro-European; as for Antoine Pinay, although a declared advocate of European construction, he kept his distance from the common market project, as this was raising concerns in French economic circles, whose outlook largely remained protectionist. Not until the formation in the wake of the parliamentary elections of 2 January 1956 of the government headed by the socialist Guy Mollet (which, in addition to Mollet himself, included two ardent pro-Europeans, Christian Pineau and Maurice Faure) would a French government again show any ambition on the European stage – although the Algerian emergency would soon come to dominate its foreign policy.

*The Suez Earthquake*

The Suez crisis, in autumn 1956, formed the point at which the European and Algerian questions overlapped, explaining its deep resonance and its profound consequences for French policy, which would emerge severely shaken from this new earthquake.[6] The origins of the crisis lay in an anti-Nasser phobia fed by the Algerian obsession of France's governing classes. In the eyes of the latter, and chief among them Mollet, Gamal Abdel Nasser, the Egyptian 'rais' – who, since ousting his rival Muhammad Naguib in 1954, had been presenting himself as the leader of pan-Arabism – was the main source of support for the Algerian 'rebels' and the only real reason for their success. This phobia was also widespread in London, where Nasser was perceived as a threat to the United Kingdom's continuing influence and military presence in the Middle East; it was even more so in Tel-Aviv, where he was seen as an existential threat to the Jewish state. Even before the crisis, then, there was a convergence of views between France, the United Kingdom and Israel regarding the desirability of overthrowing the Egyptian 'dictator', whom they willingly portrayed as a new Hitler. This, however, was rejected in Washington, where a conciliatory policy towards Nasser and Arab nationalism was still being pursued, and it was still thought that he could be persuaded to take a more pro-Western line in exchange for the financial and technical aid that he needed in order to construct the Aswan dam, the monumental project in which he had placed his hopes for the modernization and development of his country.

This went on until, in the face of Nasser's refusal to throw in his lot clearly with the Western camp (Egypt had signed a large arms deal with Czechoslovakia a few months earlier), the US administration decided on 19 July 1956 to withhold this aid, triggering a major international crisis. On 26 July, Nasser responded by nationalizing the Suez Canal, which was controlled by Franco-British interests. This action, seen as an act of liberation by the Third World, was perceived as an unacceptable challenge in the West. However, while the United States, who was keen not to alienate the Arab world, sought a somewhat unlikely negotiated solution, the French – and the influence of Mollet on UK Prime Minister Eden was decisive in this respect – set about convincing the United Kingdom that this was an opportunity for a joint military intervention; Paris, they said, was even ready to give them command over it. As for the Israelis, they saw a possible intervention as an opportunity to rid themselves of the Nasser threat. (From the beginning of 1956 onwards, links between Paris and Tel-Aviv had strengthened considerably, particularly in the military sphere: from the spring onwards, France delivered large quantities of arms to Israel, thereby becoming the Jewish state's main international backer.)

France thus took up a key position between the United Kingdom and Israel. Watching UK prevarication over the summer, the French government turned to its Israeli counterpart. The initiative came from the defence minister, Maurice Bourgès-Maunoury, with the support of Mollet and Pineau (though the Quai d'Orsay, reputedly pro-Arab, was kept in the dark). Henceforth, a plan for a Franco-British military operation, coordinated with the Israelis, was drawn up in absolute secrecy. (The latter, initially reluctant to accept the role offered to them, may have been brought around by an offer of military nuclear cooperation with France.) The plan, finalized at the tripartite meetings in Sèvres (22 and 24 October 1956), called for an Israeli attack against Egypt followed by a Franco-British intervention carried out under the dual pretext of separating the two sides and keeping the Suez Canal open to traffic.[7]

While the operation was a military success, it quickly turned into a political fiasco. On 5 November, one week after the Israeli offensive, Franco-British forces, in spite of international pressure, were landed or parachuted into the Canal Zone. However, the USSR then sent an ultimatum threatening London and Paris with nuclear reprisals if the operation continued. More importantly, the Eisenhower administration, faced with a fait accompli by its French and UK allies at a particularly delicate juncture (Eisenhower was facing re-election on November 6), put pressure on the British pound in order to force the Eden government to back down. On 7 November, the United Kingdom gave in and halted an operation that, from a military point of view, had been successful; the French had no choice but to follow suit.

The United Kingdom and France both came out of Suez equally humiliated. Faced with the rise of the Third World and the dominance of the United States and the USSR, they appeared to be in retreat on two fronts: as colonial powers in the face of independence movements, and as middle-weight powers in a world now run by the superpowers. The fact that the Suez crisis coincided with the brutal Soviet repression of the Hungarian uprising, which had threatened to weaken the USSR's dominance in eastern Europe, only served to underline this new situation, while at the same time further sullying the image of the United Kingdom and France, who were widely held responsible for having at least indirectly facilitated Moscow's intervention (Soviet tanks entered Budapest on 4 November). However, whereas the United Kingdom, following Suez, would adjust its foreign and defence policy to bring them more into line with those of the United States by relaunching the Anglo-American 'special relationship', French policy went off in the opposite direction. As far as the French government was concerned, the main lesson to be learned from the Suez crisis was that Washington had 'ditched' its two main European allies. The vital national interests of France and the United Kingdom, they believed, had been sacrificed in favour of the United States' political interests in the Arab world and the Middle East. As seen from Paris, the United States was now seeking to supplant the European powers in their traditional sphere of influence; worse still, not only had the United States failed to extend guarantees to France and the United Kingdom in the face of Soviet threats, but there had been de facto collusion between the USSR and the United States at the expense of these two countries. This reading of the Suez crisis, which gained widespread currency within the French leadership in the months that followed, also fuelled a longstanding and growing French disaffection with NATO, which was judged by Paris to be excessively dominated by the United States while providing no absolute guarantee of security for Europe. It also bolstered the determination of the country's political leadership to obtain the atom bomb: originally taken by Mendès France, as has already been mentioned, in December 1954, this decision was confirmed by Mollet straight after Suez and then by his successor, Félix Gaillard, who in early 1958 set a date of 1960 for the first French nuclear test.

Last but not least, the Suez crisis confirmed the need in French eyes to push forward with the building of Europe. It thus led to a tightening of Franco-German links, a decision taken in autumn 1956 by Mollet and Adenauer, who both shared the same reading of the crisis and agreed on the need to give Europe added weight, particularly with respect to the United States; the completion of the relaunching process begun in Messina the previous year henceforth became a priority. In this context, once the Saar question, which had been poisoning relations between the two countries, had been resolved (the treaty of 27 October 1956 stated that the Saar would be reintegrated into the FRG from 1 January 1957), this Paris-Bonn rapprochement effectively enabled the unblocking of European negotiations, which had been bogged down for several months. On 25 March 1957, the Six signed the Rome treaties, which created the European Economic Community (EEC) and the European Atomic Energy Community (EURATOM) respectively; less than three years after the failure of the EDC, the European project was once again back on track. The Paris-Bonn rapprochement also laid the foundations for a Franco-German military and strategic cooperation that was seen as a means of rebalancing the Alliance in favour of the Europeans, including in the military nuclear field, where Franco-German-Italian cooperation was secretly planned by the last governments of the Fourth Republic.[8]

The post-Suez period thus constitutes the beginning of a fundamental reorientation of French foreign policy. In some ways, the Fourth Republic had demonstrated that it was capable of radical departures, as shown by the success of the relaunch of the European project and the creation of the EEC in 1957 against the backdrop of the ongoing French economic 'miracle'. Yet the Algerian deadlock increasingly restricted the country's actions abroad; the Suez crisis had only served to intensify the Algerian conflict and accelerate its internationalization, a phenomenon that the French leadership sought to counter at all costs, in particular at the UN. As a result, relations between France and its allies, above all the United States, were increasingly affected by the deteriorating situation in Algeria.[9] This would be made clear by the Sakiet Sidi Youssef affair, in which the Tunisian village of this name was bombed on 8 February 1958 by French aircraft pursuing FLN fighters, sparking a wave of vigorous protest throughout the international community. Sakiet would be the final crisis of the Fourth Republic: the Anglo-American mediation mission (the Murphy-Beeley mission) that the Gaillard government was forced to accept under pressure from Washington, angering a section both of public opinion and of the political classes, brought about the collapse of the government in mid-April. The worsening of the situation in Algeria spelled the end for a political system that by then was falling apart. The deadlock in Algeria, diplomatic powerlessness abroad and political disintegration at home were, in spring 1958, the three interlinked manifestations of a single process, one that would bring about the terminal breakdown of the Fourth Republic and lead to the return to power of General de Gaulle.

## Notes

1. Source: Gérard Bossuat, *La France, l'aide américaine et la construction européenne (1944–1954)*, op. cit., p. 860.

2. See Denise Artaud and Lawrence Kaplan (eds), *Diên Biên Phu*, Lyon: La Manufacture, 1989.

3. Source : Gérard Bossuat, *La France, l'aide américaine et la construction européenne (1944–1954)*, op. cit., p. 856.

4. See Georges-Henri Soutou, *L'Alliance incertaine. Les rapports politiques et stratégiques franco-allemands (1954–1996)*, Paris: Fayard, 1996

5. There has been a tendency in recent studies towards re-evaluating positively French policy in this period: see William I. Hitchcock, *France Restored: Cold War Diplomacy and the Quest for Leadership in Europe (1944–1954)*, Chapel Hill: University of North Carolina Press, 1998; and Michael Creswell, *A Question of Balance: How France and the United States Created Cold War Europe*, Cambridge, MA: Harvard University Press, 2006.

6. For an analysis of this crisis, see Maurice Vaïsse (ed.), *La France et l'opération de Suez*, Paris: Addim, 1997; and Maurice Vaïsse, 'France and the Suez Crisis', in William Roger Louis and Roger Owen (eds), *Suez 1956: The Crisis and its Consequences*, Oxford: Clarendon Press, 1989.

7. See Georgette Elgey, '1956: révélations sur la crise de Suez', *L'Histoire* 202 (September 1996), pp. 88–92; and *Histoire de la IVe République*, vol. 4, *La République des tourmentes (1954–1959)*, t. II, 'Malentendu et passion', Paris: Fayard, 1997, pp. 11–244.

8. Georges-Henri Soutou, 'Les accords de 1957 et 1958: vers une communauté stratégique et nucléaire entre la France, l'Allemagne et l'Italie?', *Matériaux pour l'histoire de notre temps*, 31, (April–June 1993), pp. 1–12.

9. See Irwin Wall, *France, the United States, and the Algerian War*, Berkeley: University of California Press, 2001.

PART II

# CHALLENGING THE STATUS QUO
## (1958–1969)

# Chapter 3

# RE-ESTABLISHING FRANCE'S 'RANK' (1958–1961)

On 1 June 1958, General de Gaulle was sworn in as head of government by the *Assemblée nationale*, handing him full executive powers for six months against the backdrop of the Algerian crisis. Returning to politics after years in the wilderness, de Gaulle identified the need to restore the state's authority and bring the deteriorating situation in Algeria under control as his top priorities. However, in addition to this dual institutional and North African focus, it seemed clear both in France and abroad that his return to power would bring with it a profound transformation of the country's international role: the man who rallied the nation on 18 June 1940 held 'a certain idea of France' (as he famously wrote in his war memoirs) and hence of its position in the world. In de Gaulle's eyes, previous governments had been guilty, at the very least, of following a policy of 'abandonment' that he had resolved to end. In short, the end of the Fourth Republic marked not only the fall of a regime but also, ipso facto, that of a foreign policy.[1]

While elements of continuity with earlier orientations remained, de Gaulle's return indeed signalled a break in the foreign policy arena more than in any other. Admittedly, his priorities would, for many long months, continue to be dictated by the Algerian problem, which weighed heavily on French diplomacy. Yet as early as 13 June 1958 the General gave clear indications regarding the objectives that he was assigning to the latter beyond the resolution of the crisis in North Africa: regaining on the international stage 'a place which is rightfully ours', and once this was achieved, taking 'action which is our own action', in other words, re-establishing the 'independence' and 'rank' that had, in his view, been gravely compromised by his predecessors. This would necessarily involve a revision of the objectives and priorities of foreign policy, but also an inevitable redefinition of French power.

## The Redefinition of Power

In de Gaulle's eyes – and he had bitter experience of this from 1944–1946 – only a strong power could conduct a foreign policy in line with the national interest. The Constitution of 4 October 1958, insofar as it consisted of a rebalancing of powers in favour of the executive, was thus also crucial in refounding France's foreign policy. By ensuring the institutional pre-eminence of the president of the Republic (who held the power to nominate the prime minister and dissolve the *Assemblée nationale*) and by defining his personal prerogatives with regard to foreign policy (e.g. appointing ambassadors and negotiating and ratifying treaties) and defence (as head of the armed forces, he was the guarantor of the nation's independence and territorial integrity), the new constitution made him the uncontested authority in these areas. This was all the more so because the parliamentary majority that resulted from the November 1958 legislative elections was aligned with the presidential majority, a phenomenon that would continue to characterize the functioning of the Fifth Republic until the "cohabitations" of the 1980s and 1990s.

It is true that the institutions of the Fifth Republic did not *formally* specify that the president held sole supremacy over foreign affairs; however, in actual fact, this tended to be the case right from the outset. De Gaulle's personality, his concept and practice of power and his historical 'legitimacy' were the main factors that contributed to this unspoken rule. (To these would be added, with the presidential election of December 1965, the mandate and prestige conferred by the selection of the president through a popular vote with direct universal suffrage, which was the result of a constitutional reform introduced by de Gaulle and ratified by a referendum in 1962). The choice of relevant ministers in the government – the last of the Fourth Republic – assembled by de Gaulle when he became prime minister in June 1958 and then, from January 1959 onwards, once de Gaulle had been elected president, those in prime minister Michel Debré's government, merely served to confirm this presidential pre-eminence. Most notable among these were Maurice Couve de Murville (foreign affairs) and Pierre Guillaumat, followed by Pierre Messmer (armed forces), men who were chosen both for their talents and for their personal loyalty to the General.[2] The continuing priority given to the Algerian question and its diplomatic implications in the first three years of the Fifth Republic further reinforced this tendency to establish foreign policy de facto as a so-called *domaine réservé* (this notion of a 'presidential preserve' quickly gained currency although it was considered inaccurate by many from a constitutional point of view).[3]

In contrast to the situation that existed at the end of the war, in 1958 the General could realistically hope to build his foreign policy on a foundation of steadily recovering French power. In two key areas, the economy and defence, he benefitted from the efforts at reconstruction, albeit incomplete, that had been started by his predecessors. The French economic 'miracle' was, by the end of the 1950s, palpably real, manifesting itself most obviously in the country's sustained economic growth. Long feared by business leaders, the opening up of the country to international trade became a reality with the Treaty of Rome. Financial and monetary restructuring, meanwhile, was undertaken from autumn 1958 onwards with the Pinay-Rueff stabilization plan, which aimed to restore France's international credibility and prepare the country for the common market. Contrary to what many believed at the time, de Gaulle considered France's membership in the EEC to be necessary: in his view, French industry was overly cautious and, following his return to power, he intended to reinvigorate it as quickly as possible. As for defence, the governments of the Fourth Republic had gradually moved – albeit in great secrecy and, in some cases, with some reluctance – towards the decision to develop nuclear weapons. De Gaulle, having inherited a military nuclear programme that was already at an advanced stage of development, was unequivocal in his judgment that 'the bomb' had to form the cornerstone of an independent French defence policy. In June 1958 he decided to terminate the nuclear cooperation programme with Germany and Italy that had been set up by the last governments of the Fourth Republic and of which he disapproved; and, in July, he confirmed Felix Gaillard's earlier decision to carry out a first experimental atomic explosion at the beginning of 1960. Although France was not yet a full nuclear power, from 1958 de Gaulle acted as if it was, somehow anticipating the country's future status as a member of the atomic 'club'. Against a background of East-West crises (Berlin, Cuba) and a redefinition of relations between Western powers, this anticipated atomic status was the keystone of the reorientation of foreign policy undertaken by General de Gaulle from 1958 onwards.

## Lifting the Colonial Deadlock

Yet re-establishing France's 'rank' would first involve bringing an end to the colonial deadlock. Once back in power, de Gaulle became convinced of the inevitability of decolonization. In sub-Saharan Africa, the moves in this direction begun by the Fourth Republic were pursued further. Set up by the 1958 Constitution to replace the now defunct French Union,[4] the French Community (*Communauté française*) was quickly rendered obsolete by the accession of its members to full independence between 1959 and 1960. As a result, France's African policy, in principle at any rate, was now one of relations between sovereign states. In practice, what really counted were the personal relationships that existed between the French president and the African heads of state; meanwhile the emerging *coopération* (develop-ment policy) in effect ensured that relations between France and Africa continued to conform to what amounted to a post-, and, in some ways, a neocolonial system. Watched over closely by the Secretariat for African and Madagascan Affairs (*Secrétariat aux affaires africaines et malgaches*), which was headed at the Elysée by Jacques Foccart, and implemented by the Min-istry of Cooperation, African policy became the most important *domaine réservé* of foreign policy under the Fifth Republic, to the point that it would largely lie outside the authority of the Ministry for Foreign Affairs.

The Algerian situation was more complex. While the exact nature of his initial intentions in this respect remain open to historical debate, de Gaulle was nonetheless faced with the urgent priority from June 1958 onwards of breaking the stranglehold that the conflict continued to exercise over France's international role. The General's return to power did not put an end to the internationalization of the Algerian problem; on the contrary, Algeria still constituted a particular bone of contention, including for Franco-American relations. Even the turning point marked by the decision to grant Algerian self-determination, first announced by de Gaulle on 16 September 1959, did not end the frictions of the previous phase, with France complaining of the lack of support given by the United States, particularly at the UN. The year 1960 was a bruising one for French diplomacy at the United Nations, where a resolution by the General Assembly in December proclaimed the right of the Algerian people to independence. Only once it became clear, following the referendum of 8 January 1961, that self-determi-nation really was going to lead to independence, did the Algerian question begin to weigh less heavily on France's diplomatic outlook. The desperate attempts by supporters of French Algeria to block the process through the Algiers putsch attempt of April 1961 and the terrorist campaign carried out by the *Organisation de l'Armée Secrète*, as well as the long, difficult negotia-tions Paris conducted with the FLN, would nevertheless make things drag on for more than a year after this.

## De Gaulle's 'Memorandum Diplomacy'

Relations with the 'Anglo-Saxons' came next after the Algerian problem in the order of priorities as it stood in 1958. In de Gaulle's view, the dete-rioration of Franco-American relations was above all a result of the weak-ness – or mistakes – of the previous regime and its foreign policy. De Gaulle held the Fourth Republic responsible for having allowed itself to become locked into a relationship of dependence with respect to the United States, in spite of its declared ambition to have France formally recognized as one of the Western Big Three, as Paris had been demanding with little success ever since the creation of the Alliance in 1949–1950. The General saw the country, particularly following the Suez crisis, as politically marginalized by the Anglo-American 'special relationship' (whose real effectiveness he probably exaggerated) and militarily handicapped by its integration within NATO, an organization in which the United States and its UK sidekicks had taken all the best seats, leaving France standing in the aisles. This subordinate status was made worse in his eyes by the exclusive policy pursued by the United States with respect to military nuclear cooperation. France had been refused this whereas London – following a meeting between Dwight D. Eisenhower and Harold Macmillan in March 1957 – had succeeded in obtaining assistance from Washington in this area thanks to an amendment (taking effect in 1958) to the McMahon Act of 1946. De Gaulle therefore wanted both to reaffirm France's status as a major Western power and to restore the solidarity between France and its two main allies, starting with the United States, with whom he sought to re-establish a close relationship.

A pattern was thus established that would subsequently be reproduced at the start of each new presidency under the Fifth Republic: the new occupant of the Elysée would – initially at least – seek a significant strengthening of Franco-American ties. This began with the memorandum of 17 September 1958 addressed to the US president and the UK prime minister, in which de Gaulle called for a mechanism of political and military coordination between the three powers (and not, as has been claimed, a formal tripartite 'directorate') for the purposes of developing a nuclear strategy and managing crises on a global level:

1. The Atlantic Alliance was conceived and its functioning is prepared with a view to an eventual zone of action which no longer corresponds to political and strategic realities. The world being as it is, one cannot consider as adapted to its purpose an organization such as NATO, which is limited to the security of the North Atlantic, as if what is happening, for example, in the Middle East or in Africa, did not immediately and directly concern Europe, and as if the indivisible responsibilities of France did not extend to Africa, to the Indian Ocean and to the Pacific, in the same way as those of Great Britain and the United States. Moreover the radius of action of ships and planes and the range of missiles render militarily outdated such a narrow system. It is true that at first it was admitted that atomic armament, evidently of capital importance, would remain for a long time the monopoly of the United States, a fact which might have appeared to justify that decisions on the world level concerning defense would be practically delegated to the Washington Government. But on this point, also, it must be recognized that such a fact admitted originally no longer is justified by reality.

2. France could, therefore, no longer consider that NATO in its present form meets the conditions of security of the free world and notably its own. It appears necessary to it that on the level of world policy and strategy there

be set up an organization composed of: the United States, Great Britain and France. It would be up to this organization, on the one hand, to take joint decisions on political questions affecting world security and on the other, to establish and if necessary, to put into effect strategic plans of action, notably with regard to the employment of nuclear weapons. It would then be possible to foresee and organize eventual theaters of operations subordinated to the general organization (such as Africa, the Atlantic, the Pacific, the Indian Ocean), which could if necessary be subdivided into subordinate theaters.

3. The French Government considers such a security organization indispensable. It (the French Government) subordinates to it as of now all development of its present participation in NATO and proposes, should such appear necessary for reaching agreement, to invoke the provision for revising the North Atlantic Treaty in accordance with Article 12.[5]

While de Gaulle's memorandum echoed previous French suggestions, it was nonetheless evidence of a clear change in terms of approach and ambition. De Gaulle, in contrast to his predecessors, refused to limit France to action within the NATO framework – which he saw as too narrow and restrictive – and let it be understood that France might distance itself from the organization if his demands were not met. Although he was under no illusions as to his real chances of success (President Eisenhower's response to the memorandum was evasive to say the least), there is no doubt that de Gaulle considered that his stated objective was the right one; his entire diplomatic effort towards the West would therefore remain focused, in its initial phase, along this dual tripartite and transatlantic orientation, which the context, from 1958 to 1961, seemed to validate. The crises of the summer of 1958 in both the Middle and Far East strengthened de Gaulle's intentions: in July, London and Washington carried out a military operation in Jordan and Lebanon for which the United States used one of their bases in France without consulting French authorities; and in August, the United States – again without consulting their allies – responded to the resumption of hostilities between mainland China and Taiwan over the islands of Quemoy and Matsu by military escalation in the straits of Formosa, leading to a crisis that, as a result of the policy of 'brinkmanship' of US Secretary of State John Foster Dulles, took on a potential nuclear dimension.

These two crises allowed de Gaulle to measure the true weakness of the French position in comparison to his Anglo-American partners and, at the same time, to demand greater influence over Western decisions, as witnessed by the memorandum issued the following month. However, it was above all the second Berlin crisis (1958–1961) that allowed the French president to demonstrate the importance of solidarity between France, the United States and the United Kingdom in an affair that not only involved all three directly through their joint responsibilities regarding Germany and its former capital, but also concerned Western security more generally. This accounts for the intransigent line taken by de Gaulle from the outset in response to the ultimatum issued on 27 November 1958 by the Soviet Premier Nikita Khrushchev, which demanded that the Western powers agree to change the status of the former capital of the Reich and give up their prerogatives and military presence in Berlin.

This intransigence would be maintained by de Gaulle over all three years of the crisis and would be illustrated at the Paris summit of May 1960 (between the United States, France, the United Kingdom and the Soviet Union) by the unconditional support that he gave Eisenhower when confronted by Khrushchev following the interception of an American U2 spy plane over the USSR. In 1961, however, during the final phase of the crisis, which would culminate in August with the building of the Berlin Wall, he was alarmed by the attitude of the new US president, John F. Kennedy: since his arrival in the White House in January, Kennedy in de Gaulle's eyes had indeed been veering between the willingness to make a show of strength and the desire to open up dialogue with the USSR. Generally speaking, Western cohesion, of which de Gaulle was the main champion in this period of mounting East-West tensions, was more often than not under great pressure in the early years of his presidency. Elsewhere in the world, other events were dividing the Western powers, in particular France and the United States: as well as the Algerian affair, already referred to above, the two countries also clashed over the crises in the Congo (1960), where the French president was outraged by the intervention of the UN and the lack of solidarity between the Western powers, and Laos (1961), which was at risk of being drawn into the Vietnamese conflict, and whose neutrality de Gaulle urged Kennedy to respect. These situations all strengthened de Gaulle's belief in his tripartite scheme, along with his desire to achieve closer cooperation between the Western powers – although at the same time he remained acutely conscious of the difficulties involved in this.

## Strategic Issues

Nuclear relations between the major Western countries in this period confirm this sense of division. This was the case, first of all, from a strategic point of view. The launch of the Soviet satellite Sputnik in October 1957 – indicating that the USSR had mastered the rocket technology necessary for the development of intercontinental ballistic missiles – raised new fears regarding the future of the extended US nuclear deterrent, fears that had first appeared in the wake of the Suez crisis: how could one be sure that US nuclear reprisals would actually take place in the event of Soviet aggression in Europe if the USSR was in return capable of inflicting enormous destruction on US territory? In the United States, similar questions led a number of experts and some officials to consider a change of strategy towards a more 'flexible' response and, consequently, a lesser reliance on nuclear weapons as far as the defence of Europe was concerned. This was a worrying prospect for Europeans, who saw in this a potential weakening of the US security guarantee; the 1961 coming to power of the Kennedy administration, who right from the start were committed to a review of strategy along these lines, did little to reassure them.

Maintaining a strategic consensus between the Big Three Western powers, a major concern for de Gaulle, was also complicated by the problem of nuclear cooperation. While de Gaulle, as we have seen, was outraged at the fact that the United States was refusing France the assistance that it was now giving the United Kingdom in this area, he nonetheless had no intention of putting himself in a position of supplicant and ruled out making any concessions regarding the independence of France's future nuclear force as a price for potential US help. The United States, meanwhile, was wary of encouraging proliferation and thus stuck to a highly restrictive policy, despite being tempted from time to time to grant limited and conditional assistance to France in nuclear matters in the hope of keeping the future French *force de frappe* (nuclear strike force) within the NATO fold. The several U-turns performed by the Eisenhower and Kennedy administrations on this subject merely served to confirm in de Gaulle's eyes that France was being treated as a minor partner by the 'Anglo-Saxons', leaving him all the more convinced of the necessity of a strictly national nuclear effort. Even though de Gaulle had since 1958 made cooperation between the Western Big Three the central plank of his foreign policy, all of these elements helped to lay bare the actual limits of this cooperation.

## Towards a New Policy

While the General had, in the first instance, entertained few illusions regarding the likelihood of his memorandum of September 1958 achieving any real success, he had nevertheless continued to proclaim his desire to bring the Eisenhower and latterly the Kennedy administrations around to his idea for a new setup of the Western alliance, which was made necessary, as he saw it, by a changed strategic context; the successive attempts until 1961 to relaunch the tripartite approach were evidence of this. However, faced with the meagre results of these overtures, de Gaulle – as France's international profile grew and the prospect of a French nuclear capability drew nearer – was increasingly led first to consider, and then give priority to other approaches. In March 1959, France began modifying the terms of its participation in the Alliance with the decision to place its Mediterranean fleet, which had until then been integrated within NATO, back under strict national control. In accordance with the warning given in the memorandum, this was on the one hand a means for de Gaulle to react to the Anglo-Americans' reluctance to act upon his tripartite proposals, but also a way of registering his hostility to the NATO principle of integration, which he saw as depriving France of its freedom of political and strategic action. For these same reasons, he refused to allow US tactical atomic weapons to be based in France, as the United States was unwilling to give him the degree of control over these that he demanded, leading to the withdrawal from France of 200 US bomber aircraft. Other decisions followed: the refusal, in 1960, to include French air defences within the integrated air defence system put in place by NATO; and the veto, announced by de Gaulle in autumn 1961, in the wake of the Berlin crisis, on an increase of the US military presence in France. At the same time, the General was laying the foundations for a general reform of the organization of the nation's defences that was made necessary, in his view, by the dual prospect of the end of the Algerian conflict and the entry into operational service of France's nuclear strike force: 'The defence of France', he proclaimed to the *École militaire* in Paris on 3 November 1959, 'must be French.' The Fourth Republic had built up a sprawling military orientated towards counter-insurgency operations in distant theatres; the military policy of the Fifth Republic henceforth would be based on a more tightly focused force centred on the nuclear deterrent, which would allow France to once again become a major Western military power in Europe. The foundations of what amounted to a strategic revolution, one that would completely overturn a military institution left deeply marked, not only in terms of its organization, but also psychologically and politically, by the experience of the colonial conflicts, would be laid in 1959 with the *ordonnance portant organisation générale de la défense nationale* ('Decree relating to the general organization of national defence'), and in 1960 with the *loi-programme en matière militaire pour la période 1960–1965* ('Military planning act for the period 1960–1965').

## Relaunching Franco-German Relations

In parallel with this, de Gaulle now began concentrating on relations between Paris and Bonn, thus initiating a major reorientation of France's foreign policy with respect to Europe. Bonn had initially feared that the return of the General might have negative repercussions on Franco-German relations, which had been put back on track after the failure of the EDC and, even more decisively, in the wake of the Suez crisis. The meeting between Adenauer and de Gaulle at the General's private residence in Colombey-les-Deux-Églises on 14 September 1958, during which de Gaulle had reassured his partner of the value that he placed on relations with the FRG, had thus been a pleasant surprise for Bonn. True, the shine would be taken off this by the memorandum of 17 September, as de Gaulle had not let Adenauer in on his new initiative with its major implications for the Alliance, an initiative that in addition seemed to exclude Germany from the club of major Western powers. Yet this affair would have few lasting effects, given that de Gaulle's three-power coordination scheme – rejected by Washington mainly so as not to appear to exclude Bonn from the running of the Alliance's affairs – was having trouble getting off the ground. De Gaulle's tripartite diplomacy, in other words, had not scuppered the ambitious, although still rather vague plans with respect to Franco-German cooperation that he had laid out before Adenauer at Colombey. De Gaulle's intransigent attitude throughout the duration of the Berlin crisis – and this was no doubt one of his aims – played a decisive role in convincing Adenauer of his determination and of the importance of the Paris-Bonn relationship to the security of the FRG. Still, it would not be until the second half of 1960 that things would go beyond the initial overtures made by de Gaulle at Colombey.

By then the situation was ripe for an initiative: on the one hand, de Gaulle, having made a final – and fruitless – attempt to convince Eisenhower of the virtue of tripartitism, now very clearly saw the limits of a diplomacy that had up until this point been entirely focused on the 'Anglo-Saxons'; on the other, Adenauer was increasingly worried by the latter's lack of resolve against Khrushchev in the Berlin affair and was now openly expressing his doubts regarding the future of the US nuclear guarantee against the backdrop of an emerging 'balance of terror'. All the conditions were now fulfilled for a Franco-German rapprochement, the foundations of which would be laid at the meeting between de Gaulle and Adenauer on 29–30 July 1960 at Rambouillet, with the aim of beginning a new phase of the European project.

Admittedly, the parameters of this relaunch of Franco-German relations and European construction as envisaged by de Gaulle and Adenauer were not the same as ten years earlier, in the wake of Robert Schuman's historic declaration, which had paved the way for the creation of the ECSC. Adenauer was now very conscious of de Gaulle's strong reservations regarding the concept of European supranationalism, previously a priority for the European project's founding fathers; yet he could accept this to the extent that de Gaulle's objective was to achieve lasting reconciliation between the two countries and make close Franco-German cooperation the cornerstone of an ambitious European policy. The meeting of summer 1960 thus marked the inflection point between the diplomatic line pursued by de Gaulle for the previous two years that sought to reach a three-power agreement with the 'Anglo-Saxons' and a policy that, against the backdrop of the establishment of the Common Market and the growing power of the Europe of Six, would now emphasize relations with the Federal Republic within a renewed European setup. De Gaulle considered that the European project would henceforth need to display two major characteristics: it would, first of all, have to be a 'Europe of states', in which major decisions could only be taken within a framework of intergovernmental cooperation; while organized, this cooperation would nevertheless respect national sovereignty and would function, as de Gaulle saw it, as an 'umbrella' for the community's existing institutions. It would also need to be a 'European Europe', which is to say an entity capable of concerted political and military action on the world stage – in other words, an independent Europe, particularly with respect to the United States, whose inexorable withdrawal, in de Gaulle's view, it would eventually have to compensate for.

De Gaulle's vision, intergovernmental and European in outlook, thus represented a break both with Monnet's and Schuman's integrationist, Atlantic-focused perspectives and, more generally, with the prevailing ideas at the time of the European project's creation. De Gaulle managed to persuade Adenauer to accept this vision in spite of the personal significance that the experience and ideals of the early years of the European project held for him. All that remained was to convince the four other partners, in particular the 'small' countries (not least the Netherlands and Belgium), which were worried by the prospect of a Franco-German hegemony forming within Europe. De Gaulle invited the Six to a summit in Paris on 10–11 February 1961, resulting in the creation of a commission to study the way forward for European political union; the commission was chaired by a Gaullist diplomat, Christian Fouchet. On 19 October of the same year, France put before its partners a plan for a treaty that would establish the Six as a fully fledged political entity to be known as a 'Union of States'. The 'Fouchet plan' thus became the major issue in European diplomacy and the litmus test for the success of de Gaulle's policy, now firmly focused on Franco-German relations and Europe. Perhaps inevitably, this new focus would, from 1962 onwards, lead to a confrontation with the 'Anglo-Saxons'.

### Notes

1. For a general overview of de Gaulle's foreign policy, see Maurice Vaïsse, *La Grandeur. Politique étrangère du général de Gaulle*, Paris: Fayard, 1997; for a recent re-evaluation, see Christian Nuenlist, Anna Locher and Garret Martin (eds), *Globalizing de Gaulle: International Perspectives on French Foreign Policies (1958–1969)*, Lanham: Scarecrow Press, 2010.

2. See appendix for a table of presidents, prime ministers and foreign ministers under the Fifth Republic.

3. Translator's note: this expression, coined by Jacques Chaban-Delmas in 1959, refers to certain sectors of policy (in particular defence and foreign policy) over which it is generally accepted that the president of the Republic exercises personal authority.

4. Translator's note: created on 27 October 1946, the French Union marked the official end of the French 'Empire' by reclassifying colonies either as part of metropolitan France, as overseas departments or as overseas territories.

5. From the official translation prepared by Dulles and sent to Eisenhower on 25 September, Eisenhower Library, Whitman File. Consultable online: https://history.state.gov/historicaldocuments/frus1958-60v07p2/d45.

Chapter 4

# CHALLENGING THE ESTABLISHED ORDER (1962–1965)

It would take four years to bring a definitive end to the Algerian conflict, which eventually came with the signing of the Évian accords on 18 March 1962 and Algeria's declaration of independence on 3 July. The scorched-earth policy implemented by the Organisation de l'Armée Secrète (OAS, a far right anti-independence organization) quickly made cohabitation between the Algerian population and the European population impossible, and the latter were soon forced to return to France; meanwhile, hopes for Franco-Algerian cooperation following Algeria's independence, which de Gaulle had wanted to be a model for the new relationship between North and South, would be dashed by the intransigence of Algeria's government, in spite of a very accommodating attitude from de Gaulle. As far as the General was concerned, however, by the summer of 1962 the objective had been reached: France was free of its Algerian 'shackles' and able at last to pursue an ambitious international policy. Following the Algerian settlement, de Gaulle was able to put the finishing touches to the consolidation of the Fifth Republic and its institutions. On 28 October 1962 the referendum on the election of the president of the Republic by popular vote with universal suffrage was won, and on 18 and 25 November 1962 the parliamentary elections gave a solid Gaullist majority to the government of Georges Pompidou, Michel Debré's successor as prime minister, consigning the old party system to the past. The Fifth Republic was now firmly set upon its institutional foundations.

Thus strengthened, the new presidential system, combined with de Gaulle's aura, created unprecedented new possibilities for the expression of France's foreign policy; 1962, therefore, truly was a 'decisive year'.[1] Brimming with confidence after his consolidation of the country's institutions, de Gaulle embarked upon a new phase in French foreign policy. As well as seeking to re-establish France's 'rank', this new approach was characterized by a readiness to challenge the established international order, first within the Western grouping, and subsequently at the level of East-West relations, where de Gaulle sought to shake up the bloc system. This policy would very quickly lead to a showdown with the dominant power.

## 1962, a Decisive Year

The year 1962 was a decisive one not only for French policy but for the entire international system. Between the Berlin crisis, which reached its peak following the construction of the Wall in August 1961, and the Cuban missile crisis in October 1962, the Cold War went through its most dangerous stages. In the aftermath of this critical period, which had seen an unprecedented risk of direct confrontation between the two superpowers, the rules of the bipolar game were lastingly confirmed. In this context, two issues dominated relations between the Western powers and were of paramount concern for de Gaulle: the European question and the nuclear question; these two issues were becoming increasingly linked, for they jointly impacted on relations between Europe and the United States. Let us first examine the European question.

During the Berlin crisis, which continued throughout 1961, the policy of the US administration towards the USSR would swing markedly between the temptations of escalation and the desire to reach an accommodation, as illustrated by the meeting between Kennedy and Khrushchev in Vienna on 3 and 4 June. This inconsistency, in de Gaulle's eyes, confirmed the need to build a western Europe possessing political and military autonomy, and therefore capable of influencing US choices. This, for him, was the main objective of the Fouchet plan, under discussion by the Six since the autumn of 1961. Yet while Bonn, Rome and Luxembourg were open to this Gaullist vision, negotiations soon stalled due to reservations in Brussels and The Hague, where there was concern that the Fouchet plan not only went against the integrationist approach in European construction, but would also undermine NATO's primacy in European defence. In spite of the concessions made by the French at the end of 1961 on both these points, the unyielding Belgian and Dutch positions led the French president to harden his own stance in January 1962. Anxious to clarify the Fouchet scheme, which he thought had become diluted by a long series of modifications, he now wanted to redefine it along the lines of his own notions of a 'Europe of States' and a 'European' Europe. This formed the basis of the 'second' Fouchet plan, in which the intergovernmental nature of the European project was emphasized, while references to links with NATO were removed.

De Gaulle's objective was not to provoke a split with his partners but rather to resolve fundamental ambiguities that, as he saw it, weakened the project for political union being discussed by the Six. In the weeks that followed, French diplomacy seemed ready to make concessions, in particular over the question of how the future European defence system would fit in with NATO's role. After his meetings with Adenauer in February and with Italian Prime Minister Amintore Fanfani at the beginning of April, compromise still seemed possible. However, on 17 April 1962, negotiations between the Six ended in failure. The Belgian and Dutch foreign ministers, Paul-Henri Spaak and Joseph Luns, dug in their heels over the question of the European community. Brussels and The Hague now insisted that no progress could be made until the Six had resolved the question of UK membership in the Common Market, for which London had applied in the summer of 1961 following a historic shift in UK policy towards Europe achieved by Macmillan. The United Kingdom's candidacy had now become the major issue for the European project.

As far as the French president was concerned, the failure of the Fouchet plan had at least clarified the situation. De Gaulle pointed to the contradiction inherent in Spaak and Luns's position, which simultaneously demanded that a European community with a strong supranational character be maintained, yet also called for the participation of the United Kingdom, who was vehemently opposed to this integrationist vision of Europe. This contradiction, as he saw, merely hid the real motives of countries like Belgium and the Netherlands, namely to ensure that western Europe would remain in any case closely linked to, if not dependent upon, the United States. This could be guaranteed either by UK participation in the building of Europe (given that London remained firmly attached to the 'special relationship' with Washington) or by the retention of a community-based, even federal vision in preference to the intergovernmental model that, according to de Gaulle, was the only approach that would enable an autonomous European political entity to make its presence felt on the international scene.

It was against this backdrop that, in the spring of 1962, relations between Gaullist diplomacy and US policy, which was increasingly hostile to the 'European Europe' sought by de Gaulle, descended into open hostility. De Gaulle's vision, it was feared in Washington, could bring into question the existing status quo within the Atlantic Alliance and consequently jeopardize the pre-eminence of the United States in western Europe. Following the failure of the Fouchet plan on 17 April 1962, de Gaulle decided to raise the stakes. During a press conference on 15 May, he upbraided the proponents of a supranational Europe and denounced what he considered to be their real aim: to keep Europe beholden to the United States. His remarks sowed consternation among European integrationists, and five members of the Pompidou government belonging to the Christian Democrat MRP party resigned in protest. Faced with de Gaulle's hardening attitude, the United States also went on the offensive. This was apparent from the speech given by Kennedy in Philadelphia on 4 July 1962 in which he gave his backing to the pursuit of the European integration project (and UK participation in it), while calling for a close 'partnership' between Europe and the United States as part of a full-fledged Atlantic 'community'. The clash between de Gaulle's *grande ambition* for Europe and Kennedy's 'grand design' was now being played out in the open.

## Nuclear Issues

In this fraught context, nuclear issues were also causing increasing division between the Western powers. In a speech delivered in Athens in May 1962, US Secretary of Defense Robert McNamara outlined the new strategy of 'flexible response' that the Kennedy administration, against the backdrop of a growing 'balance of terror', wanted its allies to accept. The Europeans, however, and chief among them the French, judged this strategy to be contrary to their vital interests insofar as it would raise the 'threshold' for the use of the atomic bomb and therefore contravene the basic logic of deterrence; moreover the French resented what they saw on the part of McNamara as a clumsy dressing-down for their pretensions to nuclear independence. Following Athens, France found itself at the forefront of opposition to the new US strategy. The European issue and the nuclear issue had now become two facets of the same question of transatlantic relations, whose principal stakes involved striking a new balance between maintaining the leadership – and the security guarantees – of the United States and standing up for European interests.

The events of the closing months of 1962 would speed up the development of this dual Euro-American divergence. In spite of its happy outcome thanks to the Kennedy administration's handling of what proved to be the most dangerous American-Soviet confrontation of the Cold War, the October 1962 Cuban missile crisis would deeply influence the development of transatlantic relations. To be sure, de Gaulle had been quick to pledge France's full support to the United States in the face of the Soviet missile threat. However, having been 'informed' rather than 'consulted' by Kennedy, he drew the conclusion that Washington had been unwilling to consult its close allies over how to deal with a major crisis that potentially involved the vital interests of the latter because of its possible repercussions in Europe. France, de Gaulle concluded, would therefore have to persevere with its pursuit of nuclear independence as the keystone of Europe's security in the long term, as the continent could no longer count on unconditional guarantees from the United States. Washington, however, drew the opposite conclusion from the Cuban crisis: as far as the United States was concerned, the danger of nuclear confrontation with the USSR demanded greater centralization of strategic decision-making, which in turn meant limiting the independence of 'third' nuclear powers as much as possible. Accordingly, the aftermath of the Cuban crisis, in late 1962 and early 1963, saw a strong display of US leadership within the Western alliance, a leadership that de Gaulle increasingly saw as evidence of a desire for US hegemony.

At the end of 1962, the moment of truth was also approaching for the issue of European construction, on which the Cuban crisis also had an impact. Under discussion in Brussels, the United Kingdom's bid to join the Common Market now looked increasingly compromised. From a technical point of view, the negotiations had revealed the considerable difficulties raised by the United Kingdom's preferential links with the Commonwealth, which went against the *acquis communautaire* (the accumulated body of European Community obligations and structures), especially in the agricultural domain, seen by the French as a particular priority. In other words, regardless of political and strategic considerations, the United Kingdom's candidacy already looked unlikely to succeed on purely economic grounds. Meanwhile, the events of the closing months of 1962, especially following the Cuban crisis, were pushing France and Germany into closer partnership. Having already decided in the summer to achieve together what the Fouchet plan had called for the six European Community nations to accomplish, de Gaulle and Adenauer both saw the missile crisis and Washington's ensuing attitude as proof of the need to bring the two countries closer together in order to lay the foundations of a Europe that would be politically and strategically independent of the United States.

The meeting between Macmillan and Kennedy in Nassau, in the Bahamas (18–21 December 1962), would bring forward the moment of truth with respect to the nuclear question and, consequently, the issue of Europe as well. Following the abrupt cancellation by the Pentagon of the Skybolt missile, which was to have equipped the Royal Air Force, the United Kingdom's nuclear deterrent, whose credibility by now relied massively on cooperation with the United States, was faced with the prospect of becoming obsolete. At Nassau, Macmillan nevertheless succeeded in obtaining Kennedy's agreement to equip British nuclear submarines with American Polaris missiles as a replacement for Skybolt; London thereby received the guarantee that their national nuclear force would be maintained with assistance from the United States. However, this concession, which had to be wrung out of a US administration that was wary of others retaining an independent deterrent, came at a price: the United Kingdom's nuclear force would henceforth be placed, to a large extent, under the control of the United States. The Nassau agreement had also resulted in the revival of the American project for a multilateral nuclear force (MLF), which had first been put forward by Eisenhower's administration in 1960, and whose aim was to involve allies, in particular the Federal Republic, in taking the decision to use nuclear weapons; the goal was to reassure the Europeans over the validity of the extended US deterrent. But the MLF was also intended to solve once and for all the problem of 'third' nuclear forces, of which Washington was becoming more and more openly mistrustful; hence, under the Nassau agreement, the United Kingdom's nuclear force was to be included in the MLF.

## European Europe versus Atlantic Community

The Nassau agreement precipitated the split between de Gaulle and the 'Anglo-Saxons'. Admittedly, following the meeting in the Bahamas, Kennedy did extend the offer already made to the United Kingdom to the French, thus apparently backtracking on the United States' previous refusal to help France in the nuclear sphere. In de Gaulle's eyes, however, the offer had no real value. France's nuclear programme, he reasoned, was totally independent and now close to delivering an operational nuclear force. Polaris missiles would in any case be of no use without submarines and warheads to fit the missiles, neither of which France was able to produce in the immediate future. Above all, the integration of the French nuclear force within the MLF was ruled out by de Gaulle as it would thereby end up under US control. The General saw the Nassau agreement as further confirmation of the position of strategic dependency in which the United Kingdom now found itself with respect to the United States, in spite of Macmillan's assurances just a few days earlier at Rambouillet that he would maintain the autonomy of the United Kingdom's nuclear force at all costs.

As we have seen, irrespective of Nassau, the decision to block the United Kingdom's application to join the Common Market was probably inevitable, short of rendering the organization meaningless by the large-scale exemptions required to maintain the Commonwealth system. With Nassau, these economic considerations, which already militated against the United Kingdom's candidacy, were compounded by political and strategic considerations that led to the same conclusion: between an integrated nuclear force (like the UK deterrent following the Nassau agreement) and an independent strike force (like the future French deterrent) there was, as Couve de Murville would note, 'all the difference that exists between an Atlantic Europe and a European Europe'.

De Gaulle's announcement of France's double '*non*' to Kennedy's proposal and to the United Kingdom's Common Market application at his press conference of 14 January 1963 was an official acknowledgement of the link that had steadily become established between the nuclear question and the European question. With this announcement, de Gaulle in effect chose to turn his double refusal into an unprecedented challenge to the 'Anglo-Saxons': for Macmillan, this defeat was every bit as dramatic as the U-turn that, two years earlier, had led his government to apply for membership in the European Community; for the Kennedy administration it was a setback to their plan to bring the Alliance under control following the Cuban crisis and a humiliating rejection of Washington's efforts to set up the Atlantic 'partnership' that had become the centrepiece of Kennedy's policy. In France, de Gaulle's press conference, which amplified many of the points from the one he had given on 15 May 1962, led to consternation in Atlanticist and European circles alike. In the rest of Europe the shock wave rippled through the political classes, in particular within the Federal Republic, where hostility to Adenauer's policy, seen as being too close to de Gaulle's views, was growing in strength even among his own party. In the United States, above all, de Gaulle's decision was perceived as an outright declaration of hostility: de Gaulle's double '*non*' was interpreted as nothing short of an attack on US policy towards Europe and evidence of a desire to impose a different concept of transatlantic relations, or even to squeeze the United States out of Europe. This was the background to the battle of wills that would be played out between Paris and Washington in the early months of 1963.

### The Elysée Treaty

In spite of the controversy surrounding the press conference of 14 January and the growing opposition to Adenauer's policy within the Federal Republic, he and de Gaulle, on 22 January 1963, signed a landmark treaty on Franco-German cooperation at the Elysée palace. The culmination of the rapprochement between the two countries that had begun in 1960, it was above all, as stated above, a consequence of the failed Fouchet plan of spring 1962. Calling for close cooperation between Paris and Bonn, particularly in the military sphere, the Elysée Treaty established the Franco-German relationship as the kernel of the projected 'European' Europe.

This further increased existing concerns in Washington, where the treaty was seen as yet another challenge laid down by de Gaulle, whose objective, it was believed, was to make the Federal Republic 'choose' Paris over Washington and create a Franco-German bloc capable of challenging US leadership. In the early months of 1963 the Kennedy administration thus set about neutralizing the new Franco-German entente. The first act occurred when the Bundestag in May 1963 voted a preamble to the law ratifying the Elysée Treaty, a text that restated the Europeanist and Atlanticist orientations of German policy. With the encouragement of Washington and European activists – among them Jean Monnet – the parliamentary majority in Bonn thereby disowned Adenauer by stripping the Franco-German treaty of much of its political substance. In June 1963, hot on the heels of this vote, the US president made a visit to the Federal Republic that was intended to show his hosts the primacy of US-German relations. True, the considerable resonance of this visit with the German public did not surpass the equally remarkable success achieved by de Gaulle during his state visit to the Federal Republic in September 1962; still, Kennedy did manage to leave a lasting impression, as witnessed by the famous phrase '*Ich bin ein Berliner*' pronounced during his trip to Berlin.

Coming on top of this, the replacement in autumn 1963 of Adenauer by the strongly Atlanticist Ludwig Erhard allowed the United States both to re-establish its long-term influence over German politics and to counter the Gaullist effort to create a 'European', Franco-German Europe. De Gaulle could only look on and wait for more favourable times: Franco-German relations, previously so promising, now moved into a phase of relative stagnation, although the inherent validity of the Elysée Treaty would not be brought into question by either party in the years that followed.[2]

While Washington had clearly succeeded in countering his policy, de Gaulle was not prepared to let the United States press home its advantage and impose its vision of an 'Atlantic Community' or, less still, an Atlantic Europe, which would signal the end of his European ambitions. This accounts for his attitude towards the multilateral force, which the United States was now actively promoting: even though de Gaulle (who was convinced that 'nuclear weapons are not for sharing') did not believe that the proposed MLF, if created, would have any real military substance, he still judged the scheme to be politically dangerous, as it would consolidate Europe's perceived dependence on the United States. In addition, the involvement, however minor, of West Germany in the decision to use nuclear weapons was, in his eyes, a dangerous possibility given the likely hostile Soviet reaction. He therefore strove to prevent the MLF from becoming a reality and, in particular, to dissuade the Federal Republic from participating in it. His attitude would pay dividends: when the administration of Lyndon B. Johnson (who succeeded Kennedy following the latter's assassination in November 1963) finally abandoned the project at the end of 1964, their decision was in no small part due to the opposition of de Gaulle's France.

Even though, due to the failure of the Fouchet plan, de Gaulle had not succeeded in imposing his vision of European construction, he was nevertheless determined to contain supranationalism and at the same time defend French interests within the Common Market. A European Community (EC) crisis began to brew up in autumn 1964 when the General threatened to withdraw from the Common Market faced with his partners' reticence regarding the setting-up of the Common Agricultural Policy (CAP), which in his view was an absolute priority (de Gaulle finally got his way at the end of the year). The crisis erupted in earnest in spring 1965, when the president of the EC Commission, Walter Hallstein, used the need to make financial arrangements for the CAP as a pretext to advance his federalist vision by proposing that the Community should have its own fiscal resources, an idea that de Gaulle viewed as unacceptable, if not an outright provocation. As a response, on 30 June 1965 the French government suspended all involvement in the activities of the European Community. Although he did not seek to break up the Common Market, being well aware of the interest France had in its continued existence, de Gaulle intended to use this 'empty chair' strategy as a way of putting an end to what he saw as the 'drift' towards federalism within Community institutions.[3]

## Beyond the Bloc System

With the relative failure of his Franco-German and European ambitions, the nature of de Gaulle's international priorities would steadily change from 1964–1965 onwards. The questioning of the West-West established order now gave way to a Gaullist policy that was increasingly focused on the quest for East-West dialogue and, beyond this, the promotion of France's influence in the Third World. As France steadily consolidated its economic prosperity and re-established its international prestige, de Gaulle's diplomacy developed a new grand ambition: to go beyond the bloc system. To bring the East-West status quo into question, to loosen the bonds of the bipolar game and release Europe from the grasp of both blocs – in short, to overcome 'Yalta': these were the new objectives of a grand policy that was not solely about affirming France's 'grandeur' or 'rank' in a narrow sense, but was instead part of what Stanley Hoffmann has eloquently termed a 'global revisionism' that aimed to challenge the basic rules of the bipolar international system.[4] The Cuban crisis and its fallout had revealed the new risk now faced by the Europeans, namely that the two superpowers, as partners/adversaries in the 'balance of terror', would strike a deal to perpetuate their grip over the old continent on the grounds of strategic stability. The Partial Test Ban treaty signed in Moscow in August 1963 was confirmation in de Gaulle's eyes that Moscow and Washington were creating the conditions for a new 'Yalta' based on the emerging nuclear parity between the two superpowers. France would thus have to take the lead in opening up relations with the East if Europe was to avoid the consequences of an exclusively American-Soviet understanding.

The circumstances seemed favourable. The ousting of Khrushchev in 1964 marked the end of a relatively adventurist period in Soviet policy, thus offering the prospect of more stable relations with the USSR. At the same time, there was a glimmer of hope that the popular democracies in eastern Europe might be able to assert themselves more strongly in relation to Moscow, as shown by the policy of 'independence' followed by Nicolae Ceausescu's Romania. Overall, the bonds of the bipolar system seemed likely to loosen. From 1964, de Gaulle thus set about intensifying bilateral relations with the eastern bloc countries, beginning with the USSR, to which Minister of the Economy Valéry Giscard d'Estaing made an important visit in January of that year. De Gaulle hoped to find new markets for French exports and also take the opportunity to show off France's technological prowess and thus bolster the country's international standing. The March 1965 agreement to supply the French SECAM colour television system to Moscow, who had chosen it in preference to the German PAL, was a promising start in this respect.[5]

## Détente, Entente and Cooperation

De Gaulle, however, had bigger plans. By taking a pragmatic approach to improving East-West relations, he sought to establish the conditions needed for 'détente', 'entente' and 'cooperation'. The French president would present the broad outlines of this ambitious vision on 4 February 1965 during a press conference held twenty years to the day after the Yalta conference, which de Gaulle had always – no doubt taking a degree of historical liberty – seen as the quintessential symbol of the 'carving-up' of Europe. Denouncing the closed logic of confrontation that had prevailed for two decades between the blocs, the General proposed to go beyond it in order to put an end to the division of the old continent and promote the emergence of an undivided Europe stretching 'from the Atlantic to the Urals'. In addition to this, he set out his idea of how such a context might potentially offer a definitive solution to the German question, hitherto kept in deadlock by the very nature of the bloc system. As early as 1959, de Gaulle had referred to German reunification as the 'normal destiny of the German people' and enunciated the necessary preconditions, in particular Germany's final renunciation of nuclear weapons and recognition of its borders (first and foremost the Polish border). In his February 1965 press conference, he went on to outline a scheme: a pragmatic and gradual rapprochement between the two Germanys within a renewed pan-European framework as well as a continued European project would, he declared, make it possible, in the long term, to envisage Germany returning to a form of unity with the agreement of neighbouring countries:

> It is clear that any real peace, and by necessity any fruitful relations between West and East, will be impossible to establish so long as an anomalous situation persists in Germany, with all the concerns this raises and the challenges it sets. It is no less obvious that, short of going to war so that one side or the other might impose its solution, and mindful of the reasons for constantly bringing this problem before the conscience of the world's nations, this same problem will not be resolved through a confrontation between the ideologies and forces belonging to the two camps that face each other across the world today. What needs to be done can only possibly be achieved, one day, through the agreement and concerted action of peoples, who have always been, are now and will remain above all concerned with the destiny of their German neighbour, that is to say, the peoples of Europe. That they should seek first to examine together, then to resolve in concert, and finally to guarantee jointly the solution to a question that belongs essentially to their continent: this is the only path allowing Europe to rise again, the only bond that would allow the continent to remain in a state of balance, peace and cooperation from one end to the other of the territory granted it by nature.[6]

This vista opened up a vast new horizon for Gaullist diplomacy, one where the bloc-based order could now be challenged. De Gaulle's ambition was set in a long-term perspective (he spoke of 'a generation') and had a clear rationale (escaping from the 'zero-sum game' between East and West in which Germany found itself caught). It was nevertheless realistic: de Gaulle's ambition to move beyond blocs consisted in recognizing, in practice at least, the current situation in Europe and Germany in order one day to be able to go beyond it. But in so doing de Gaulle found himself at odds with the other Western powers over a number of points: over the German question, as the Gaullist approach argued that détente, followed by entente and cooperation, were the necessary preliminaries to a possible reunification of the country, and not the other way around; and over the East-West problem more generally, insofar as the same approach brought the very notion of a Western bloc into question and, consequently, the whole rationale behind the US strategy of containment.

This new Gaullist challenge, as a result, caused concern both in Bonn, where some – wrongly – suspected the General of in fact wanting to perpetuate the division of Germany by means of an agreement between Paris and Moscow, and in Washington, where many – just as erroneously – saw in his proposed pan-European structure the threat of a security system that would shut the United States out of the old continent.[7] An aggravating factor in Washington's view was that de Gaulle, while pursuing his offensive against the bloc system, was simultaneously leading the charge against US hegemony. Hence at the same press conference de Gaulle attacked the role of the dollar, questioning its value as the international reserve currency, and called for a return to a monetary system based on the gold standard; this 'assault' on one of the symbols of US power was seen as a new affront in the United States. Yet although all were careful to pour scorn on the remedy he suggested, the accuracy of his diagnosis was hardly contested; de Gaulle, moreover, based his argument on the considerable reserves accumulated by the Banque de France (the result of the country's flourishing foreign trade), a situation that contrasted sharply with the growing deterioration in the United States' account balance. De Gaulle's questioning of the established Western order, in other words, was based on a new set of power relations in which the fresh dynamism of Europe contrasted with the United States, the limits of whose power were now becoming visible as a result of its military engagement in Vietnam.

By vigorously condemning US involvement in Southeast Asia – in particular following the escalation launched by the Johnson administration with the bombing of North Vietnam at the start of 1965 – de Gaulle, in fact, added a powerful new card to the diplomatic hand held by France in this part of the world. During Kennedy's presidency, de Gaulle had warned the United States about the dangers of their growing involvement; he could now build on the proven accuracy of his diagnosis (and on France's earlier experience in the war in Indochina) in order to increase France's influence. With de Gaulle's decision to officially recognize the People's Republic of China (PRC) in January 1964 and the establishment of diplomatic relations with Peking, French policy in Asia was interpreted in Washington as a new challenge to the United States. Once more, however, de Gaulle was in fact merely acknowledging a reality (the existence of communist China) that his predecessors, who had considered opening relations with the PRC since 1950, had been unable to recognize openly owing to the Cold War context and, above all, their dependence on Washington (this reality would eventually also dawn on the United States, as would be illustrated some years later by Richard Nixon's trip to China).

Looking beyond Asia to the Third World as a whole, it was on a global scale that de Gaulle now sought to assert the presence of a France whose 'hands were free', as he put it, a France that intended to make 'the liberty, equality and fraternity of peoples' the foundation of 'a different order' in world affairs. It would be hard to give a better description – one that derived from the very motto of the French Republic – of the inherently universalist vision in which de Gaulle, from 1964–1965 onwards, had resolved to set France's international policy. A series of developments, including France's role in the first United Nations Conference on Trade and Development (UNCTAD) in spring 1964, the General's tours of Latin America (the United States' 'backyard') in spring and autumn 1964 and French condemnation of US intervention in the Dominican Republic in spring 1965, all provided de Gaulle with opportunities to assert this new long-term focus of French foreign policy. It would only be a matter of time before the inevitable clash with the dominant power occurred.

## Notes

1. This is the term used by de Gaulle's chief of staff at the Elysée from 1962 to 1967, Étienne Burin des Roziers, *Retour aux sources. 1962, l'année décisive*, Paris: Plon, 1986.

2. See Benedikt Schoenborn, *La Mésentente apprivoisée. De Gaulle et les Allemands (1963–1969)*, Paris: PUF, 2007.

3. See Piers Ludlow, 'From Words to Actions: Reinterpreting de Gaulle's European Policy', in Christian Nuenlist, Anna Locher and Garret Martin (eds), *Globalizing de Gaulle: International Perspectives on French Foreign Policies (1958–1969)*, op. cit.

4. See Stanley Hoffmann, 'De Gaulle et le monde: la scène et la pièce', in *Essais sur la France*, Paris: Seuil, 1974.

5. On this see Marie-Pierre Rey, *La Tentation du rapprochement. France et URSS à l'heure de la détente*, Paris: Publications de la Sorbonne, 1991.

6. Extracts of a press conference given by General de Gaulle, 4 February 1965.

7. On these aspects of the situation, see Frédéric Bozo, 'France, "Gaullism", and the Cold War', in Melvyn P. Leffler and Odd A. Westad (eds), *Cambridge History of the Cold War*, Cambridge: Cambridge University Press, 2010, vol. 2.

# Chapter 5

# The Apogee of de Gaulle's Grand Policy (1966–1969)

On 19 December 1965, de Gaulle was re-elected as president of the Republic. Granted, a second round of voting had to take place, with the left-wing candidate, François Mitterrand, winning more than 45 per cent of the vote: de Gaulle now had to reckon with an opposition that was capable of making its voice heard and marshalling its forces for such elections (Mitterrand, in fact, would adroitly use his having taken de Gaulle to a second ballot as the starting point of his long road to power). The General nevertheless became the first president of the Fifth Republic to be elected by a popular vote with direct universal suffrage; against the backdrop of the increased 'presidentialization' of the new regime, this naturally conferred added legitimacy upon him. De Gaulle's foreign policy could only emerge from this election in strengthened form, although (with the exception of the European crisis, which had lurked in the background of the debates) it had not really been a major campaign issue. The majority of the French people were essentially behind the foreign policy of de Gaulle, who from then on was free to pursue his project of restoring the country's 'rank'. He was able to do so based on France's renewed military and economic strength. The country had been a full nuclear power since the operational deployment of its nuclear deterrent in autumn 1964, and it was now also a leading economic power: France's growth rate (an average of 5.8 per cent per year for the decade) was one of the highest among industrialized nations, and the economy was steadily opening up to the outside world, increasing its competiveness and export figures, intensifying efforts in scientific research and technological development and modernizing its industrial base. De Gaulle, in other words, had the means to pursue the grand policy he desired: a middleweight power, yet one possessing global standing, France was now able to make a different voice heard on a planetary scale.

### 'The End of Subordination'

In the wake of the presidential election, the priority was to resolve the crisis in the European Community. Beyond the question of the CAP and its finances, the pretext for France's 'empty chair', the nub of the crisis concerned the functioning and future development of the Community system. While de Gaulle's aim was not to bring into question the basic premises of the Common Market – and in particular the CAP – from which France benefitted considerably, French diplomacy did seek through the empty chair crisis to steer the European project as a whole in a direction more closely aligned with its own vision: the objective pursued by Paris was indeed to obtain a renegotiation of the adoption of majority voting for Community decisions, a change scheduled under the Rome Treaties to take force on 1 January 1966.

After six months of deadlock between France and its five partners, a way out of the crisis began to emerge in January 1966: Paris would stop asking for the treaties to be modified in order to block majority voting, a demand that the 'Five' found unacceptable; in return, the latter countries would be prepared to recognize that, when it came to the most important decisions, the 'vital interests' of a member-state would justify the need to achieve unanimity. The result was the 'Luxembourg Compromise' (30 January 1966), a common declaration by the Six that did not bring any legal modifications to the existing legislation but brought its spirit more into line with the Gaullist viewpoint. Politically at least, French diplomacy had achieved its goal, namely to neutralize the federal vision of the Community project and block the ambitions of the Commission.

### The 'Withdrawal' from NATO

It had seemed unwise to set off an Atlantic crisis while the European crisis was still ongoing. With the Luxembourg Compromise, however, de Gaulle was now able to take a decision on the question of NATO, as he had resolved to do following his re-election. For several years, as de Gaulle had hinted in his memorandum of September 1958, France had gradually reduced its participation in the Alliance's integrated military and command structures. Faced with what he now saw as an attempt to strengthen US hegemony within the Alliance by further reinforcing military integration (not least through the MLF), de Gaulle's policy took a harder line, at the risk of growing French isolation within NATO. Throughout 1965, the nuclear issue had further widened the gulf between French and US conceptions. France blocked the formal adoption by the Alliance of the strategy of 'flexible response' and opposed Washington's willingness, following the abandonment of the MLF, to create structures for nuclear coordination and planning within NATO, which France considered to be mere window-dressing. Given this context, the United States was expecting a decision from de Gaulle on NATO in the near future; they had even begun preparing for a potential French withdrawal by drawing up plans for the redeployment of US troops stationed in France to other European countries.[1]

It was clear by the beginning of 1966 that a deadlock had been reached. Paris could not tolerate what it perceived as the development of the Alliance towards ever-greater integration and consolidation of US domination; conversely, the allies could not afford to let France block their decisions. The denouement of the crisis seemed close at hand; de Gaulle, though, wanted to retain an element of surprise regarding the exact timing and nature of his decision, which he referred to only in vague terms at a press conference on 21 February. On 7 March, he announced his intentions to Johnson: the end of the integration of French forces still under NATO command as of 1 July 1966 and the departure of all foreign forces based in France by 1 April 1967. Predictable as this decision was, it nevertheless provoked uproar among the rest of the Alliance, first and foremost in the United States, in spite of Johnson's willingness to avoid further confrontation (as he saw it, if the United States was seen to drag its feet now it would only serve de Gaulle's interests). In France, while the decision did not shock public opinion, it did give rise to profound unease in pro-European and Atlanticist circles. France's withdrawal was the subject of a debate in the *Assemblée nationale* in April, during which a motion of censure was proposed by the socialist SFIO and Christian-democrat MRP opposition but overwhelmingly rejected. While Mitterrand took the opportunity to denounce de Gaulle's foreign policy as 'poujadism of universe-wide dimensions',[2] the French communist party did not join in with this condemnation of Gaullist policy with which, fundamentally, it agreed.

De Gaulle's decision above all marked the return of France to a situation of national independence that he had always seen as being hampered by Atlantic integration; in his view, it was essential to guaranteeing the autonomy in decision-making required for a nuclear power. Yet de Gaulle's motives went beyond a simple desire to satisfy national pride through a 'policy of grandeur'. The NATO decision was first and foremost the consequence of his partners' refusal to consider the transformation of the Alliance that he had been demanding for years in order, most importantly, to have the 'European reality' recognized within it. This refusal forced him to take action: for de Gaulle, France's withdrawal would serve to reassert the objective of establishing a west European politico-military autonomy that this move sought in some ways to prefigure. Yet the March 1966 decision was also the logical outcome of France's ongoing policy of challenging the East-West status quo, which meant, first and foremost, challenging the bloc system within the Alliance. Paris hoped that this would lead to similar developments within the Eastern bloc along the lines of a loosening of the grip exerted by the Soviet Union over its sphere of influence. In other words, the decision over NATO, taken a few weeks before de Gaulle's visit to the USSR, formed part of the ambitious East-West policy that the French president now planned to implement.

Remarkably, while the March 1966 decision constituted a political turning point, it did not lead in the military sphere to a major split between France and the Alliance. Although France had left NATO's integrated structure, it still remained a full member of the Alliance. De Gaulle was keen to keep up the existing collaboration with France's main allies as far as European defence was concerned; he gave instructions to this effect to his armed forces chief of staff, General Charles Ailleret, who had the task of negotiating an agreement with the SACEUR, at this time US General Lyman Lemnitzer. The Ailleret-Lemnitzer agreement, which was signed on 27 August 1967, in effect laid the foundations of a new relationship of military 'cooperation' between France and its allies, to replace the former situation of 'integration'. Paradoxically, France's military role in Western defence – namely to act as a reserve force for the NATO armies in the central European zone – in many respects became more important following de Gaulle's decision. To be sure, this was to a large extent obscured, both domestically (for the sake of the sacrosanct Gaullist notion of 'independence') and internationally (as a result of the allies' staunch condemnation of de Gaulle's move). In the final analysis however, withdrawing from NATO's integrated military structure would allow France to find its own place within the Alliance and become a 'satisfied' ally after two decades of frustration.

## Planetary Diplomacy

In spite of this, de Gaulle's visit to the USSR (20–30 June 1966), where he was given a triumphal welcome just weeks after his decision over NATO, inevitably gave rise to fears in Western capitals regarding where this decision would lead. Was the French president trying to reach a deal with the USSR to the detriment not only of the Atlantic Alliance and Western defence interests, but also of Germany and its possible reunification? De Gaulle, now fully committed to his posture of defiance towards the United States and its allies, was certainly happy to raise such fears. Yet the Gaullist vision of 1966 was no longer that of a Franco-Soviet 'alliance de revers' as in 1944. While de Gaulle took the same stance as Moscow in condemning the US escalation in Vietnam and US policy in the Third World more generally, he was not, as Moscow would have liked, willing to precipitate the United States' disengagement from Europe, even though he anticipated this eventuality in the long term; for him, there was no question of pursuing a French policy of de facto neutrality. As regards the German question, while there were points of convergence between France and the USSR with respect to some of its aspects (e.g. borders and nuclear weapons), de Gaulle was not willing to write off German unity by recognizing the German Democratic Republic (the GDR, i.e. East Germany) as the USSR demanded; instead, he defended the principle of German self-determination against the wishes of the Soviet government, who were desperate to have the country's division officially recognized.

There were, then, limits to any Franco-Soviet entente and these became very clear at the time of de Gaulle's visit to the USSR. Still, the new Franco-Soviet relationship was now the centrepiece of the Gaullist policy of détente, entente and cooperation that was reaching its zenith in this period. Following de Gaulle's visit, this policy led to a phase of intensified French engagement with eastern Europe, where France hoped to regain some of the influence it had wielded before the interruption of the war and the ensuing division of Europe. Basing its approach on the policy of challenging the status quo that it had pursued within the Western bloc, France sought to encourage similar developments in the Soviet bloc. De Gaulle's diplomacy thus became very active in the east, particularly towards Poland and Romania, which the French president visited, respectively, in September 1967 and May 1968.

De Gaulle's radical ambition went beyond the borders of the old continent, asserting itself in the Third World as well. Now a major plank of French policy, this Gaullist variant of anti-imperialism stemmed more from a desire to balance the role of the United States, who risked sliding into the 'arrogance of power' (the phrase used by Senator J. William Fulbright), than from the anti-American ideology widely attributed to the General. True, his sometimes virulent rhetoric could (most likely intentionally) leave room for some doubt regarding his underlying motives. In his speech given in Phnom Penh on 1 September 1966, for instance, de Gaulle denounced the 'murderous' illusions of the recourse to force in Vietnam and predicted that the US war machine would fail in the face of the will to self-determination of the Vietnamese people, whose nationalism it would merely serve to inflame (arguably, it was not so much de Gaulle's moral condemnation of the United

States' involvement in Vietnam as his prophecy of their inevitable defeat that struck a sore point at a time when many in the United States had increasing doubts as to the justification for the war and its eventual outcome).

## The Six-Day War

De Gaulle's motives were very similar when it came to his policy in the Middle East at the time of the June 1967 Six-Day War. The war, once again, pitted him against US policy, which he saw as one of unconditional support for Israel. The reasoning behind his advice to the Israelis not to launch a pre-emptive attack following the closure of the Gulf of Aqaba by Nasser lay in his geopolitical analysis of the conflict: Israel, he judged, was not under threat, given its crushing military superiority, while another war in the Middle East could this time lead to a global confrontation involving the United States and the USSR; such a war, at any rate, would only aggravate the Israeli-Arab problem by creating a new Palestinian exodus following Israel's likely conquest of new territory. The ensuing conflict would largely confirm this analysis, with the exception of the predicted superpower confrontation. Hence the line taken by de Gaulle once war effectively broke out in June 1967 and in the aftermath of the conflict: weapons shipments to 'front-line' countries (in other words Israel, whose main arms supplier was France) were suspended and a negotiated solution was to be sought through the four major powers (France, the Soviet Union, the United Kingdom and the United States) on the basis of Resolution 242, which was adopted on 22 November 1967 by the UN Security Council.

To be sure, since the end of the Algerian War, de Gaulle had begun to modify the balance of French policy in the Middle East by seeking to extricate himself from the overly exclusive relationship with Israel that he believed he had inherited from the Fourth Republic, while at the same time trying to regain a foothold in the Arab world. However, his attitude regarding the Six-Day War was not the result of a premeditated plan to woo Arab states, nor did it stem from an anti-Zionist (let alone anti-Semitic) inclination that some accused him of harbouring on account of his famous reference to the Israelis as an 'elite people, sure of themselves and domineering' made during a press conference (27 November 1967). In his view, the rebalancing of French Middle Eastern policy that he had begun several years earlier was not about France severing its links with Israel or disregarding the latter's security, nor was it about seeking Arab friendship at any price. His attitude was instead dictated by his reading of this third Arab-Israeli war and by the overall spirit of his foreign policy, characterized by its rejection of the confrontation between the two blocs and its defiance of the United States. Still, the Six-Day War did mark a new departure for France's policy in the region – one that de Gaulle's successors would take further down the road towards a full-fledged Arab, if not pro-Arab policy.[3]

The year 1967 marked the apogee of de Gaulle's challenge to the established international order and American hegemony. His July speech in Montreal, during which he famously proclaimed the rallying cry '*Vive le Québec libre!*', pushed his argument with the United States into uncharted rhetorical territory, unleashing a storm of fury in the United States and English-speaking Canada. Although probably a spontaneous outburst, this phrase amounted to no less than a historical indictment against the 'Anglo-Saxons'. At the very least, it marked a turning point for the politics of Gaullism; the party's majority had been badly shaken in the hard-fought parliamentary elections of March 1967, with some members, following the example of Valéry Giscard d'Estaing, now denouncing de Gaulle's 'solitary exercise of power'. Meanwhile, although public opinion was still mostly behind de Gaulle in spite of his confrontation with the United States, doubts were beginning to surface regarding certain aspects of his policy, in particular in the Middle East. The support of the French people was no longer unconditional.

## The Shock of 1968

The year 1968 was one of crisis in de Gaulle's foreign policy. The student protests, followed by the political and social unrest that spread to the whole of the country in May, were evidence that the French public were growing tired of the priority that de Gaulle had been giving to foreign policy. While the policy of 'grandeur' had so far contributed to a certain sense of national cohesion, French society was increasingly impatient to enjoy the fruits of economic growth and a fairer distribution of resources, and less impressed by a grand policy for which the public no longer had much appetite. However, the consequences of May 1968 on foreign policy were above all material in nature: the social crisis and its aftermath led to a financial and monetary crisis that undermined the foundations of the very concept of national independence that was so emblematic of Gaullist foreign policy. The crisis of the franc in November 1968, during which US authorities would end up supporting the French currency on the international markets, was a symbol of this new situation. This was a far cry from the days of the 'assault' on the dollar, which had been backed by the considerable monetary reserves built up by the Banque de France.

Yet while de Gaulle now had significantly less room for manoeuvre on the international scene given this troubled situation at home, he was still not prepared to alter his foreign policy. Buoyed up by the strong Gaullist majority achieved in the parliamentary elections of 23 and 30 June 1968, he even sought to reassert its major objectives. The unexpected replacement of Prime Minister Georges Pompidou by Maurice Couve de Murville signalled that de Gaulle intended to bring affairs back under his own control, while the arrival in the Quai d'Orsay of the loyalist Michel Debré indicated a desire to pursue the same foreign policy. A staunch defender of national independence, the job given to Debré was above all to prevent the 'drift' that de Gaulle so feared, in particular with respect to European and Atlantic affairs.

However, the crisis in de Gaulle's foreign policy also stemmed from an international context that was increasingly placing limits upon this policy, especially with respect to East-West relations. The latter had, over the last few months, gone down a different route from the one desired by de Gaulle. True, his main Western partners, in particular the United States and the Germans, were now convinced – in part thanks to his own policy in this respect – of the need for détente with the East: the former expected it to pay dividends in Vietnam and to bring about a process of strategic arms control; and the latter, urged on by Willy Brandt, the social-democrat foreign minister in the grand coalition now in power in Bonn, sought to promote a dialogue with the countries of the East, including the GDR. In many respects, West Germany's emerging *Ostpolitik* shared the same vision as de Gaulle's policy. Yet Washington and Bonn's conversion to détente did not mean that they had come round to the Gaullist vision of overcoming 'Yalta'. Unlike de Gaulle, France's main Western partners wanted to manage East-West relations on a bloc-to-bloc basis. Building on the denunciation of de Gaulle's policies and France's 'withdrawal' from NATO, the United States managed to impose its vision of an active Alliance role in East-West relations. By declaring that East-West dialogue was one of NATO's core missions, the Harmel Report, adopted in December 1967 (and named after Belgian Foreign Minister Pierre Harmel, who had taken the initiative), was clearly underpinned by a bipolar approach to détente that de Gaulle rejected (France, as a result, would only give lukewarm support to it). Meanwhile, French diplomacy could only stand by and watch as Bonn moved rapidly towards a fully fledged *Ostpolitik*, one of the main premises of which was acknowledging the role of military alliances in East-West dialogue. France was at risk of losing its place as the primary interlocutor with the Soviet camp, but also of seeing reinforced the very East-West status quo that de Gaulle's vision had sought to counter.

French diplomacy was also concerned about what it saw as a rush by West Germany to regain its position in eastern Europe, particularly from an economic point of view; in French eyes the German move indeed risked triggering a hardening in the Soviet position if Moscow felt that its influence over the popular democracies was under threat. In contrast to the hopes he had entertained a few years earlier, de Gaulle now realized that under no circumstances was the USSR prepared to loosen its grip over its satellites. During his visit to Poland in 1967, the communist leader Władysław Gomułka had conveyed to him how little room for manoeuvre the Eastern countries actually possessed. The invasion of Czechoslovakia by Warsaw Pact forces on 21 August 1968 brought a shocking confirmation: though he was no less severe in his condemnation of the Soviet move than his Western allies, de Gaulle saw it, first and foremost, as a product of the persistence of the very bloc system that he condemned. Yet the crisis only caused a brief interruption to the process of détente: Moscow was now reassured regarding its ability to maintain its sphere of influence in spite of a reduction in tension, so once what both sides were soon merely calling 'an accident on the road to détente' was safely behind them, the crushing of the 'Prague Spring' paradoxically confirmed the new dynamic in East-West relations. The latter, however, was now taking a different route from that which de Gaulle had advocated.

## Towards Normalization

The last months of de Gaulle's presidency were nevertheless marked by the continued pursuit of the main objectives of his foreign policy, namely challenging the bloc system – an aim he once again restated in September 1968 – and maintaining France's position of independence within the Atlantic Alliance. The French also stayed out of the Nuclear Non-Proliferation Treaty (NPT), signed in July 1968, which they denounced as discriminatory on the grounds that it formally bore the mark of the superpowers' tendency to impose their own rules. (France nevertheless announced that, in practice, it would apply the treaty provisions and refrain from encouraging nuclear proliferation.) Still, France's Western partners noticed a move towards 'normalization' in Gaullist diplomacy, which now seemed less blunt in tone. This was felt particularly strongly in Washington: while the US government was well aware that they would not see a fundamental shift in French policy, they nonetheless wanted to put the Franco-American quarrels of previous years behind them. De Gaulle was receptive to their approaches, as witnessed by the improvement in relations between Paris and Washington in the last months of the Johnson presidency and, even more so, in the wake of Richard Nixon's coming to power in January 1969.

The new US president, who made no secret of his admiration for de Gaulle, was quick to visit Paris in February 1969, and sought to restore normal relations between the two countries. On their side, the French felt that the new president, along with National Security Advisor Henry Kissinger, was a partner for dialogue who understood their policy, without necessarily approving of all of its aspects; the United States, meanwhile, judged that the French, while retaining their own views, in particular over the Atlantic Alliance, were no longer trying to impose them on the other allies. In short, this Franco-American rapprochement, which did not lack a certain warmth, was based on a mutual acceptance of the other side's position.

As far as other matters were concerned, the only new initiative in the closing months of de Gaulle's presidency related to European policy. De Gaulle was keen to relaunch the idea of a political Europe that had been sidelined since the failure of the Fouchet plan; following the renewed French veto that he had placed on a fresh UK application to join the European Community in May 1967, despite its having been actively supported by the Five, he was also conscious of the difficulty he would have in closing the door permanently to the United Kingdom. In February 1969, using UK Ambassador Christopher Soames as an intermediary, de Gaulle sent out discreet feelers to London regarding the idea of a relaunch of the Europe project based on a four-way entente (France, the United Kingdom, the Federal Republic of Germany, Italy). Yet de Gaulle's initiative was soon torpedoed by the Foreign Office, who thus got their 'revenge' for the two vetoes placed by de Gaulle on the United Kingdom's candidacy.

With the exception of this episode, the last months of de Gaulle's diplomacy were characterized by continuity. When the General resigned on 29 April 1969, following a lost referendum on regionalization on which he had staked his political career, France's foreign policy consisted essentially in defending the achievements of Gaullist policy in the face of an established East-West order that was proving to be durable. For the next twenty years, the persistence of that order would remain the defining problem faced by French foreign policy, increasingly torn apart as it was between its denunciation of the status quo and its accommodation to it.

## Notes

1. See Frédéric Bozo, *Two Strategies for Europe: De Gaulle, the United States, and the Atlantic Alliance, 1958–1969*, Lanham, MD: Rowman & Littlefield, 2001; and 'Chronique d'une décision annoncée: le retrait de l'organisation militaire (1965–1967)', in Maurice Vaïsse, Pierre Melandri and Frédéric Bozo (eds), *La France et l'OTAN (1949–1996)*, Brussels: Complexe, 1996.

2. Translator's note: Mitterrand's disparaging reference concerned Pierre Poujade, a populist politician whose isolationist views had won him some support under the Fourth Republic.

3. See the still perfectly valid analysis provided by Samy Cohen, *De Gaulle, les gaullistes et Israël*, Paris: Moreau, 1974.

# Part III

# MANAGING DE GAULLE'S LEGACY
# (1969–1981)

# Chapter 6

# OPTING FOR CONTINUITY (1969–1974)

De Gaulle's voluntary departure in spring 1969 ended a period of more than a quarter of a century during which his actions (or his opinions) had dominated the nation's public life, and it raised questions as to what would become of his legacy. As none of the possible candidates to succeed him possessed his historical stature, the General's retirement necessarily raised the issue of the prolongation – or possibly the abandonment – of his work. While the imprint left by de Gaulle seemed profound, there was no guarantee that it would prove lasting; a return to the institutional practices and diplomatic orientations of the past, perhaps encouraged by developments in internal politics, could not be ruled out. The outcome of the spring 1969 presidential election would thus have a significant bearing on the future evolution of the Fifth Republic, both as regards its political structure and its foreign policy.

It quickly became clear, however, that continuity would prevail. On his election as president of the Republic in June 1969, having beaten the centrist candidate Alain Poher, who in many ways represented the old 'system', Georges Pompidou, de Gaulle's close associate and his prime minister from 1962 to 1968, very much took up the mantle of heir to the General, in spite of the distance that had grown between the two men in the aftermath of the May 1968 crisis. Immediately ruling out any revision of the existing institutions or foreign policy directions, Pompidou would defend the major political choices his predecessor had made and would (if one looks past the inevitable shifts in tone and adaptations) reveal himself to be the continuator – and at times the intransigent defender – of de Gaulle's work.

## The European Dynamic

Admittedly, the new president's foreign policy, less abrupt and more open to dialogue, at least contrasted in style with that of his predecessor. Except during the final stages of his illness (he died in April 1974), Pompidou did not, unlike de Gaulle, use confrontation as an instrument of diplomacy. Now deprived of de Gaulle's charisma and prestige, French diplomacy became more concerned with arguing its case rather than simply asserting its position. This said, had the General himself not already toned down the most acerbic aspects of his foreign policy after 1968?

Still, Pompidou's idea of France's role and power in the world was not identical to de Gaulle's. While he, too, was attached to the notion of 'independence', he understood the notion in a more pragmatic sense than his predecessor. To be sure, he accepted the General's legacy in military matters, in particular by pursuing and developing France's nuclear programme. Yet Pompidou – whose presidency coincided with the apogee and the end of the 'Trente Glorieuses', France's thirty years of extraordinary postwar growth – believed that the pursuit of a grand policy abroad could not simply be built upon a narrow, almost regal vision of power: it would also, in his eyes, require the strengthening of the nation's economic and social foundations, which the crises of 1968 had revealed to be shaky. The surprise devaluation of the franc in August 1969 was, in Pompidou's view, a necessary precondition; as the old economic order fell apart and the dynamics of international rivalry took over in this area, his experience and personality would lead him to give priority to economic and monetary issues – without neglecting all the others, though.

This, at least to some extent, explains the only real difference between de Gaulle and Pompidou, which was discernible in their policy concerning European construction. While in the eyes of de Gaulle, the latter was primarily a means of asserting France's 'rank', for Pompidou it was the condition upon which the country's power was predicated, especially when faced with a Germany whose growing political power, particularly with respect to East-West relations, was increasingly bolstered by economic dynamism. Pompidou, therefore, believed that it was necessary to launch a new phase of European construction. De Gaulle, as we have seen, had grown conscious in the latter stages of his presidency of France's isolation within the community of Six; for Pompidou, France's negative attitude with respect to the major EEC issues – in particular the United Kingdom's membership – was quite simply no longer tenable in 1969. Having in part owed his election victory to his wooing of centrists, to whom he had made assurances in this respect, Pompidou formed an openly pro-European government. With Jacques Chaban-Delmas as prime minister and Maurice Schumann at the

Quai d'Orsay, both of whom were pro-European Gaullists, Pompidou set out to implement an ambitious yet pragmatic policy aiming to put the European project back on track. This policy would, between 1969 and 1972, achieve an undeniable degree of success, if only in comparison with the deadlock of the preceding period.

## The Relaunch of the European Project

With the arrival of Pompidou, European construction once again became a priority, first and foremost in its political dimension, upon which the project needed, in his eyes, to refocus its attention. As expected, the new president acted quickly to remove the veto that de Gaulle had twice placed on the United Kingdom's candidacy. Admittedly, it would be a mistake to exaggerate the extent to which this initial action constituted a clear break with the past: de Gaulle himself had become convinced in the closing stages of his presidency that the United Kingdom would, sooner or later, have to join in with the European project, a project that would, at the same time, need to prioritize its political objectives. Like de Gaulle, Pompidou saw the United Kingdom's involvement as an insurance policy against the EEC's drift towards supranationalism, which he wanted to counter.[1]

The end of France's opposition to UK entry into the EEC, hitherto a major bone of contention with the Five, was a prerequisite to the relaunch desired by Pompidou. With an eye on the summit of the Six that he had called for (it would take place in The Hague on 1–2 December 1969), the new French president made the triptych of 'completion, deepening, and widening' the rallying cry of his European policy. For Pompidou, the 'completion' of the EEC was the sine qua non of any eventual expansion, or 'widening': there could be no question of admitting new members as long as the future of the Common Agricultural Policy and its financing, which had been left hanging in the air since the crisis of 1965–1966, remained undecided. As he had hoped, Pompidou's new openness towards Europe allowed him to gain the support of the Five on the latter point and, on 22 December 1969, agreement was reached over CAP financing, to take effect from 1 January 1970.

Now that 'completion' had been achieved, the path lay open for the negotiation of the 'widening' and 'deepening' of the European Community, which Pompidou envisaged as parallel processes. As far as widening was concerned, preliminary negotiations regarding the membership of Denmark, Ireland, Norway and the United Kingdom opened in Luxembourg on 30 June 1970. On 18 June, the general election in the United Kingdom had brought the Conservatives back into power, led by the pro-European Edward Heath. Heath's excellent relations with Pompidou would henceforth play a crucial role in pushing forward these difficult negotiations, signalling a

Franco-British rapprochement, the like of which had not been seen since the war. When, in spring 1971, the talks were still dragging on – the result of the need to preserve the *acquis communautaire* – and beginning to raise substantive problems (the role of the British pound, the United Kingdom's financial contribution, agricultural imports from New Zealand), face-to-face meetings between Heath and Pompidou in Paris on 20 and 21 May 1971 were able to unblock the situation. On 23 June in Luxembourg, negotiations with the four candidate nations were successfully concluded and, on 22 January 1972, the membership treaties were signed in Brussels. (The Norwegians would later renounce their membership following a referendum.) For Pompidou, the favourable outcome of the United Kingdom's application and the widening of the Community constituted real successes, although they brought with them new risks: while France had regained its leading role in the European project, its future was now dependent on Heath's attitude – and most of all that of his successors – towards Europe.

Deepening, a necessary accompaniment to widening, would prove more difficult. The French president was faced with the same contradictions as his predecessor: how was it possible to reconcile wanting a strong Europe with preserving French independence? Pompidou was in favour of pursuing economic and monetary cooperation as a means of achieving European unification and, at The Hague summit, the principle of an economic and monetary union had been approved. Yet the implementation of this project quickly came up against serious difficulties. Pompidou wanted to keep cooperation in this area on a strictly intergovernmental basis; this led him in spring 1970 to oppose the report written by Luxembourg's Prime Minister Pierre Werner, judging the latter's vision to be excessively integrationist (the report would be shelved in December of that year). The US dollar crisis (Nixon suspended its convertibility into gold on 15 August 1971) and continuing Franco-German monetary disagreements complicated things further. Following the Smithsonian Agreement negotiated between Nixon and Pompidou in Washington on 18 December 1971, a Franco-German rapprochement in March 1972 nevertheless resulted in the European 'snake in the tunnel', which set limits on the fluctuation between EEC currencies and was the first step on what would be a long road towards economic and monetary union.

As far as the project's political dimension was concerned, Pompidou, to be sure, was strongly in favour of the emergence of a European identity and of the Six gaining collective influence on the global stage. He was nonetheless hostile to any supranational 'drift' in this area as well. His vision was directly descended from the notions set out ten years before by de Gaulle in the Fouchet plan, as can be seen from his proposal that regular meetings between European foreign ministers should resume, something that had not happened since 1963. In his view the new system of foreign policy coordination (European Political Cooperation, or EPC), first set out in a report written by the Belgian diplomat Étienne Davignon (adopted on 24 October 1970) and gradually implemented by the Six and then the Nine, ought to be kept both external to the community's formal institutions and strictly intergovernmental. While the new mechanism certainly represented progress, it also revealed how difficult it was to reconcile an actively pro-European stance with the defence of national sovereignty; nevertheless, up until 1973 at least, the Six and then Nine, led by France, Germany and the United Kingdom, would, through EPC, demonstrate an ability to assert a collective position on the international stage that was truly unprecedented.[2]

*Europe and the Superpowers*

Like de Gaulle before him, Pompidou considered that the first area in which a European identity needed to emerge was the continent's relations with the superpowers, first and foremost the United States. The European factor, as had been the case in the previous period, would thus play an important role in Franco-American relations during most of the 1970s. For a while, it was a positive role: the years between 1969 and 1972 were a period of exceptionally fair weather in Franco-American relations. As seen above, the improvement had begun in the closing months of de Gaulle's presidency, before settling in firmly under Pompidou thanks to a favourable international context marked by the emergence of détente in Europe and between the superpowers. Nixon saw this rapprochement as a return to a normal situation after the mis-understandings of the preceding years; he even regarded Pompidou as the spokesman for a Europe that was naturally keen to assert itself on the inter-national scene. For Nixon, the establishment of a 'special relationship' with France (the expression, normally reserved for the United Kingdom, was effectively used by his national security advisor, Henry Kissinger) was an important element in the redefinition of transatlantic relations, which had become inevitable against the backdrop of the continuing war in Vietnam and diminishing US involvement in Europe. In spite of the protests staged during Pompidou's visit to the United States in February 1970 by pro-Israeli campaigners opposed to his policy towards the Arab world, in particular the sale of Mirage aircraft to Libya, the rapprochement between Paris and Washington grew steadily over the first three years of his presidency. Pom-pidou's meeting with Nixon and Kissinger in the Azores (13–14 December 1971) marked one of its high points. By negotiating on behalf of the Six an exit to the monetary crisis triggered by the United States on 15 August (leading soon afterwards to the Smithsonian Agreement), Pompidou acted as Europe's leader, however fragile the resulting compromise may have been.

The most remarkable feature of the Franco-American rapprochement was arguably the shift that then took place in the attitude of the United States towards France's nuclear force, which had long been the major bone of contention between the two countries, along with monetary issues. Cooperation in this area was first proposed by Washington in the utmost secrecy in May 1971; the US offer having been taken up with interest, if cautiously, by the French, this cooperation would in the end prove satisfactory to both parties. Although owing to US legislation the procedure remained tightly regulated and the scope limited to certain defined areas, the US nuclear assistance (which would long remain secret though it did not impinge on French nuclear independence) demonstrated the exceptional improvement in relations between the two countries and showed that Washington at last recognized France as a major strategic partner. This, after all, had been de Gaulle's objective all along.[3]

## Consolidating the Legacy

Continuity was also visible in other aspects of Pompidou's diplomacy, where de Gaulle's legacy was further consolidated. This was certainly the case as far as East-West relations were concerned. The president was keen to develop Franco-Soviet relations, which he saw as essential to France's international standing and, to some extent, to its security. Admittedly there were, once again, some differences in approach compared to his predecessor: while Pompidou wanted to pursue the rapprochement initiated by de Gaulle, at the same time he was rather more wary with respect to a USSR that was now displaying all the characteristics of a superpower, particularly in the strategic domain where, as the 1970s went on, it would achieve parity with the United States. Franco-Soviet relations nevertheless intensified, assisted by the good relationship between Pompidou and Leonid Brezhnev, who exchanged visits on a more-or-less yearly basis. The convergence between their views on major international questions (e.g. the Middle East and Vietnam) gave real substance to the dialogue between Paris and Moscow; this dialogue was now a central feature of French diplomacy, which was eager to prevent the United States and West Germany from exercising sole control over the process of détente with the USSR. However, while Pompidou was prepared to give Franco-Soviet relations greater political weight than de Gaulle had been, he also wanted to make the limits of this process clear. Hence, although the protocol signed during his October 1970 Moscow visit established 'political cooperation' between the two states by making provision for regular meetings between their foreign ministers, Pompidou refused to sign a 'treaty of friendship' as proposed by the USSR; he did not wish to appear to lag behind the FRG in this area (Bonn had signed an important treaty with Moscow in August 1970).

On a more fundamental level, France and the USSR were far from sharing the same understanding of détente. To be sure, in a clear departure from de Gaulle's position, Pompidou was sceptical of the notion of a Europe 'from the Atlantic to the Urals', the limits of which had been shown by the Czechoslovakian crisis of 1968, and he judged that the process of détente should be progressive; yet like de Gaulle, he rejected any approach that might lead to further consolidation of the bloc system. The USSR, by contrast, was now actively seeking a form of international recognition of the European status quo. So while Pompidou in October 1969 had accepted the Soviet proposal for a conference on security and cooperation in Europe (CSCE), this was on the condition that it would examine human rights issues as well as cultural exchanges between East and West, not to mention contact between their populations more generally, all of which the French saw as being likely to help loosen the Soviet grip on eastern Europe. Furthermore, whereas Moscow had, from 1971 onwards, accepted the principle of negotiations over mutual and balanced force reductions (MBFR) between the Warsaw Pact and NATO, pressed for by the latter since 1968, Paris remained firmly opposed to these talks, considering that they risked consolidating the two military blocs and threatening France's independent status.

Pompidou's East-West diplomacy occasionally found itself in a difficult situation with respect to the Federal Republic, which, thanks to the context of détente, now had more room for manoeuvre in this sphere. While he supported the policy towards the East followed by Chancellor Willy Brandt (1969–1974) and his advisor Egon Bahr – a policy that contributed to the general move towards détente that he so desired – Pompidou, like his American and British counterparts, kept a close eye on West German initiatives in that realm, which in his view could eventually lead the FRG to loosen its ties with the West, and even begin drifting towards the East in the hope of keeping open the prospect of reunification. Pompidou hoped to keep the FRG's *Ostpolitik* contained within the framework of Franco-German relations and the wider European project and thus to prevent the Germans from going it alone in their relations with the East. Hence his staunch defence of the four-power prerogatives over Germany and Berlin (which a worried Quai d'Orsay saw as having been neglected in the 1970 treaty between the USSR and the Federal Republic), leading Paris to insist that the four powers' rights be respected as part of the negotiations over the status of Berlin, which resulted in the quadripartite agreement of 3 September 1971.[4]

## The Middle East

Faced with the high stakes involved in the Middle East, Pompidou's attitude was essentially a continuation of the policy of balance adopted by de Gaulle. While attentive to the views of the Arab world, he had no intention of breaking with Israel; at the beginning of his presidency, he even seemed open to the idea of warmer Franco-Israeli relations. The 'Boats of Cherbourg' affair of December 1969 (in which the Israelis spirited away five French-built missile boats ordered prior to the Six-Day War) had only limited consequences for bilateral relations; although officially the arms embargo still held, France secretly continued to supply spare parts for Israel's Mirage jets. Yet in the years that followed Israel became increasingly unhappy with Pompidou's approach to the Arab-Israeli problem, leading to increasingly strained relations between the two countries. Pompidou, like de Gaulle, was anxious to avoid the bipolarization of the Arab-Israeli conflict; his priority was for the 'Big Four' (United States, USSR, France, United Kingdom) to hold talks on this issue, talks that effectively began in early 1969 – in spite of Washington's reluctance – and dragged on fruitlessly until September 1971. In contrast to US policy, French diplomacy stressed the need for a 'global' solution based on a strict interpretation of UN Security Council Resolution 242 and Israel's return to its pre-1967 borders. Paris also strove to win the Six over to the French approach in the context of the nascent EPC (for which the Middle East, along with East-West relations, represented an area of prime importance), finally persuading them to sign a joint document in May 1971. Yet the document hardly concealed the lack of substantive unity among the Six, thus increasing Pompidou's scepticism as to Europe's ability to become a fully fledged international actor, particularly in the Middle East.

In parallel with this, an 'Arab policy', such as de Gaulle had only roughly sketched out in his time, was taking shape under Pompidou, who was pushed in this direction by some of his advisors, including the Elysée's general secretary, Michel Jobert, as well as certain pro-Arab personalities such as Philippe de Saint-Robert. France under Pompidou was shoring up its positions in relation to the Arab states of the Middle East, capitalizing on the prestige gained from de Gaulle's attitude in 1967. This policy was focused in particular on a country that had broken away from UK influence, namely Iraq, whose vice-president, Saddam Hussein, made an official visit to France in June 1972; France thus managed to maintain its oil interests in the country in spite of the nationalizations announced by Baghdad. The French also began looking towards the Gulf monarchies, in particular Saudi Arabia, with King Faisal making a trip to Paris in May 1973. This developing French policy married the defence of material interests (e.g. oil supply and arms sales) with aspirations to a major political role in the region; these aspirations were based on the idea that France, thanks to its unique, independent position, could offer Arab countries like Iraq an alternative to exclusive alignment with one of the superpowers.[5]

Lastly, Pompidou was convinced of the need for a grand Mediterranean policy that would allow France to renew its links with the Maghreb and at the same time implement a policy of cooperation with the Third World in a region that was both geographically close and strategically vital. As the largest power bordering on the Mediterranean, France was not prepared to cede this space to the two superpowers: so went the main argument presented by Paris in justification of its sale in December 1969 of arms to Colonel Muammar Gaddafi's Libya (Paris also insisted that Libya was not, strictly speaking, part of the Middle Eastern 'front-line' states to which its embargo on arms deliveries applied). This decision nevertheless provoked strong reactions abroad, not only (unsurprisingly) in Israel, but also in the United States where, as has already been mentioned, the protests that Pompidou had to confront somewhat marred his official visit in February 1970. In other spots, Pompidou's Mediterranean policy met with mixed success: cooperation with Tunisia improved, as did relations with Morocco, which since 1965 had been strained by the Ben Barka affair (King Hassan II paid an official visit to France in February 1970); relations with Algeria, however, remained tense, owing in particular to a dispute stemming from the nationalization in 1971 of French oil companies' operations in the country.

## 'The Era of Uncertainties'

In contrast to these first three years, the premature end of Pompidou's presidency coincided, to use his own expression, with the beginning of the 'era of uncertainties'.[6] The departure of Chaban-Delmas as prime minister in summer 1972 and his replacement by Pierre Messmer were as much a sign of Pompidou's wish to reassert his authority as they were of a growing political uncertainty exacerbated by his illness – an uncertainty that even the clear majority won by the government in the parliamentary elections of March 1973 did little to dispel. In terms of foreign policy, the last year of Pompidou's truncated term (he died on 2 April 1974) saw a visible hardening of French positions, due not only to developments on the international scene, but also to the influence of the president's own personal role. For while Jobert, whom he appointed as foreign minister in spring 1973, embodied a return to the uncompromising style of French foreign policy seen in the Gaullist era, Pompidou would continue to take full responsibility for running diplomacy right until the very end.

The year 1972 was a turning point in European affairs as well. The disappointing result of the 23 April referendum on enlarging the Community was a political setback for Pompidou (although the 'yes' campaign won 68 per cent of the votes, abstention was running at almost 40 per cent, meaning that less than a third of the electorate actually voted in favour). It signalled the end of three years of intense activity on the European front, during which the Community had become the major focus of French foreign policy; public opinion now seemed less interested in pursuing the process of integration, especially if this involved a loss of French sovereignty. True, the widening of the Common Market to include Denmark, Ireland and the United Kingdom from 1 January 1973 was now a done deal, but the viability of a Europe of nine member states had yet to be proved.

To be sure, coming three years after The Hague, the Paris summit (19–21 October 1972), which had been prepared in minute detail by Paris, Bonn and London, appeared to have been a great success; all parties involved achieved the results they wanted and seemed to agree on the two ambitious objectives that the Nine had set themselves for the end of the decade, namely to achieve economic and monetary union and to establish a fully fledged European Union. And yet, while this declaration of intent – which caused a sensation following the summit – seemed to suggest that a major step forward had indeed been made in the political dimension of European construction, it was, in a fact, a reflection of the many uncertainties surrounding the latter; Pompidou, for his part, saw the notion of a European Union as having the advantage of being rather vague as to the form – whether federal or confederate – of the future European entity, whose creation he in fact regarded as rather hypothetical. Agreement among the Nine over exactly how European institutions should be strengthened in order to accommodate the widening and deepening of the Community was indeed elusive; France wanted a strictly intergovernmental approach, rejecting any increased role for the Commission or Parliament and opposing any moves to create closer links between EPC and the existing Community institutions.

Meanwhile the European project was beginning to stall in the economic and monetary domain against the backdrop of the dismantling of the Bretton Woods system. The rather half-hearted way in which the United States approached the implementation of the December 1971 Smithsonian Agreement, along with monetary divergence between the European countries, soon threatened European monetary cooperation. The June 1972 exit of the British pound from the recently created 'snake in a tunnel', followed by renewed disagreement between Paris and Bonn in the summer, made the prospect of economic and monetary union seem all the more distant, although it was again referred to at the Paris summit in October. The monetary crisis worsened in the months that followed, leading in February 1973 to a fresh devaluation of the US dollar, followed in March by the floating of the US currency. Forced to support the German recommendation of a joint float of European currencies against the dollar, Pompidou, who was anxious to preserve agreement among the Europeans despite the effects of the dollar crisis, could see just how little room for manoeuvre France possessed; meanwhile, the increasing German monetary preponderance, thrown into light by the failure of Bretton Woods, reflected the FRG's growing economic power and financial health. By making the process of European construction more necessary, but also more difficult than ever, the worldwide monetary (and before long economic) crisis placed France in a conundrum.

### 'The Year of Europe'

In this context, from 1973 onwards the European project once more became a bone of contention between the United States and its allies, leading to a re-emergence of transatlantic misunderstandings and a new deterioration in Franco-American relations. This again hinged on the issue of how to reconcile a strong European identity with keeping a strong transatlantic relationship. Starting in 1973, the United States, having put Vietnam behind them at the Paris Peace Accords in January, sought to regain control over the Atlantic Alliance, whose cohesion in its view was threatened by mounting commercial rivalries and the growing climate of East-West détente. Nixon and Kissinger wanted to reassert American leadership while at the same time ensuring that the emerging European identity would not bring the Atlantic community into question. These were the motives behind Kissinger's sensational speech of 23 April, in which he proposed to make 1973 the 'Year of Europe' and to adopt a new 'Charter' of transatlantic relations.

From the outset, Kissinger's proposal was received with some scepticism, particularly in Paris. At a time when the European countries were struggling to assert their political and economic cohesion, French diplomacy saw the US initiative as an attempt to place a still fragile European identity under US authority. This scepticism was understandable given that US policy was increasingly moving towards unilateralism, particularly in the economic sphere; French scepticism was further encouraged by Kissinger's distinction between the 'regional' interests that he attributed to the Europeans as opposed to the 'global' interests of the United States and by the fact that his initiative could be interpreted as part of the internal political manoeuvring surrounding the Watergate affair. In short, the 'Year of Europe', as seen from Paris, looked suspiciously like a resurgence of the United States' quest for hegemony and, as a result, as a threat to French (and European) political independence.

This accounts for the attitude taken by Pompidou and Jobert when presented with Kissinger's initiative. At the Franco-American summit held in Reykjavik (31 May–1 June 1973), where the atmosphere was very different from what it had been in the Azores a year and a half earlier, Pompidou made his reservations very clear: he showed scepticism regarding the idea of a Euro-Atlantic declaration and he rejected any linkage between the economic and political dimensions of transatlantic relations (which the United States, as part of its policy of 'burden sharing', was seeking to forge in order to obtain commercial concessions in exchange for its continuing military protection of the European continent); and he postponed discussion of the US proposal for a summit between the United States and the Nine until a later date. The French, in fact, had resolved to turn around the whole question of the 'Year of Europe' as it was understood by the Americans: hence Jobert's efforts over the summer of 1973 to obtain a declaration of European identity from his partners as a preliminary step towards redefining transatlantic relations. The United States was surprised and irritated by this unexpected French move, though it was, at the same time, anxious to avoid exacerbating a delicate situation.[7]

Transatlantic relations were not the only source of friction between Paris and Washington. French diplomacy was becoming increasingly concerned by the direction in which détente between Moscow and Washington was heading. Pompidou and Jobert saw it as confirming de Gaulle's fears regarding the Americans' dual propensity (which was not as contradictory as it seemed) on the one hand to disengage from European security and, on the other, to govern it jointly with Moscow. One year after the signing of the Strategic Arms Limitation Treaty in Moscow (SALT, 26 May 1972), which officially enshrined a situation of nuclear parity and codified the balance of terror between the superpowers, the signing of the joint US-USSR agreement on the prevention of nuclear war in San Clemente (22 June 1973) confirmed, in their eyes, this growing tendency for the superpowers to maintain an exclusive dialogue at the expense of European interests. In spite of its rather limited ambit, the San Clemente agreement was used by Paris as an opportunity to denounce the 'condominium' that they claimed the two superpowers were trying to establish, demonstrating the need for Europe to assert itself strategically. Meanwhile, US-Soviet détente and the deepening of German-Soviet relations were increasingly pushing relations between France and the USSR into the background. Now that détente had become the watchword in East-West relations, the relationship between Paris and Moscow no longer seemed so exceptional, even though close contacts were still maintained.

As we have seen, against the backdrop of a triumphant détente, French diplomacy (as was also the case among the FRG's other Western partners, including the United States) kept a close eye on Brandt's *Ostpolitik*. Somewhat paradoxically, the French were also wary about Bonn's Atlanticism; in short, Paris feared any overly pronounced German-Soviet or German-American rapprochement in equal measure, judging both to be prejudicial to the assertion of western European unity. France's policy contained its own share of contradictions: by opposing all aspects of détente that had a 'bloc-to-bloc' character (refusing, for instance, to participate in the Mutual and Balanced Force Reductions [MBFR] talks begun in Vienna in October 1973), France ran the risk both of finding itself marginalized and of being perceived as a defender of the East-West status quo while at the same time continuing to proclaim that it wanted to overcome 'Yalta'. These contradictions were visible in the speech delivered by Jobert in Helsinki on 4 July 1973, at the opening of the Conference on Security and Cooperation in Europe (CSCE), in which he refused to accept Europe being turned into 'a special zone, an open range where external forces can balance each other out':

> We will proclaim, therefore, that the situation in Europe, a legacy of the rivalries of the past, must not deprive any of the states brought together here of their sovereign equality and the rights which come from it, of the inviolability of their borders, or of their protection against any use of force or any interference in their internal affairs. This will not, let us be clear, be a particularly spectacular act, as the public, even more so than us ourselves, believes that these principles go without saying. Reminding ourselves of them will at least prevent states from moving further apart from each other and show them that Europe is not some special zone where international law does not apply fully. For Europe cannot be such a special zone, an open range where external forces can balance each other out, a space given over to these rivalries. Those who think this is the case are mistaken in their analysis, for sooner or later this idea will no longer be tolerated, once the peoples of Europe have understood the danger of remaining passive. Several countries have seen fit to begin negotiations in another capital over arms reduction in Europe [an allusion to the MBFR talks]. I do wish – without any real conviction – that this may be in their interests, as this is not the right way for us to move towards a more real form of security, more truly European and determined by Europe, for it is obvious that it will be defined and controlled from outside.

## The October War

The October 1973 war in the Middle East served as a catalyst for all these tendencies and led to a general stiffening of French policy in the final months of Pompidou's presidency. 'Does trying to get back into one's own home really constitute unprovoked aggression?' Jobert asked two days after the joint Egyptian and Syrian attack against Israel. Jobert's uncompromising position was spurred on by Pompidou himself, who saw the latest Israeli-Arab conflict as merely confirming de Gaulle's analysis of the situation in

1967. Even more than the Six-Day War, the October War would see France pitted against the United States. Paris would, it is true, be prepared to make a show of unity with Washington when the crisis threatened to deteriorate into a confrontation with the USSR. However, the disagreement between them over the subject of the Middle East was deep-seated. Over the coming months, France (but also the United Kingdom) would therefore find itself left out of the various US attempts to achieve a partial resolution of the conflict – none of which French diplomacy approved of in any case – and the country would be barred from taking part in the December 1973 Geneva Conference. All of these developments led the French to redouble their efforts to establish themselves as the primary interlocutors for the Arab world in the face of American policy and pull the other Europeans along with them. As far as Paris was concerned, the October War, which had almost led to a confrontation between the superpowers, had at the end of the day once again revealed their mutual collusion. As had been the case during the Cuban crisis in 1962, Washington, by ordering a nuclear alert during the night of 24–25 October 1973 in order to dissuade the USSR from launching a direct intervention, had taken crucial decisions without consulting their allies. The crisis and its consequences, as a result, only served to reinforce fears of a 'condominium' and to encourage the French to play the European card, as illustrated by the publication by the Nine of a joint declaration on the Middle East on 6 November 1973.

Treated as a 'nonperson', in Jobert's words, Europe was proving more vital than ever. At the WEU assembly on 21 November, the French foreign minister made the case for an autonomous European defence system, something that had up until now been regarded with scepticism by Pompidou. To be sure, the Middle East crisis led to an increased sense of European self-awareness, culminating in the Copenhagen summit (14–15 December 1973), where the Nine issued a 'declaration of identity' and resolved to launch a 'Euro-Arab dialogue'. Yet the crisis also quickly revealed the fragility of this dynamic. Proof of this was provided by Pompidou's failure to persuade his partners to accept holding regular European summits – an idea put forward by Jean Monnet – the first of which would have been the Copenhagen meeting. Above all, the Europeans, whose solidarity was being sorely tested by the OPEC embargo and the ensuing oil crisis, were unable to stand up to US pressure; this was illustrated by the Washington energy conference (11–13 February 1974), during which Jobert, issued with strict instructions by Pompidou, found himself alone, 'betrayed', as he saw it, by his European partners, in the face of the United States' decision to establish a cartel of consumers, which the French regarded as no less than a 'Western bloc' directed against the Arab oil-producing countries.

The French were disillusioned: behind the façade of a Euro-Arab dialogue – which in fact amounted to little more than wishful thinking – the Europeans, they observed, preferred the energy protection offered to them by the United States. By 1973–1974, Pompidou's attitude towards European matters had become characterized by pronounced scepticism, even cynicism; faced with what he saw as a lack of practical means and, especially, of political will on the part of his fellow Europeans, Pompidou's priority was to defend French interests. The floating of the franc, starting on 19 January 1974, was an illustration of this deliberate – and perhaps inevitable – falling back on the 'national' option that the fragmentation of the world order seemed to encourage in all areas. Despite the hopes and ambitions of the years between 1969 and 1972, the pursuit of the European project simply did not appear to be a viable response to this emerging disorder.

This apparent reversion in French foreign policy to a form of prickly Gaullism was as much due to the new international circumstances as it was to the intransigent refusal by Pompidou, now gravely ill and aware that the end was near, to accept any compromise that might in his view jeopardize the future of France's 'rank' and the long-term possibility of a strong Europe. This resulted, in the wake of the Washington energy conference, in a Franco-American confrontation of a degree unprecedented since de Gaulle. It was made all the more bitter by the fact that Franco-American relations had seen spectacular improvement up until 1972–1973, and that, ever since, Pompidou had been left with the impression that protestations from the United States of goodwill towards France and Europe had not translated into action. This impression was likely justified in the nuclear domain, where relations between the two countries were now stalled in spite of the proposal made by Nixon in Reykjavik to widen existing cooperation. When de Gaulle's successor died, then, France was once again alone in defending the idea of a more independent Europe faced with the United States' enduring dominance.

## Notes

1. See Maurice Vaïsse, 'Changement et continuité dans la politique européenne de la France', in Association Georges Pompidou, *Georges Pompidou et l'Europe*, Brussels: Complexe, 1995.

2. On this, see Daniel Möckli, *European Foreign Policy during the Cold War: Heath, Brandt, Pompidou and the Dream of Political Unity*, London: I. B. Tauris, 2009.

3. On this, see Pierre Melandri, 'Aux origines de la coopération nucléaire franco-américaine,' in Maurice Vaïsse (ed.), *La France et l'Atome. Études d'histoire nucléaire*, Brussels: Bruylant, 1994; and Maurice Vaïsse, 'Les "relations spéciales" franco-américaines au temps de Richard Nixon et Georges Pompidou', *Relations internationales* 119 (2004), pp. 345–362.

4. See Georges-Henri Soutou, 'La France et l'accord quadripartite sur Berlin du 3 septembre 1971', *Revue d'histoire diplomatique* 1 (2004), pp. 45–73.

5. See David Styan, *France and Iraq: Oil, Arms and French Policy in the Middle East*, London: I. B. Tauris, 2006.

6. See Éric Roussel, *Pompidou*, Paris: Lattès, 1994.

7. For an analysis of this episode, see Pierre Melandri, 'Une relation très spéciale : la France, les États-Unis et l'année de l'Europe, 1973–1974', in *Georges Pompidou et l'Europe, op. cit.*; and Marc Trachtenberg, 'The French Factor in U. S. Foreign Policy during the Nixon-Pompidou Period (1969–1974)', *Journal of Cold War Studies*, 13: 1 (winter 2011), pp. 4–59.

# Chapter 7

# THE EDUCATION OF A PRESIDENT (1974–1981)

The election of Valéry Giscard d'Estaing in May 1974 once again raised the question of continuity in French foreign policy. To be sure, the first non-Gaullist president of the Fifth Republic was to some extent shaped by his experience of serving under the governments of de Gaulle and Pompidou as economy and finance minister (1962–1966 and 1969–1974). However, by defining himself as 'liberal, centrist and European', Giscard, who attributed his election to a desire for 'renewal' and 'change', appeared set to distinguish himself from his predecessors as far as foreign policy was concerned. Giscard's economic liberalism, tinged with a globalism that was at times almost irenic, seemed a long way from the cold realism from which de Gaulle's vision of international relations derived. His centrism, meanwhile, harked back more to the Fourth Republic than to the Fifth, more to Antoine Pinay than to Georges Pompidou. Finally, Giscard's Europeanist persuasion made him appear closer in outlook to a Jean Monnet than to a Charles de Gaulle (Giscard was, in fact, a member of Monnet's Action Committee for the United States of Europe). In short, Giscard's arrival at the Elysée seemed to signal a period of renewal at the top level of the state and also, consequently, in the key directions of France's foreign policy.

Yet Giscard, during his election campaign, had promised to defend 'the dignity and independence' of France and he would, in effect, reprise the principal policy orientations of his predecessors. Aside from the style and personal touches that 'VGE' brought to foreign policy, his actions in this area would adhere closely to the framework laid out by the founder of the Fifth Republic. Foreign policy-making under Giscard would more than ever reflect presidential pre-eminence, all three occupants of the Quai d'Orsay under his rule having been professional diplomats. By his own admission Giscard's presidency would, as far as foreign policy was concerned, bear

many of the hallmarks of an apprenticeship, thus demonstrating the enduring power of the legacy he had inherited. So, did this president who, in
his own words, had been 'elected at a young age' and thus needed 'to pull
himself up to match the stature of his predecessors', actually succeed in
doing so?[1]

## The Challenges Faced by the West

Marked along its way by the impact of two oil shocks (in 1973 and 1979),
Giscard's seven-year term would, right from the start, play out in a context
of global crisis. When he came to power just after the first oil crisis, the
West remained in a fragile state: against the backdrop of an energy crisis
whose effects were still being felt, low growth, rising inflation, a disinte-
grating international monetary system and the temptations of protection-
ism were challenges faced by all the Western nations. Giscard's arrival in
spring 1974 also coincided with a change in the leadership of the four main
Western countries over the space of a few months: Heath lost the elections
in March, Pompidou died in April, Brandt resigned in May and Nixon's
resignation would come in August, in the wake of the Watergate scandal. In
this context of crisis and changing leadership, Giscard's diplomacy turned
its attention towards the way in which the Western world was organized and
the challenges it faced.

When he looked at the issues confronting the West (issues that to a large
extent justified the global approach to problems that he wanted to promote),
Giscard, from the very start of his presidency – and in contrast to the intransigence shown by his predecessor at the end of his life – wished to present
the image of a man open to solutions arrived at in concert with his partners.
The positions that he had adopted as finance minister in the last months of
Pompidou's presidency had already hinted at this: it was precisely because
Pompidou had considered him too willing to accept compromise that Giscard had not been sent to the Washington Energy Conference in February
1974. Yet while Giscard's diplomacy would indeed be more forthcoming than
that of his predecessor when it came to such questions as energy and the
international monetary system, the principal parameters of French policy in
these key policy areas remained by and large unchanged.

As far as energy policy was concerned, Giscard adopted a more conciliatory style and made concessions towards his Western partners; yet he did
not, in any fundamental way, bring the position inherited from Pompidou
into question. While the creation of the International Energy Agency (IEA)
in November 1974 within the framework of the OECD was a success for
US diplomacy, the United States nonetheless sought to reach an accom-

modation with France over this issue. At the Franco-American Martinique summit (14–16 December 1974), the French president and his US counterpart Gerald Ford reached a compromise: though France did not wish to be a member of the Agency, Paris accepted the European Community's participation in it, and the United States accepted Giscard's idea (suggested in October 1974) of starting a dialogue between exporters, industrialized importers and non-industrialized importers of oil. On monetary issues, by contrast, the French made the majority of the concessions to the United States in the negotiations that were carried out throughout 1975 over the statutes of the International Monetary Fund (IMF), reform of which had become necessary owing to the widespread floating of currencies. While the French would have liked to keep the prospect of a return to a fixed parity system open, they had to accept the reality of floating exchange rates and the end of the Gold Standard (Jamaica Agreement, January 1976).

The West in this period also confronted challenges that were political in nature, whether as a result of Third World activism or of the USSR's increasing involvement on the 'periphery'. In this context, organizing relations between the major Western powers (i.e. the United States, western Europe and Japan, which was now an increasingly influential member of the 'club') was at the top of the list of priorities. This led Giscard – who was eager to establish direct personal contacts between leaders – to launch a major diplomatic initiative in this direction at the Rambouillet summit (15–17 November 1975), which brought together the heads of state or government of the United States, Japan, Germany, France, the United Kingdom and Italy. Even though this new formula for coordination between the Western powers (joined by Canada at the Puerto Rico summit the following year) was unable in the short term to prevent the outcome of the Jamaica talks (unsatisfactory in France's view), it was an undeniable success for Giscard's diplomacy and marked the beginnings of a key institution: the Group of Seven (G7). The strengthening of multilateralism, which Giscard's diplomacy had thus helped to achieve – first and foremost within the Western grouping – was now emerging as one of the major themes of French foreign policy.

## The Birth of the European Council

Strengthening the institutional architecture of the West also involved reinforcing the European project, which was a priority for Giscard's diplomacy from the outset.[2] A convinced pro-European, VGE believed that western Europe needed to assert itself as a decision-making centre alongside the United States and Japan. Like Pompidou, he saw the construction of Europe as a multiplier of French power. Admittedly, he did not place as much emphasis on the United Kingdom's role as his predecessor had done; yet the United Kingdom's whole outlook on Europe had in any case been brought into question with the departure of Heath, ending the close ties built up between Paris and London over the last few years. The return to government of the Labour Party, who sought to renegotiate the terms of the United Kingdom's participation, marked the beginning of a long period of crisis in relations between the United Kingdom and the Community. By contrast, the emphasis placed by Giscard on Franco-German relations would be sustained throughout his seven-year term; based on a very close personal relationship with the new German Chancellor Helmut Schmidt – like Giscard, a former finance minister – this Franco-German priority would, in the years that followed, result in a decisive consolidation of the Paris-Bonn relationship.[3]

Continuity with his predecessors was also in evidence when it came to Giscard's vision of European institutions. While he had no intention of revising or weakening the EC *acquis*, his vision was predominantly inter-governmental; in Giscard's view, only states and their governments possessed the legitimacy required to exercise leadership at a European level. The new French president was nevertheless determined to strengthen and give structure to the EEC: hence the strong institutional element present in the European relaunch that, in close coordination with Schmidt, he undertook and pushed forward at the Paris summit (9–10 December 1974). Reprising the proposal for regular European summit meetings that Pompidou had put forward unsuccessfully in autumn 1973, the Paris conference instituted the European Council at the level of heads of state and government, thus consolidating the Community institutions and the workings of the EPC beneath a single intergovernmental 'hat'. While some concessions were made to a more integrationist approach, these remained limited to the extension of majority voting within the Council (which would rarely be applied), and the election of the European Parliament by direct universal suffrage. Although the latter was deemed unacceptable by the Gaullists, who fought against it, its effects would be slight due to the limited increase in the Parliament's powers that accompanied it. Overall, the decisions taken at the Paris summit, driven by Giscard's diplomacy, achieved a lasting balance between the various European institutions, laying the foundations for future developments.

Further to reinforcing Community institutions, Giscard sought to push forward European integration on the economic and monetary front. Faced with the monetary disorder raging across the globe, Europe in his view had to become a buttress of stability. When the franc, which had rejoined the 'snake in a tunnel' in July 1975, had to leave it once more in March 1976 as a result of inflationary pressures, Giscard wanted to look again at the project for an economic and monetary union. He therefore proposed a system whose scope would be wider than that of the 'snake in the tunnel': the new mechanism in his view should not simply stabilize exchange rates, but actually work towards achieving convergence between Europe's economies. Circumstances at the beginning of Giscard's term were not conducive given the troubled international monetary situation; France and Germany's economic policies, in addition, were moving apart as a result of the economic stimulus measures introduced by Prime Minister Jacques Chirac (1974–1976). Yet things changed with the arrival of the government of Raymond Barre (1976–1981) and the implementation of austerity policies that reassured the Germans and offered the prospect of increased economic convergence between the two countries. The initiative was seized by Giscard and Schmidt in April 1978, leading the following year to the creation of the European Monetary System (EMS), which the Franco-German pairing played a key role in establishing. Although it did not constitute an economic and monetary union in the full sense, the EMS was nevertheless successful insofar as it put Europe back on the path to exchange-rate stability while introducing a new unit of account, the ECU (European Currency Unit). The creation of the EMS rested on a Franco-German compromise: France accepted economic 'rigour' while Germany recognized the need for increased monetary solidarity.[4]

## The Ottawa Declaration

The second half of 1974 saw a noticeable improvement in transatlantic relations, helped by the arrival of a new president in the White House and the changes of leadership in the major European countries, all eager to have closer ties with Washington. As far as Franco-American relations were concerned, Giscard's arrival heralded a spell of fairer weather, as was clearly visible at the Martinique summit in December 1974 where Giscard and Ford, putting aside the arguments of the previous months (in particular the row over energy), inaugurated a much-improved bilateral relationship. There was also a distinct change of tone with regard to defence and security issues, where a desire to lower tensions was manifest on both sides: hence cooperation between France and NATO was celebrated in Martinique as 'an important factor for security in Europe'. The adoption by the Atlantic Alliance in June 1974 of the Ottawa declaration – negotiations over which had been blocked by the convulsion in Franco-American relations during the closing months of Pompidou's presidency – finally put to rest the psychodrama of the 'Year of Europe'; in particular, at Ottawa, the contribution of France's nuclear deterrent to Atlantic defence received recognition for the first time. The following month, Giscard announced a review of French military policy, emphasizing the importance of Franco-American relations in defence matters. Meanwhile, Paris and Washington decided, rather more discreetly, to continue and to widen the nuclear cooperation begun under Nixon and Pompidou.[5]

This desire for closer Franco-American ties in the first phase of Giscard's presidency came as the concept behind France's defence posture was undergoing significant change. Whereas for years nuclear weapons had been France's main priority, Giscard was keen to make up the ground lost in the area of conventional forces. Accordingly, the *loi de programmation militaire* passed by the French parliament in 1976 emphasized the need to strengthen conventional military power and build solidarity between France and its allies. The Valentin-Ferber agreement of July 1974 was an important step in that direction, extending as it did cooperation between France and NATO to the whole of the French 1st Army, and not just the 2nd Corps as the 1967 Ailleret-Lemnitzer agreement had stipulated. In the nuclear domain, too, procedures for coordination in the event of tactical nuclear weapon use were agreed in 1975 between the French armed forces' chief of staff, General Guy Méry, and the SACEUR, General Alexander Haig; meanwhile a review of the French concept of a tactical nuclear 'final warning' (*ultime avertissement*) was undertaken with the aim of making it more compatible with NATO doctrine.

Significant as they were, however, none of these shifts fundamentally brought the major orientations of France's NATO policy into question. In terms of public declarations, France under Giscard was admittedly more concerned with affirming its solidarity with allies (starting with Germany) than it had been in the past, which was seen by some as a departure from the Gaullist doctrine. True also, the possibility of an 'extended sanctuarization' (in other words a widened French nuclear umbrella, mentioned officially in 1976), along with hints of a possible French participation in NATO's 'forward battle', triggered a fierce debate in France. Yet this was primarily due to domestic politics: following Chirac's resignation in August 1976 and the creation of the Rassemblement pour la République (RPR) that September to replace the UDR, the Gaullists increasingly positioned themselves as the protectors of the true Faith against a president they criticised for his supposed 'Atlanticism'. In concrete terms, closer cooperation between France and NATO in no way brought the principle of France's 'autonomy of decision', and the sacrosanct 'non-integration' in effect remained the cornerstone of French alliance policy.[6]

The early days of Giscard's seven-year term coincided with the apogee of détente, as symbolized by the culmination of the Conference on Security and Cooperation in Europe and the signing of the Helsinki Final Act (1 August 1975). From the outset, Giscard sought an understanding with the Soviet Union and made the pursuit of détente a permanent feature of French foreign policy, thus consolidating the legacy of de Gaulle and Pompidou in this area. The new president had a highly personal vision of East-West relations. Having travelled to the USSR in 1964 in his capacity as economy and finance minister, Giscard was convinced that the political antagonism between the two blocs could be overcome through economic exchanges. This conviction caused him to believe that the ideological rivalry between the two blocs could be brought to an end, and, during his visit to the Soviet Union in October 1975, it would even lead him to place a wreath on Lenin's mausoleum, an act that would spark a long controversy. Giscard, in fact, demonstrated a willingness to go further than his predecessors (de Gaulle having been more of a realist, Pompidou less trusting) in pursuing Franco-Soviet understanding. At the Franco-Soviet summit in Rambouillet (4–7 December 1974), he gave Leonid Brezhnev assurances of his commitment to the relationship with Moscow: he confirmed his desire to establish a permanent Franco-Soviet dialogue on the basis of the 1970 protocol (there would be four other summits during his presidency, in 1975, 1977, 1979 and 1980); he accepted the idea that the CSCE final meeting should take place at summit level (something Moscow eagerly wanted), causing the other Western leaders, who were reticent, to follow suit; and, even though this remained one of French diplomacy's main objectives, he assured the Soviet premier that he understood the USSR's 'concerns' regarding the emergence of a European defence system. The tone of Franco-Soviet relations was thus set very early on by Giscard, and it would subsequently change very little.

### France and the South

Relations between North and South were a crucial dimension of the 'global' approach to economic and political problems that Giscard sought to promote. Giscard was convinced that a redefining of relations between industrialized countries and the countries of the Third World following the oil crisis was inevitable and considered that the best way forward was through institutionalized dialogue at summit level rather than through confrontation. Having inherited the policy of openness towards the Third World begun by his predecessors, he believed that France's role was to act as a mediator between the proponents of a system of unconstrained economic liberalism and those who favoured government intervention. After launching the idea of a tripartite dialogue on energy issues in October 1974, Giscard made a considerable personal investment in what would become a plan for a wider North-South conference; and, unlike his main Western partners who were less enthusiastic, he joined the calls for a New International Economic Order (NIEO). His efforts over the following year to convince his main interlocutors in the Third World (Iran, Algeria, Morocco, Zaire) of the project's merits were rewarded in December 1975, when the Conference on International Economic Cooperation (CIEC, often referred to as the 'North-South Conference') opened in Paris. Bringing together eight industrialized nations and nineteen developing nations, it dealt with energy and related issues, such as raw materials, financial problems and development. Launching the conference constituted a success for Giscard's diplomacy; as far as concrete achievements were concerned, however, the picture was mixed. By June 1977, the process begun in 1975 had resulted in little more than a restatement of some vague principles and a set of very real disagreements; by 1978, North-South dialogue had ceased to be a priority for French diplomacy, in spite of the supposed 'trilogue' (between Europe, Africa and the Arab nations) announced in 1979, which was greeted with general scepticism.

The failure of this North-South dialogue and the limited success of French initiatives in this area were symptomatic of the project's inherent contradictions. While the French had been able to provide the NIEO with an institutional framework, they were not able to define what it actually stood for. Faced with the demands of the Third World, France remained, first and foremost, a Western power weakened by the crisis; while perhaps more conscious than its partners of the need to guard against the risk of a North-South split, France was hardly any better prepared than they were for a revolutionary worldwide economic 'new dawn'. In short, France had a North-South diplomacy rather than an actual North-South policy.[7] At any rate, North-South relations, for France, were increasingly embedded in the relationship between the European Community and developing countries; in that framework, France advocated granting assistance to the poorer countries in the ACP zone through a revenue stabilization scheme applying to raw materials exports (implemented by the Lomé Convention of February 1975, followed by Lomé II in October 1979).

### France's 'African Estate'

This left what is routinely referred to as the 'pré carré africain', the former colonial possessions in Africa that France in many ways still regarded as its own 'private estate', and over which it sought to exercise exclusive influence. Giscard's relations with Africa would prove close; it weighed heavily upon his political fate when his image became tarnished by his compromising associations with the 'emperor' of the Republic of Central Africa, Jean-Bedel Bokassa, despite having decided to depose the latter in September 1979 (in Operation Barracuda). Besides the president's personal predilection for the continent noir, Giscard's term was, in fact, emblematic of France's increasingly controversial 'African policy'. When he arrived at the Elysée,

Giscard had, it was true, set about 'modernizing' Franco-African relations: not only did he desire an African policy that would encompass more than just the community of French-speaking former colonies, but he was also anxious to institutionalize and multilateralize this policy by means of annual Franco-African summits; he also abolished the *secrétariat général pour les Affaires africaines et malgaches*, empowering the Ministry of Cooperation. Yet African policy would remain very much part of the president's personal *domaine réservé*; controlled from the Elysée by René Journiac (who had been Foccart's deputy for seven years) up until his accidental death in 1980, it still essentially dispensed with traditional diplomatic circuits. French policy in Africa was characterized more than ever by military interventions carried out by the former colonial power, whether in support of regimes it sought to protect, or quite simply to defend its own interests. Such operations were carried out in Zaire, first by proxy (through the provision of transport for a Moroccan intervention in 1977) and later directly (with France's intervention in Katanga in 1978), in Mauritania (1977) and in Chad (1978 and 1980).

Giscard's presidency coincided with a period of growing international interest in Africa; the continent was increasingly coveted by outside powers not only for its natural resources but also as a 'peripheral' arena for East-West rivalry, which the prevailing climate of superpower détente was increasingly pushing towards the South. France positioned itself as a power guaranteeing stability and the West's influence in an area where this was under threat. This was, in fact, the main cause of the brief deterioration in 1977–1978 in relations with the Soviets, who were moving their pawns forward on the African chessboard. Africa, in short, allowed France to play a strategic game on a scale that suited it, on familiar ground and at minimal cost.

### France's Arab and Middle East Policies

Giscard's presidential term was also notable for consolidating policy towards the Arab states. Admittedly, relations with the Maghreb states (already made difficult by long-standing issues and further complicated by the Western Sahara dispute) did not see the improvement Giscard had hoped for, despite his visit to Algeria (April 1975) and generally good relations with Morocco and Tunisia. So it was in the Middle East that this policy really found its feet. Giscard turned out to be a staunch defender of the Palestinian cause (about which he would later admit to having known virtually nothing before arriving at the Elysée); the meeting between French Foreign Minister Jean Sauvagnargues and the leader of the Palestine Liberation Organization (PLO), Yasser Arafat, on 21 October 1974 in Beirut, followed by Giscard's reference in his press conference of 24 October to a Palestinian 'homeland' (*patrie*), marked a clear strengthening of French policy in this respect, confirmed the following year with the opening of an office of the PLO in Paris. Sticking with its 'global' approach to the Israeli-Arab conflict in spite of the fact that the idea of separate settlements was gaining ground, French diplomacy was not happy with the terms of the Israeli-Egyptian peace treaty signed in Washington on 26 March 1979 following the Camp David negotiations of the preceding year, in particular bemoaning the fact that the Palestinian question was left unresolved by the Israel-Egypt separate peace treaty. Following on from Pompidou's policy, Giscard managed to crystallize a common European position by having a declaration on the Middle East largely based on French ideas adopted by the European Council in Venice on 13 June 1980, an ambitious document that once again distanced the Nine from US diplomacy in this region.

After a slight improvement in the first two years of the new presidency in spite of French initiatives regarding the Palestine question, subsequent Franco-Israeli relations inevitably suffered from Giscard's pro-Palestinian policy and, more generally, from France's evolving Middle Eastern policy. The mounting number of points of friction between the two countries, especially following the arrival in office of Prime Minister Menachem Begin in 1977, led to a distinct deterioration in their relations. By the end of Giscard's seven-year term, the shift begun by de Gaulle in 1967 had produced a policy that was more and more clearly pro-Arab.

Of course, Middle Eastern policy during Giscard's presidency was also affected by economic and commercial considerations. Following the October 1973 war and the first oil crisis, the search for secure energy supplies played an increasingly important role in defining French positions in the region. Likewise, the focus on the country's balance of payments and external trade led the French government to try to target markets where the pursuit of a policy seen as pro-Arab was potentially beneficial. One of the economic areas that allowed France to position itself in these promising markets was the public-works sector, leading to large export contracts throughout this period. France's arms industry, meanwhile, was becoming increasingly dependent on this region once the 1967 arms embargo imposed on front-line states was lifted in August 1974. French arms sales in the Middle East in turn helped to consolidate the country's defence industry, which increasingly relied on exports to fund its programmes. The nuclear industry would also prove highly active in the region, in spite of the proliferation risks involved, although these would begin to be taken into consideration from 1976 onwards, with the creation of a presidential council for nuclear export policy (*Conseil de politique nucléaire extérieure*).

In addition to its traditional areas of influence, such as Syria, Egypt and Lebanon (the latter torn apart by civil war from 1975 onwards), France under Giscard increasingly turned towards the oil-rich Gulf monarchies (especially Saudi Arabia, now France's main oil supplier), as well as Iraq, as Pompidou had begun to do. The strategic geopolitical position, oil wealth and modernizing outlook of this secular Arab country seemed particularly promising to the French government, while the Iraqi regime saw a partnership with post-Gaullist France as a means of counterbalancing Soviet influence. As prime minister, Chirac established a personal relationship with Saddam Hussein, who was then emerging as the regime's strongman, inviting him to Paris in 1975 and himself going to Iraq in 1974 and 1976. In addition to civilian and military contracts, close technological cooperation developed between the two countries, including in the sensitive area of nuclear technology. This continued under Raymond Barre's government, culminating in the controversial supplying to Baghdad in 1980 of the Osirak reactor. Iran, with whom Giscard's diplomacy sought close relations, was not neglected either (until the Islamic revolution toppled the Shah in 1979), with large civilian contracts, the planned supply of nuclear reactors and Iranian financial investment in Eurodif (the uranium enrichment plant at Tricastin in southern France). The Middle East was increasingly opening up new horizons for French foreign policy.

## The Deterioration of East-West Relations

For France, however, the most crucial issues still centred on the old continent. The last years of Giscard's presidency coincided with a noticeable deterioration in East-West relations, globally at first, then within Europe itself. This shift in an international context that had hitherto been dominated by détente had a major impact on Giscard's foreign policy from 1979 onwards. Giscard's policy, from then on, became more 'Gaullist', reasserting France's specific position within the Western grouping and once again promoting French independence vis-à-vis the blocs. After an improvement in Franco-American relations in the first half of Giscard's term in office, the second half saw them worsen once again, especially following the arrival of Jimmy Carter's administration in January 1977. Carter's unpredictable shifts in policy direction worried the Europeans, especially the French and the Germans, whose analyses converged on their assessment of US policy. The new US administration's strong activism on the issue of human rights in the Soviet bloc was seen in Paris and Bonn as counterproductive; Giscard saw Carter's approach as overly 'ideological' and liable to compromise relations with Moscow for no real gain. Like Schmidt, Giscard preferred a more discreet approach in these matters.

Furthermore, US policy seemed ambivalent when it came to strategic issues. The incoming Carter administration's willingness to review the ongoing SALT II negotiations – something that Moscow was unhappy with – made the Europeans nervous. The Germans feared that what they regarded as a crucial process of arms control could be compromised. At the same time, as illustrated by Schmidt's important October 1977 speech in London, they were critical of the fact that the US-Soviet strategic negotiations tended to overlook the specifics of the European theatre and the new threat of the Soviet medium-range SS 20 missiles. In the meantime, the U-turn performed by Carter over the Enhanced Radiation Weapon (ERW), or 'neutron bomb', dealt a severe blow to his credibility (Carter had initially called for ERW deployment in spite of Schmidt's reservations, before finally abandoning the idea in 1978, causing major domestic difficulties in the FRG). In this context, French policy had to strike a delicate balance; its aim was to work towards maintaining a strategic equilibrium while at the same time preserving détente in Europe, and to contribute to strengthening Western security while defending France's independence within the Alliance. Caught between a US administration now set on deploying new weapons systems and a Federal Germany that favoured negotiation in order to remove the threat posed by the SS 20s, Giscard sought to forge a middle path. Keen to take the position of his German partner into account, he summoned, with Schmidt's agreement, a summit meeting of the leaders of the Alliance's four great powers, the first of its kind. At the Guadeloupe summit (5–6 January 1979) Carter, Giscard, Schmidt and UK Prime Minister James Callaghan reached a compromise: the Western Alliance would negotiate with the Soviets in order to obtain the removal of the SS 20s, but if negotiations failed, the United States would deploy Pershing II and cruise missiles in western Europe. Yet although the French played a part in achieving this compromise, they resolved, based on their special position within the Alliance, not to associate themselves formally with the 'Double-Track Decision' taken by NATO in mid-December 1979.

In late December 1979, the Soviets launched a military intervention in Afghanistan that threatened to deal a fatal blow to détente. Giscard rejected a bloc-based response, which he saw as likely to exacerbate tensions; he was growingly critical of US policy, which, like Schmidt, he judged as veering towards unnecessary escalation. This may explain the most controversial foreign policy decision of his presidency, namely his meeting with Brezhnev in Warsaw in May 1980. This was a very personal decision, taken against the advice of his foreign minister, Jean François-Poncet, and in spite of the United States' desire to present a united front against the USSR following the invasion of Afghanistan. Giscard's decision came out of his reading of the Afghan crisis as a misstep by the Soviet leadership, for whom a 'way out' had to be provided; but it was also an expression of his disapproval of the United States' reaction (including a call for economic sanctions and for the boycott of the 1980 Moscow Olympics), which he saw as potentially spelling the end for détente in Europe. While he was subsequently criticized for what appeared as a mere policy of appeasement, Giscard in fact displayed firmness in his head-to-head talks with Brezhnev (Schmidt would himself go to Moscow soon after Giscard's Warsaw trip). However, the fact remained that, with the Soviet Union refusing to give ground and skilfully turning Giscard's initiative to its own advantage, his action inevitably seemed to mark an acceptance of Moscow's fait accompli in Afghanistan. The same was true of his attitude towards events in Poland in the aftermath of the strikes in Gdansk in summer 1980: emphasizing the risk of Soviet intervention against the growing Solidarnosc movement, Giscard, in the opening weeks of 1981, declared that it was necessary to 'take geographical and strategic realities into account', thus appearing to condone Soviet domination in eastern Europe. Unusually, Giscard's controversial positions on international matters would have a certain bearing on domestic politics during the presidential election campaign of 1981.

## The Unfinished Business of European Construction

Faced with a deteriorating international political situation and the economic consequences of the second oil crisis, the strengthening of European cohesion appeared more desirable than ever. Yet with hindsight, with the exception in 1979 of the launch of the EMS and of Greece's accession to European Community membership (which was to a large extent the result of the strong support of Giscard), the final phase of VGE's presidency was characterized by great expectations rather than concrete actions. To be sure, the Venice declaration, as already mentioned, showed that there was convergence between the Nine regarding Middle Eastern issues; yet beyond this, international developments and the deterioration of East-West relations left Europe little room to assert itself. This situation led Giscard, at the very end of his term in office, to once again reflect on how to strengthen the Community's international profile and improve European political cooperation, including in defence matters, while at the same time retaining the room for manoeuvre of Europe's major states, which he saw as vital. Yet Giscard's European yearnings remained unfulfilled.

The key development in this period, then, was the strengthening of the Franco-German partnership, helped by the close understanding between Giscard and Schmidt and their shared analysis of the international situation. This Franco-German convergence was reflected in the common declaration on Afghanistan issued on 5 February 1980 by Giscard and Schmidt, which condemned the Soviet invasion while calling for détente to be maintained in Europe. This shared vision was now leading the two countries to consider strengthening their cooperation in the areas of security and defence. Yet for the time being it would result in little more than a plan to jointly build a main battle tank, confirming that the differences between the two countries' military policies – in particular their respective roles within NATO and their respective positions regarding nuclear weapons – continued to constitute an obstacle to such cooperation (the tank project would later be abandoned). A fully fledged Franco-German strategic partnership, in other words, was still a long way off; time seemed to have run out for a French president who perhaps only realized the importance of increased Franco-German cooperation in this area too late in the day.[8]

The legacy left by Giscard and Schmidt in the area of Franco-German relations would nevertheless be taken up by their successors (Schmidt would leave office a year and a half after Giscard). France, it is true, was not able to 'catch up' with the Federal Republic in this period, as had been desired by Giscard, who saw economic equilibrium between France and Germany as an essential objective. Yet the two countries were becoming increasingly interdependent and the launch of the EMS in 1979 could only encourage their convergence. As a strategically independent power, France could also boast of its international status in comparison to a still-divided Germany; French nuclear power, in a sense, compensated for the strength of the deutschmark. Be that as it may, the foundations of enhanced Franco-German cooperation had been laid by the end of the 1970s. If the de Gaulle-Adenauer period had been one of ambitious projects that never came to fruition, the Giscard-Schmidt period was one of pragmatic – albeit incomplete – deepening.

France was 'recognized, by East and West alike, as an independent and responsible power'; this was the satisfied assessment that the outgoing president gave of his own policy on the eve of the presidential election of April–May 1981. While this statement was designed for domestic political consumption, it nevertheless reflected the fact that Giscard, in the closing stages of his presidency, had indeed followed a 'Gaullist' line of challenging the bloc system, strengthening Europe, and, above all, defending his country's independence. Faced with mounting danger in the East, Giscard chose to increase military spending, with the result that France was the only NATO member to achieve the objective of a 3 per cent yearly rise in long-term conventional defence spending; yet he had come a long way from his initial eagerness to develop closer ties with NATO, and the end of his presidency would serve to confirm the value of France's independent position within the Alliance. A similar emphasis on national independence was to be found in the president's declarations at the tail end of his term in office regarding the prospects of European political union, which he described during a televised interview on 27 January 1981 in terms of 'a structure flexible enough so that the voice of Europe would not necessarily be the most timid one' – in other words so that France's voice would not be drowned out. Having initially based his foreign policy on a multilateralist approach that had not been its dominant characteristic in the past, Giscard, then, ended his presidency with an unmistakeably Gaullist reassertion of the primacy of national independence.

## Notes

1. Valéry Giscard d'Estaing, *Le Pouvoir et la vie*, vol. II, 'L'Affrontement', Paris: Cie 12, 1991, p. 9.

2. On this, see Serge Berstein and Jean-François Sirinelli (eds), *Les Années Giscard. Valéry Giscard d'Estaing et l'Europe (1974–1981)*, Paris: Armand Colin, 2006.

3. See Michèle Weinachter, *Valéry Giscard d'Estaing et l'Allemagne. Le double rêve inachevé*, Paris: L'Harmattan, 2004; and Hélène Miard-Delacroix, *Partenaires de choix? Le chancelier Helmut Schmidt et la France (1974–1982)*, Bern: Peter Lang, 1993

4. See Robert Frank, 'Les problèmes monétaires et la création du SME', in Serge Berstein and Jean-François Sirinelli (eds), *Les Années Giscard*, op. cit.

5. See Valéry Giscard d'Estaing, *Le Pouvoir et la vie*, vol. II, op. cit., pp. 183–191.

6. See Frédéric Bozo, *La France et l'OTAN. De la guerre froide au nouvel ordre européen*, op. cit., pp. 109–122; and Pierre Melandri, 'La France et l'Alliance atlantique sous Georges Pompidou et Valéry Giscard d'Estaing', in Maurice Vaïsse, Pierre Melandri and Frédéric Bozo (eds), *La France et l'OTAN (1949–1996)*, op. cit.

7. See Marie-Claude Smouts, 'Valéry Giscard d'Estaing et le nouvel ordre économique international: une diplomatie plus qu'une politique?' in Samy Cohen and Marie-Claude Smouts (eds), *La Politique extérieure de Valéry Giscard d'Estaing*, Paris: Presses de la Fondation nationale des sciences politiques, 1985.

8. See Georges-Henri Soutou, 'L'anneau et les deux triangles: les rapports franco-allemands dans la politique européenne et mondiale de 1974 à 1981', and Maurice Vaïsse, 'Valéry Giscard d'Estaing: de la défense de l'Europe à la défense européenne', in Serge Berstein and Jean-François Sirinelli (eds), *Les Années Giscard*, op. cit.

# Part IV

# THE END OF THE COLD WAR
# (1981–1995)

# Chapter 8

# NEW COLD WAR, NEW DÉTENTE (1981–1988)

François Mitterrand's victory in the presidential election of 10 May 1981, further consolidated by the triumph of his Socialist Party in the parliamentary elections of 14 and 21 June, marked a major turning point in the country's political history. After almost a quarter of a century in opposition, the Left found themselves in charge for the first time since the foundation of the Fifth Republic. Soon, however, the consequences of this shift in terms of foreign policy seemed bound to be limited. True, the new occupant of the Elysée had, in the early years of the Fifth Republic, taken a resolutely anti-Gaullist stance with regard to the functioning of institutions and foreign policy alike. Yet de Gaulle's adversary in the presidential elections of 1965 had travelled a long road since then; in the process of taking control of the Socialist Party throughout the 1970s and then of taking power in 1981, he had, in real terms, come to accept the major choices made by his predecessors against a backdrop of consolidation, among the political classes and public opinion alike, of a broad national consensus regarding foreign policy. Once again, therefore, continuity was the order of the day in spite of the 'change' that Mitterrand had called for in his candidacy. Moulding the functioning of institutions to his own vision and making full use of his presidential prerogatives in foreign policy, the new president set out to 'pick up the legacy', albeit with a view to 'gradually bringing about its evolution'.[1] Both the domestic political context, which would (until 1986 at any rate) offer him unchallenged political authority, and the international situation, namely the final phase of the Cold War, seemed to validate this choice. Right from the start of his first term of office, then, the first socialist president of the Fifth Republic would position himself very much as the continuator of Charles de Gaulle.

## France and the 'New' Cold War

Mitterrand's election came against the backdrop of worsening East-West relations; with the Euromissile crisis, the Soviet invasion of Afghanistan and the situation in Poland, a 'new' Cold War was settling in. The new French president displayed a willingness to break with his predecessor in this area. Mitterrand, in the build-up to the presidential elections, had criticized Giscard's policy towards the USSR following his meeting with Brezhnev in Warsaw and derided him as a 'little telegraphist' for bringing back false news that a Soviet retreat from Afghanistan was about to start. Having accused Giscard of having wanted to preserve détente with the USSR at the price of appeasement (a criticism that had paid dividends in the elections), Mitterrand, once in office, maintained a very firm attitude towards the East; for two years, he would position himself as the steadfast ally of the United States in the face of renewed Soviet 'expansionism'. A centre-right president who wanted to preserve his understanding with the USSR was thus succeeded by a left-wing president who was ready to face down Moscow. The fact that his government, headed by the Socialist Prime Minister Pierre Mauroy, included four communist ministers for the first time since 1947 arguably encouraged him in his intransigent stance towards Moscow as a means of demonstrating the PCF's lack of influence on foreign policy. Yet while the domestic situation led Mitterrand to visibly distance himself from his predecessor's East-West policy and display his freedom of manoeuvre with respect to the French communists (who in any case had resolved to follow the government line, not the party line), the differences between Mitterrand and Giscard were, in the final analysis, more concerned with emphasis than with their fundamental views regarding the Soviet threat, the importance of the Western Alliance or France's security interests.[2]

For more than three years, Mitterrand nevertheless made his firm stance towards the USSR the central tenet of his diplomacy; he was even determined to carry out a 'detox' (*cure de désintoxication*) of Franco-Soviet relations. While maintaining low profile contact with Moscow, the new president decided to freeze all top-level relations between France and the USSR, suspending the principle of holding regular summits (adopted under Georges Pompidou) until the strategic balance had been re-established in Europe; French diplomacy under Mitterrand wanted to 'wean' France of the overly close relationship that in his view had developed with the USSR during the 1970s. Mitterrand saw the clarification of France's position regarding the threat of the SS20s as a prerequisite; breaking with the reticence shown by his predecessor on this subject, he declared France's support for NATO's 'Double-Track Decision' in clear terms, while at the same time continuing to reject out of hand the idea that French nuclear weapons should be included in the negotiations under way between Washington and Moscow over Intermediate-Range Nuclear Forces (INF).

Mitterrand's support did not mean that Paris was aligning itself with Washington's position. As the INF negotiations, which opened in 1981, dragged slowly on, throughout 1982 the French president promoted the idea of a compromise position between the unlikely 'zero option' proposed by Washington and the unacceptable 'freeze' called for by Moscow, both of which, in his view, were evidence of the reluctance of either superpower to negotiate seriously. Yet as the likelihood of such a compromise receded and the date set for the deployment of the US systems in 1983 drew closer, Mitterrand was keen to emphasize France's solidarity with its allies, in particular the Federal Republic, which formed the central issue in the politico-strategic stand-off between East and West. This was the thrust of his speech to the Bundestag on 20 January 1983; at the start of a crucial year in the Euromissile crisis, this speech marked a turning point for France and the Alliance: for the first time since the 1960s, the former became involved in the military-strategic debates of the latter. Delivered a few weeks before the Federal Republic's March 1983 general elections (which would be won by Helmut Kohl's CDU-FDP coalition), the Bundestag speech, which Mitterrand subsequently described as the most important of his first seven-year term, would also mark the beginning of his long political friendship with Kohl and lead to the relaunch of a strategic Franco-German partnership that would continue to grow stronger over the following years:

> Ladies and Gentlemen . . . Our peoples hate war, they and the other peoples of Europe with them have suffered from it more than enough. French thinking is governed by one simple idea: war must remain impossible and those who might consider it must be dissuaded from doing so. Our analysis and our conviction, that of France, are that nuclear weapons – the instrument, whether one likes or deplores the fact, of that dissuasion – remain the guarantee of peace as long as there exists a balance of forces. All things considered, it is only that balance which can lead to good relations with our neighbours and historical partners, the countries of Eastern Europe. It has been the sound basis of what has been termed détente. It has enabled you to put into effect your Ostpolitik. It made possible the Helsinki agreements. But the maintenance of that balance means, in my view, that there must be no depriving whole regions of Europe of a parry to nuclear weapons specifically aimed at them. Anyone banking on 'uncoupling' the European and American continents would, in our opinion, call in [sic] question the balance of forces and so the maintenance of peace. I think, and I will say, that 'uncoupling' is dangerous in itself, and it is my earnest hope that the Geneva negotiations will lead to the averting of a danger that weighs singularly upon the non-nuclear weapon[-armed] European partners. . . . Peace is only possible through negotiation. It is for those who negotiate to prepare the way to the [sic] indispensable harmony. It suffices for one, not to say two, of the partners to refuse this for agreement to become impossible. The conditions of

the necessary balance must, therefore, be maintained, with the assurance, for the peoples concerned, that they will not find themselves under the burden of foreign domination.[3]

## Mitterrand and Reagan

Relations between Mitterrand and the new US President Ronald Reagan, who arrived in the White House in January 1981, were to a large extent determined by the context of the 'new' Cold War. From the outset, Mitterrand sought to reassure Reagan that socialist France was solidly anchored in the West. Washington's initial concerns regarding the consequences that the presence of communist ministers in government might have for France's foreign and defence policy were allayed when Mitterrand met with Vice-President George H. W. Bush at the Elysée on 23 June 1981. The new French president also gave a token of Atlantic loyalty to his American counterpart by informing him of a major counter-espionage operation being carried out against the USSR by the French intelligence services (known as the 'Farewell' affair, after the codename of their Soviet informant).[4]

Faced with the looming Soviet threat, Reagan found in Mitterrand a determined ally whose strategic stances were greatly appreciated. Although they appeared so utterly different, these two men were able to establish a relationship of mutual confidence; Franco-American solidarity, in fact, had rarely been so strong since the Cuban crisis. As well as the positions adopted by Mitterrand in the Euromissile crisis, the United States was quite happy with his defence policy. Based on the domestic consensus that had existed in this area since the French Communist Party, soon followed by the Socialists, had accepted France's nuclear posture in the late 1970s, Mitterrand was determined to give priority to France's deterrent while still pursuing efforts to modernize conventional forces, resulting in the creation in 1983 of the *Force d'action rapide* (FAR) (Rapid Reaction Force). Without bringing into question France's special position within the Alliance (which he now accepted completely), Mitterrand displayed a willingness from the very beginning of his presidency to increase cooperation with NATO, symbolically hosting a NATO ministerial meeting in Paris in spring 1983 for the first time since 1966.

Yet no French alignment with the United States in the 'new' Cold War would follow – far from it. In spite of the strategic understanding that prevailed between the two countries, other aspects of East-West relations constituted so many bones of contention between France (and very often Europe, too) and the United States. Hence France refused the policy of sanctions against the USSR into which Washington sought to lead its allies, denouncing it as a manifestation of an imperial notion of US leadership, and rejecting the logic of an 'economic Cold War' inherent in such a policy. These disagreements would reach a head in 1982 when, following the declaration of martial law in Poland (13 December 1981), the United States stepped up its campaign. The G7 summit held in Versailles in June 1982 (the sumptuous nature of which, at Mitterrand's behest, was meant to show the 'respectability' of socialist France in the eyes of the other Western powers) became the theatre of a head-on clash over this issue; the quarrel continued in the following months over plans for a Euro-Siberian gas pipeline, the construction of which the United States attempted to block by exerting unprecedented pressure on the Europeans, who were nevertheless determined not to give in.

As the G7 summit held in Williamsburg in May 1983 showed, French efforts to oppose Reagan's attempts to 'globalize' the new Cold War by stepping outside the geographical framework or mandate of existing institutions (NATO, CoCom, G7) met with limited success. France also tried to act as a counterweight to 'reaganomics', whose effects, prompted by high interest rates and an overvalued US dollar, were proving damaging for Europe and disastrous for the developing world. Yet the country's poor economic situation and the lack of European cohesion on this issue meant that France possessed no real means to impose its views, whether in the monetary domain or in that of North-South relations. The latter were another point of friction with an increasingly 'imperial' US superpower. Washington disliked the Third-Worldist declarations made by Mitterrand in Mexico on 20 October and then at the North-South conference in Cancún on 22 and 23 October 1981; the United States, above all, was irritated in 1981–1982 by French policy in its 'backyard', namely France's political backing (in concert with Mexico) of left-wing guerrillas in El Salvador, and its support, however symbolic, for the Sandinista government through a modest arms shipment to Nicaragua. However, by the spring of 1982 these quarrels had been settled, as Mitterrand did not wish to spoil his relations with the United States for the sake of an issue that he judged to be of secondary importance, in spite of calls for action from his minister of external relations Claude Cheysson and his advisor Régis Debray.

## North-South Relations, Africa and the Middle East

France's approach to North-South problems did not fundamentally change in 1981. Aside from adopting a more radical rhetoric than that of his predecessor, Mitterrand reprised the main existing policy directions in this area and stuck to what France's economic situation allowed. France's development-aid budget, which he had intended to increase from 0.36 per cent of GDP to 0.7 per cent at the end of his term in office, would in fact peak at 0.56 per cent in 1986.[5] African policy, which Mitterrand, like his predecessors, would make a presidential *domaine réservé*, very quickly showed signs of continuity that surprised those who had hoped for change just as much as it did those who had feared it. The resignation at the end of 1982 of the minister for cooperation, Jean-Pierre Cot, who had been in favour of deep change in this area, sealed victory for the latter group. The Chad crisis, which Mitterrand had inherited from his predecessors, was emblematic of the tribute that African policy would have to pay to realism under his presidency. In the face of Libya's constant machinations and in spite of his reluctance to order military intervention in Chad, Mitterrand was obliged to carry out Operation *Manta*, launched in August 1983 with the objective of putting a stop to Colonel Gaddafi's meddling south of the 15th Parallel (Mitterrand's controversial meeting with Gaddafi in Crete, in November 1984, resolved nothing, and in February 1986 a new operation, *Épervier* [Sparrowhawk] was launched).

Continuity also prevailed with respect to the Maghreb. Mitterrand wanted to improve relations with Chadli Benjedid's Algeria, which he wanted to turn into a model for North-South relations (hence a gas contract signed with Algiers in 1982 averaged at 25 per cent above the mean price for gas paid by France on the world markets); yet he also sought to maintain a balance with Hassan II's Morocco in spite of the controversy surrounding the human rights situation in the country.

In the Middle East, meanwhile, Mitterrand's desire for change quickly became tinged with realism. While he was very critical of France's 'Arab policy' of the past years that, in his eyes, was mainly a cover for commercial interests, Mitterrand was nevertheless anxious to maintain good relations with the Arab world, which had a strong advocate in the form of Cheysson – and he could not easily ignore economic and geopolitical realities. These realities not only pushed him towards making overtures to the Gulf monarchies (King Khalid of Saudi Arabia was the first head of state received by Mitterrand, in June 1981, and the kingdom would be the destination of the president's first state visit in September), they also encouraged him to maintain France's military support for Iraq, which had launched a war against Iran in 1980. Despite having initially wanted to reconsider French policy regarding arms exports, in particular to the Middle East, and while feeling no particular affection for the regime in Baghdad, Mitterrand nevertheless decided in the summer of 1981 to continue French arms deliveries to Iraq. (He refused, however, to rebuild the Osirak reactor, which had been destroyed by an Israeli air raid in June 1981.) Encouraged by the Gulf monarchies, who saw Saddam Hussein's Iraq as a bulwark against the threat posed by Ayatollah Ruhollah Khomeini's Iran following the 1979 Islamic revolution, and having received at least implicit backing from the United

States, Mitterrand's France quickly became a crucial source of military support for Baghdad, even resulting in a form of de facto co-belligerence when in 1983 Paris agreed to 'loan' to Iraq French Super Étendard aircraft armed with Exocet missiles.

The attitude adopted by Mitterrand towards the Arab-Israeli conflict was also tinged with realism. A long-standing friend of the Jewish state, and generally considered to be pro-Israeli, Mitterrand wanted to build closer relations with Tel-Aviv by reviewing what he saw as an excessively unbalanced French policy; hence his state visit to Israel (the first by a French president) in 1982. Keen to encourage peace between the Arabs and the Israelis, be it through separate treaties or simply through progressive steps, he clearly expressed his support for the Camp David process, in contrast to his predecessor. Yet faced with the bogging down of the peace process and the stalemate over the Palestinian problem, he soon toned down the shift in French policy. His speech to the Knesset (4 March 1982) – though notable for its daring choice of venue – was, in some respects, very much a continuation of prior French doctrine: the need for the Palestinians, and in particular the PLO, to recognize Israel's right to existence and security; and the need for Israel to recognize the right of the Palestinians to have their own state 'when the time came'. Unsurprisingly, this position was not welcomed by Israeli Prime Minister Menachem Begin.

While he had no desire to bring into question his support for Israel and its security, events pushed Mitterrand into taking an increasingly clear stance as a defender of the Palestinians. Operation 'Peace for Galilee', carried out by Israel in Lebanon in June 1982, which Mitterrand condemned in no uncertain terms, even forced him to become their protector, with French forces evacuating Yasser Arafat from Beirut, then under siege by the Israeli army, in August 1982. The following year, the French navy was involved in a second evacuation of the Palestinian leader, now caught in a pincer movement by Syrian forces in Tripoli, in northern Lebanon (December 1983). The French president was gambling on the political future of the head of the PLO, judging that, when the time came – and on the condition that Israel's right to security was fully recognized by the PLO – he would become a necessary partner in a peaceful resolution of the Israeli-Palestinian conflict.[6]

In spite of these markers laid down for the future, events on the ground nevertheless showed the narrow limits of France's influence in the Middle East. This was particularly clear in Lebanon, with the Beirut barracks bombings, in which 58 French soldiers serving with the Multinational Force were killed on 23 October 1983, along with 238 US servicemen, leading to the French withdrawal in spring 1984. More generally, France henceforth found itself obliged to adopt a low profile in this highly polarized region where, in addition to Israeli disapproval (owing to French support of the Palestinians) it was now confronted with open hostility from two major players: Iran (because of French support for Iraq) and Syria (because of France's defence of Lebanese sovereignty). The wave of terrorist attacks that France would suffer on its own territory in the months and years that followed would only serve to highlight the limited room for manoeuvre that it possessed, forcing the country to perform a balancing act in its policy towards Lebanon and the region.

### France, Germany and Europe

By early 1984, the first phase of Mitterrand's diplomacy was drawing to a close. On 22 November 1983, the Bundestag approved the deployment of US missiles pursuant to the 'Double-Track Decision'. For Mitterrand, the resulting restoration of the strategic balance meant that France could now re-establish a 'normal' relationship with Moscow, which he would visit in June 1984. While willing to renew the tradition of Franco-Soviet relations (and, like his predecessors, look to the East for a counterweight to an all-powerful United States), the French president was nevertheless unwilling either to weaken Western cohesion or to sacrifice principles, as illustrated by his reference to the fate of Soviet dissident Andrei Sakhorov in the toast that he offered in the Kremlin in the presence of Soviet Premier Konstantin Chernenko on 21 June. Anticipating a drop in East-West tensions, French diplomacy from 1984 onwards began to move towards a 'new détente'. This would be confirmed in October 1985 by the success of Mikhail Gorbachev's visit to France, the new Soviet leader's first trip to the West. Having taken office the previous March, the general secretary of the Soviet Communist Party used this occasion to demonstrate the total change of style, if not yet of substance, that he intended to bring to the USSR's foreign policy. The visit made by the Polish head of state, General Wojciech Jaruzelski, to Paris in December 1985, meanwhile, reflected Mitterrand's sense that favourable developments were now underway in Poland also. (This sparked a controversy: Prime Minister Laurent Fabius expressed his 'discomfort' at this visit by the man who had ordered the 'state of war' in Poland a few years before.) As subsequent events would show, Mitterrand's intuition would soon be confirmed.

In this rapidly changing East-West context, the European Community, which had thus far not been a very high priority for Mitterrand, returned to the fore. As the grip of the bloc system seemed to begin to loosen and, as we shall see, Franco-American disagreements continued, particularly over the GATT multilateral trade negotiations and the Strategic Defense Initiative (SDI, or 'Star Wars'), relaunching European construction was increasingly seen in Paris as a necessity. From 1983–1984 onwards, the European project, centred on a close Franco-German relationship, would gradually become the central plank of Mitterrand's policy. Against the backdrop of change in the USSR and a new climate of détente from 1985 onwards, this pro-European choice would increasingly form part of Mitterrand's plan to overcome the East-West deadlock.

The European option pursued by socialist France starting in 1983–1984 was also dictated by economic imperatives. By 1982, the effects of an economic stimulus policy that France had pursued on its own (attacks on the franc, stalled growth) led Mauroy's government to announce a switch to 'rigour', as recommended by the Minister of Economy and Finance Jacques Delors. In spite of the severe measures taken starting in mid-1982, the economic results at the end of that year remained poor and threatened to force the withdrawal of the franc from the EMS. In spring 1983, Mitterrand had to choose between two policies: one was promoted by Minister of Research and Industry Jean-Pierre Chevènement and Minister of Social Affairs Pierre Bérégovoy, both of whom supported the modernization of French industry through lower interest rates, a policy that they believed would bring in new investment but would involve unpegging the franc from the mark; the other, put forward by Mauroy and Delors, focused on defending the franc and fighting inflation. On 21 March, following the third devaluation of his presidential term so far, Mitterrand chose decisively in favour of the latter option, and of keeping the franc firmly within the EMS. While this decision in many ways put an end to the 'socialist experiment' and confirmed that it was no longer possible to pursue an economic policy that ran counter to that of France's partners, it also, more importantly, marked the rejection of French isolation within Europe and thus constituted the founding act of a European policy that would never subsequently be abandoned.

### The Franco-German Partnership

The economic choice made in March 1983 made it possible to give new momentum to the European project, which had previously been paralysed by the crisis over the United Kingdom's financial contribution. Following the European Council summit in Athens (5–6 December 1983), Mitterrand, who was getting ready to take over the six-month presidency of the Community on 1 January 1984, believed that the time was right for this relaunch. He appointed a close friend and associate, the lawyer Roland Dumas, as minister for European affairs (Dumas would replace Cheysson as foreign minister a few months later) and he began a tour of Europe's capitals. Some results were achieved at the European Council meeting in Brussels on 19–20 March 1984, but UK Prime Minister Margaret Thatcher remained utterly determined to reduce her country's contribution to the EU budget. Mitterrand, in turn, was determined to mobilize all the means at his disposal in order to unblock this stalemate, starting with the support that Germany's Chancellor Kohl had resolved to give him. This firm Franco-German front proved decisive at the European Council meeting held in Fontainebleau on 25 and 26 June 1984. Having been unable to drive a wedge between Mitterrand and Kohl, Thatcher was forced to accept the Franco-German proposal for resolving the issue of the UK contribution or face the risk of shutting the United Kingdom out of the process of building the Community. In the wake of Fontainebleau, the European process at long last regained a powerful forward momentum, raising hopes that negotiations over widening the Union to include Spain and Portugal could soon be concluded and, more importantly, making further deepening a possibility thanks to the setting up of the Dooge committee on strengthening the European Community; furthermore, Paris and Bonn reached an agreement regarding the appointment of Delors as president of the European Commission on 1 January 1985.

Europe was now moving away from its earlier 'Europessimism'. A French initiative announced in April 1985 (which soon became a Franco-German initiative) led to the launch by seventeen European countries in July of that year of the Eurêka programme; extending beyond the EC boundaries, Eurêka aimed to allow Europe to rise to the technological challenge set by Ronald Reagan's 'Star Wars' project. Following the submission of the Dooge report in March, at the Milan European Council (28–30 June 1985), the Europeans heads of states and governments – notwithstanding opposition from the United Kingdom, Denmark and Greece – decided to hold an intergovernmental conference at the end of the year. This resulted in the signing by the Twelve (including Spain and Portugal) in February 1986 of the Single European Act, which was greeted by Mitterrand as a 'compromise for the sake of progress'. Although the Single Act did not live up to French hopes, it did succeed in revitalizing the European project, thanks in particular to the prospect of having a single market by 1992, a prospect exploited by Delors to accelerate this process.

During this same period, transatlantic issues once again tested European cohesion. In the face of the strong pressure exerted by the United States on its partners, France sometimes found itself isolated. This was the case with SDI, with the United States' attempts to make the Europeans mere technological subcontractors for a project that Mitterrand judged contrary to their strategic interests; it was also the case regarding the GATT talks, with Washington's demands for the opening of a new cycle of negotiations in which the CAP risked coming under threat. At the May 1985 G7 summit in Bonn, Mitterrand received virtually no support from his partners, including Kohl, in his attempts to oppose Reagan on these two issues.

Difficulties with the United States added further impetus to the search for greater European and Franco-German cohesion, particularly over strategic questions; 1985–1986 saw a push towards rapprochement between Paris and Bonn in that sphere. First mooted in 1982 by Mitterrand and Schmidt, and then Kohl, this rapprochement began to take shape following Mitterrand's Bundestag speech. The speech, held on the twentieth anniversary of the Elysée Treaty, had been used by Mitterrand as an occasion to make solemn declarations of Franco-German solidarity; the following year, the image of Mitterrand and Kohl standing hand-in-hand at Verdun offered a powerful illustration of the Franco-German rapprochement. It would result in particular, at the beginning of 1986, in the pledge by the French President to consult the German chancellor in the event of pre-strategic nuclear weapons being used in the context of a possible conflict on German soil. While some sticking points remained between the two countries on these questions, the Franco-German relationship, thanks to the close understanding between Kohl and Mitterrand, was once again becoming the driving force behind the political and strategic advances now under way in Europe. With the 1984 relaunch of the WEU, whose members had set themselves the objective of defining Europe's security identity (Rome, 26–27 October 1984), these advances could take place within a concrete political framework.

## Cohabitation and the New Détente

The parliamentary elections of March 1986, which were won by the Gaullist and centre-right coalition formed by the RPR and the UDF (Union pour la démocratie française, the centrist and centre-right party created by Giscard in the 1970s), resulted in a political and institutional situation of cohabitation never before seen under the Fifth Republic. As the cohabitation got under way, its consequences looked particularly uncertain with regard to diplomacy and defence, where responsibilities would have to be divided between the president of the Republic and the government. But what sort of division would this be, and along what lines? While the idea of a joint exercise of power seemed the best option as far as the national interest was concerned, political logic nonetheless dictated that there would be competition at the highest level of the state. The initial arrangement between Mitterrand and the neo-Gaullist prime minister, Jacques Chirac, for sharing out duties involved the appointment to key posts of personalities who belonged to the latter's majority but were accepted by the former on the grounds of their professional competence: hence a career diplomat, Jean-Bernard Raimond, until that point France's ambassador to Moscow, was appointed as foreign minister; and the former head of the French Atomic Energy Commission, André Giraud, a technician, went to defence.

In the early days, at least, this arrangement did not go smoothly, leading on occasions to serious incidents, in particular when the government failed to pass on to the Elysée certain pieces of diplomatic correspondence. These incidents would, however, become less frequent with time and the building of a less confrontational relationship over these matters between the Elysée and the prime minister's office at Matignon. To be sure, both sides would continue to present themselves to public opinion as the main decision-making centre for foreign policy, thus confirming that competition existed at the highest level in that sphere. Yet the fact remains that, in spite of some tense moments, the experience of cohabitation did not prevent France from speaking with a single voice. Admittedly, this period was peppered with arguments over precedence and protocol between the president and the prime minister, particularly at the G7 summit in Tokyo (May 1986) and European Council meetings (The Hague in June and London in December 1986), which left observers from abroad perplexed and amused. Yet on the main issues at hand, the two protagonists generally managed to agree in substance thanks to mutual concessions. Thus Chirac had the Single European Act ratified by his parliamentary majority and, in spite of his earlier statements, gave up on his demands for a renegotiation of the conditions of Spain and Portugal's membership in the European Community; and Mitterrand, for his part, decided not to oppose the opening of the Uruguay Round of GATT talks in autumn 1986. Henceforth, the two protagonists, while not necessarily agreeing on all issues, were keen to project a united front in order to hide any disagreements that could be played upon abroad and so weaken France's position in major international negotiations or bilateral relations.

The international crises that France had to confront in this period likewise tended to promote convergence on which stance to adopt based on the traditional options of French policy – around which there was, in fact, broad consensus. Mitterrand and Chirac thus agreed, in April 1986, to deny the use of French airspace to US aircraft heading for Libya to participate in a raid against Gaddafi, an operation that the French disapproved of. While policy over issues relating to terrorism was jealously guarded by the government (1986 saw a new wave of terrorist attacks in France, and the country was still confronted with the problem of hostages held in Lebanon), the diplomatic background to these problems, namely Middle East policy, was not the subject of any major disagreements between the Elysée and Matignon. France's support for Iraq was maintained in spite of attempts to rebalance policy towards Teheran, attempts that were abandoned in 1987 owing to continuing tensions with Iran over the Lebanese hostage crisis.

*Presidential Pre-eminence*

While it saw the consolidation of a new climate of East-West détente, the international context between 1986 and 1988 was dominated by security and defence issues, which allowed Mitterrand to assert his presidential pre-eminence. Presenting himself as the guarantor of the national interest, the president sometimes forcefully opposed the prime minister and, more particularly, the defence minister. The regal domain of military policy served to illustrate this: hence without obstructing the new *Loi de programmation militaire* drawn up by the government in 1987 – and voted for by the Socialist Party – Mitterrand blocked the development of a new mobile nuclear-missile system, which he considered contrary to the French deterrence concept and unacceptable to public opinion. The deterrent concept itself became the subject of a hushed but sustained debate behind the scenes of the cohabitation. Accusing the government of adopting an inconsistent tone with regard to nuclear doctrine, Mitterrand ironically positioned himself as the protector of the Gaullist dogma against his nominally Gaullist prime minister. Chirac thus had to abandon the idea of French participation in the SDI programme, a possibility to which he had declared himself open before the election but one that the president ruled out categorically. Above all, emphasizing the preservation of the national consensus that existed around this issue, Mitterrand opposed Chirac's and above all Giraud's willingness to move French nuclear strategy closer to the US doctrine of flexible response, even threatening, at the beginning of 1988, to make public opinion the ultimate arbiter of this debate.

The nuclear debate was inextricably linked to the issue of disarmament, which had now come to dominate the international agenda. Following the Reagan-Gorbachev summit in Reykjavik (October 1986), a fear of Euro-American 'decoupling' gripped the leaders of the major European countries. The Intermediate-Range Nuclear Forces Treaty signed in Washington in December 1987, which brought the Euromissile affair to a close and paved the way to nuclear disarmament, elicited a sceptical reaction in France and in Europe more generally. Mitterrand, however, took a different view. Faced with the doubts towards the emerging INF agreement expressed by Chirac's government (whom he accused of losing sight of the principle of independence underpinning France's strategic posture) and anxious to take into account the attitude of the Germans (who were increasingly in favour of reaching an agreement), Mitterrand managed to impose his views, pledging France's support for the 'zero option'. Generally speaking, Mitterrand in this period proved more willing than Chirac to bank on the possibility of a new détente with Moscow, to which he paid another visit in July 1986. Wagering on Gorbachev's sincerity and on his chances of success, Mitterrand welcomed the return of superpower dialogue and wanted to encourage a détente that might one day make Europe's bloc system a thing of the past. By contrast, Chirac's government, up until 1987 at any rate, was more wary of Gorbachev, whom it suspected of pursuing the same objectives behind a new façade (Chirac visited Moscow in turn in May 1987 and he returned with a more positive view of the Soviet premier and his policy).

In this changing East-West context, French policy aimed to strengthen Franco-German cooperation, an issue that was the subject of broad consensus within the executive. The Franco-German partnership, in the wake of the Single European Act, increasingly saw itself as the driving force behind renewed European integration, as can be seen from the revival of plans for economic and monetary union, which was the subject of the Genscher Memorandum of February 1988 and the Delors Report of April 1989. In the areas of security and defence, too, the progress made in Franco-German cooperation was put on show in the large-scale joint military exercise '*Moineau Hardi*' ('Kecker Spatz', or 'Bold Sparrow'), in which the French Rapid Reaction Force was put through its paces (September 1987), and at the celebration of the 25th anniversary of the Elysée Treaty, on 22 January 1988, during which Mitterrand and Kohl announced the creation of a Franco-German Security and Defence Council. More generally, Franco-German cooperation now increasingly seemed to form the basis of the emerging west European strategic identity that Paris had sought to promote for many years, as could be seen in the 'Platform on European Security Interests' adopted at the prompting of the Chirac government by the members of the WEU in The Hague, in October 1987.

Mitterrand's re-election against Chirac in the second round of the presidential election on 8 May 1988 signalled his triumph in the tug of war of a cohabitation that had to all intents and purposes turned into a pre-election campaign. Foreign policy, over which Mitterrand had clearly reasserted his authority, helped him achieve victory by showing that he had been able to impose his will on his rival. In this sense, Mitterrand's re-election may be seen, in this area at least, as a vote for continuity and consensus, both of which the socialist president had managed to embody – of all people – against a neo-Gaullist challenger who personally claimed to incarnate General de Gaulle's legacy. Yet this continuity precisely demonstrated the strength of this legacy – although it would soon be put to the test by the rapid march of history.

## Notes

1. In the words of Hubert Védrine, *Les Mondes de François Mitterrand. À l'Elysée (1981–1995)*, Paris: Fayard, 1996, p. 89.

2. See 'Mitterrand, la diplomatie française et la nouvelle guerre froide', in Frédéric Bozo (ed.), *Relations internationales et stratégie. De la guerre froide à la guerre contre le terrorisme*, Rennes: Presses universitaires de Rennes, 2005.

3. Translation taken from: United States Arms Control and Disarmament Agency, *Documents on Disarmament 1983* (Washington, United States Government Printing Office, 1986) pp. 23-24.

4. See Pierre Favier and Michel Martin-Roland, *La Décennie Mitterrand*, vol. I, *Les Ruptures (1981–1984)*, Paris: Seuil, 1990, pp. 94–99.

5. See Pierre Favier and Michel Martin-Roland, *La Décennie Mitterrand*, vol. I, op. cit., pp. 321–322.

6. For further analysis, see Jean-Pierre Filiu, *Mitterrand et la Palestine*, Paris: Fayard, 2005.

# Chapter 9

# THE END OF 'YALTA' (1988–1995)

Although his second seven-year term began with the twin themes of national consensus and continuity in foreign policy, themes he had exploited during his election campaign, François Mitterrand would, a little more than a year after his comfortable re-election, be forced to confront the most momentous upheaval in international affairs since 1947. Forty years after France's reluctant entry into the Cold War, the 'end of Yalta' was no easier to deal with. With the east European revolutions of autumn 1989 and the fall of the Berlin Wall, followed in October 1990 by German reunification and in December 1991 by the break-up of the USSR, French foreign policy would lose all the familiar bearings that it had relied on for the past forty years. True, the tearing-up of the bloc system was a vindication of the notion of moving on from 'Yalta' that had underpinned this policy since de Gaulle; yet it also brought its major orientations into question, for the international context that had driven them had now disappeared. France now had to give up the comfortable situation that it had enjoyed during the Cold War, a situation that had allowed it to make the denunciation of the bipolar world order the central tenet of its diplomacy while at the same time reaping the benefits that this order brought in many respects.

So did France, at this juncture, seek at all costs to maintain the status quo? Confronted with the prodigious speed with which history was unfolding and the uncertainties that this brought, Mitterrand, it is true, chose to exercise caution. In so doing, of course, he ran the risk of giving the impression that his policy was focused on maintaining the established order, leading to the controversies that have long surrounded the decisions taken in 1989–1991. These decisions have often been presented as mere attempts to slow down, or even oppose developments that were inevitable, beginning with German reunification. However, with the benefit of hindsight and access to the relevant archives, Mitterrand's management of the end of 'Yalta' must today be seen in a very different light. French policy in this period did not aim at defending the established order, nor did it ever consist in seeking to hinder German reunification.[1] All things considered, Mitterrand would play the part of a 'middle-man' between the 'world before the Wall' and the 'world after the Wall' rather well.[2]

## German Reunification, European Unification

The upheavals of 1989 occurred against a backdrop of French and European euphoria. At the start of a new presidential term, and helped by a promising economic outlook and an international situation characterized by the spread of détente and the progress of democratic ideals in Europe, Mitterrand's France sought to present itself as a role model. The bicentenary of the French Revolution, celebrated with great pomp in July 1989 against a backdrop of east European revolutions, served as a fanfare for the role that France claimed to play in the world. During the series of international meetings that took place amid the festivities, French diplomacy was in a position to highlight its principal motives: its membership of the club of major Western powers (with the G7 summit in the Grande Arche at La Défense, Paris's business district, on 14–16 July); its support for developing countries (with the invitation issued by Paris to leaders of the South in parallel with the G7 summit, and a new French initiative on debt reduction); and, last but not least, détente and openness towards eastern Europe (with Mikhail Gorbachev's visit to France on 4–6 July and the decision by the G7 to provide assistance to Poland and Hungary).

Policy towards the East was the main international priority at the beginning of Mitterrand's second term. The cohabitation having ended with his re-election in May 1988 and the election of a presidential parliamentary majority in its wake, Mitterrand once again exercised almost sole control over foreign policy; as has usually been the case under the Fifth Republic, the new prime minister, Michel Rocard (1988–1991), a moderate socialist, had little influence on it. At a time when Gorbachev's diplomacy was breaking with the old patterns of Soviet policy, Mitterrand was determined to see France move back into a leading position in the emerging 'new' détente between East and West. On the advice of Roland Dumas, whom he had once again appointed at the Quai d'Orsay, Mitterrand, gambling that the USSR under Gorbachev would no longer be willing to use force in its sphere of influence and believing that France should return to its historical role in the region after many years of absence, ordered a vast programme of visits to the countries of eastern Europe (with the exception of Romania, where a visit was deemed politically impossible under Ceausescu's rule). After first receiving Hungary's reform-oriented communist leaders, then visiting the USSR once again in November 1988, Mitterrand went to Czechoslovakia in December, meeting the leading dissident Vaclav Havel in the French embassy, before going in January 1989 to Bulgaria and, in June 1989, to Poland, by then fully engaged in its transition to democracy. There was one imperfection in this picture of a new and ambitious French policy to the East, however: the absence of close coordination with the FRG, despite this having been previously considered by Paris and Bonn with a view to the creation of a shared *Ostpolitik*. Had it been implemented, a joint Franco-German policy towards the East would likely have been a positive contribution when the Berlin wall came down.

## German Reunification

The fall of the Berlin Wall on 9 November 1989 was a huge surprise for Paris just like for the rest of the world; in less than a year it would give rise to a unified Germany (3 October 1990). So did Mitterrand's policy following the fall of the Wall really consist, as many have subsequently argued, in slowing down, if not actually preventing this outcome? By no means. At the end of July 1989 – when such a scenario still seemed most unlikely – Mitterrand had been the first major international leader to speak openly about this possibility. German reunification, he had publicly declared, would be 'legitimate', provided that it did not come about 'using forceps' but was achieved 'peacefully and democratically'. Mitterrand's attitude over the following months consisted of two simple precepts that derived from this early statement: an acceptance of the principle of German reunification, and a desire to see it carried out within a European and international framework.[3]

Admittedly, French public opinion spontaneously showed itself to be more in favour of a return to a unified Germany than some sections of the political and media classes, some of whose representatives appeared sceptical and even fearful at the prospect of this sudden 'return of history'.[4] As a man of his generation, Mitterrand (he was born in 1916, the year of Verdun) harboured his own doubts and anxieties, often expressing over these crucial months his fear of a 'return to 1913', namely a Europe dominated by nationalism and irredentism that in his view would result if the process of German reunification (and the exit from the Cold War more generally) were not managed properly. The rapid acceleration of events, from the late autumn of 1989 (when Helmut Kohl gave his Ten-Point Plan speech in the Bundestag on 28 November) to the winter of 1990 (when Gorbachev gave East German Premier Hans Modrow the go-ahead for reunification on 30 January), rightly preoccupied international leaders, who were anxious to avoid a dangerous destabilization of Europe. Mitterrand was concerned about the possible consequences that a forced march towards German unity – which he thought the USSR would have trouble accepting at this point – might have on Gorbachev's ability to remain in power, which he saw as the absolute condition on which a peaceful transition to a 'post-Yalta' world depended.

Yet at no time did French diplomacy seek to hamper German reunification, either by invoking the rights and responsibilities of the four powers who guaranteed Germany's status (the United Kingdom, France, the Soviet Union and the United States) or by seeking to re-establish an *alliance de revers* with Gorbachev's USSR or an *entente cordiale* with the United Kingdom, where Margaret Thatcher was openly hostile to reunification. Mitterrand was perfectly aware of just how pointless and counterproductive such moves would be; and it is hard, with hindsight, to think that he would have been willing to take the risk of bringing into question forty years of Franco-German reconciliation and cooperation in the vain hope of preventing German reunification (a process that de Gaulle had described thirty years earlier as part of the 'normal destiny of the German people'), especially given that he himself had continuously declared the legitimacy of the Germans' right to self-determination.

Admittedly, Mitterrand found it uneasy to 'communicate' during these crucial months, thus running the risk of being misunderstood in Germany; hence, he refrained from delivering a 'big speech' or making a 'grand gesture' (such as standing beside Kohl at the ceremonial opening of the Brandenburg Gate in December 1989) that the Germans – who still had the image of Kohl and Mitterrand standing hand in hand at Verdun in their minds – might have expected from the French president on such an occasion. This attitude was most likely carefully calculated; during the closing weeks of 1989 and the first few weeks of the following year, Mitterrand's priority was indeed to hold Kohl back from rushing headlong towards the kind of reunification 'using forceps' that he wanted to avoid (in other words, a reunification without regard for the international context). Yet as a result, he could not prevent certain actions from being interpreted as attempts to place obstacles in the path of German unity, such as his meeting with Gorbachev in Kiev on 6 December, or his visit to East Germany on 20–22 December. This failure to 'communicate', no doubt, accounts for the brief deterioration in relations between Paris and Bonn over these few weeks.

It was nevertheless a desire to place the reunification process within a firm framework, and not some far-fetched attempt to derail it, which explains Mitterrand's attitude. While he saw reunification per se as the Germans' own business, he believed that its international consequences did affect Germany's neighbours, and the four powers in particular. The role played by France in the 'Two Plus Four' negotiations, which began in March 1990 and would result in the treaty that definitively settled the German question (Moscow, 12 September 1990), was in accordance with this belief. Still faithfully adhering to the doctrine first set out by de Gaulle in 1959, French diplomacy concentrated in particular on the question of borders, in other words the Oder-Neisse line, which Mitterrand wanted a reunified Germany to accept unequivocally. His insistence was given a cool reception by Kohl for domestic political reasons; this led to a short-lived crisis in relations with Bonn before the chancellor acquiesced to his partner's demands. In other respects, the French role in the 'Two Plus Four' negotiations was more secondary. Without pressing the issue unduly, France subscribed to the aim of keeping a unified Germany inside the Atlantic Alliance, an objective that the United States had made its priority from December 1989 onwards; Mitterrand, in fact, helped convince Gorbachev to accept it during his visit to Moscow on 25 May 1990 (the final agreement of the Soviet leader on this matter, obtained by Kohl in July 1990, removed the last hurdle to the signing of the Moscow Treaty two months later).

## European Unification

Yet Mitterrand's real priority with respect to a unified Germany lay elsewhere. After four decades of reconciliation and cooperation with the Federal Republic, the French president naturally concluded that the solution to the German question was to be found in the continued pursuit and strengthening of the European project, a conviction that was shared by the German chancellor. It was now a matter of turning into fact what had, up until the fall of the Berlin Wall, simply been an abstract formula, at most a long-term prospect. In the wake of the fall of the Wall, which had occurred during France's turn at occupying the six-month presidency of the European Community in the second semester of 1989, Mitterrand's main concern was therefore to make sure that the likely forthcoming reunification of Germany would not jeopardize the vital pursuit of European unification; in his view, it would even be necessary to accelerate the latter even if this meant appearing, in German eyes, to be trying to hold back the former. The difference in priorities between Bonn and Paris was clear when the Twelve met over dinner at the Elysée on 18 November 1989 to discuss events in eastern Europe and what the Community's response to them should be (economic aid, help towards democratic transition): tellingly, the question of German reunification was barely mentioned on that occasion. At that juncture, the European Council meeting in Strasbourg (8–9 December 1989) seemed to present a decisive deadline for action. Mitterrand wanted to set a firm timetable for putting in place an Economic and Monetary Union (EMU), plans for which had been relaunched by Paris and Bonn in 1988–1989; but Kohl remained doubtful, baulking for domestic political reasons at committing himself to effectively starting a negotiation over EMU before the German elections in 1990. Mitterrand nevertheless kept up the pressure. His tenacity paid off: in Strasbourg, Kohl accepted the call for an intergovernmental conference (IGC) to begin at the end of 1990, as Mitterrand had wanted. In parallel to this, the chancellor obtained the support of the Twelve for the principle of German unity. Although there was no formal quid pro quo between German reunification and European unification, the linkage between the two was quite obvious, and it marked the culmination of four decades of Franco-German reconciliation and cooperation in the context of the European project.

To be sure, the views of France and Germany in this crucial phase of European integration were not identical. While Paris wanted above all to hasten the implementation of EMU, Bonn's priority was to accelerate political unification. While the former was difficult to accept for the Germans, who saw it as spelling the end for the deutschmark, the latter inspired similar foreboding in Paris, where the federalist approach traditionally favoured by Bonn was regarded with suspicion. Faced with the insistence shown by Kohl, who was backed by Delors, Mitterrand realized that he would not be able to oppose a fresh reform of European institutions; however, he did hope that he could prevent the political union that would accompany EMU from taking an excessively integrationist turn. In discussing political union, he wanted to give priority to promoting the EU as an actor on the international stage, something that could only be based on intergovernmental decision-making. A compromise emerged along these lines at the Dublin I and II European Council meetings in April and June 1990, where it was agreed that in parallel with the IGC devoted to EMU, the Twelve would hold an IGC on political union. These two conferences were launched concurrently in Rome in December 1990; negotiations went on throughout 1991 and resulted in December of that year in a treaty that was approved in outline form, and subsequently signed by the Twelve at Maastricht in February 1992.

The Maastricht Treaty, which instituted the European Union, was the culmination of projects set in motion more than twenty years before. As well as reaching agreement on a future common currency, the Twelve adopted a Common Foreign and Security Policy and restated their long-term objective of developing a system of European defence. This leap forward in the building of Europe was a success for Mitterrand's diplomacy: in spite of the inevitable compromises and ambiguities that were present in the treaty, the result obtained at Maastricht lived up to French ambitions. Above all, the Maastricht Treaty signalled the successful conclusion of a Franco-German dynamic that German reunification had, in spite of a few short-lived episodes of friction, never seriously brought into question, and if anything had given renewed impetus. For Mitterrand's France, the end of the Europe of 'Yalta' meant, first and foremost, the birth of the Europe of Maastricht.

## The Elusive New World Order

France's place within the new international system was also undergoing change outside Europe; some difficult adjustments had to be made there as well. With the end of the Cold War and the political thaw in the East, the spread of democracy was now becoming a major issue worldwide – nowhere more so than in Africa. The situation to which France had become accustomed since decolonization was now changing rapidly, leading to some hard choices for Paris. In the case of Algeria, which had been shaken by riots that were harshly repressed in October 1988, Paris pledged its support to the regime of Chadli Bendjedid, which was now – cautiously – engaged in a programme of democratic reform (a new constitution was adopted in February 1989 and, in March, Mitterrand made a visit); the aim was to prevent a slide into repression by the regime on the one hand, and the taking of power by the Islamists on the other. This meant treading a narrow tightrope, however. The Islamists continued to grow in strength following the legalization of the Islamic Salvation Front (*Front Islamique du Salut*, FIS) in autumn 1989; after claiming victory in the municipal elections of June 1990, they won an overwhelming majority in the parliamentary elections of December 1991, leading the army in the first few months of 1992 to remove Chadli from office, declare the election void and outlaw the FIS. The country found itself on the brink of civil war.

In sub-Saharan African, meanwhile, even France's seemingly everlasting 'African estate' was not immune from the country's need to reassess its major foreign policy orientations. Yet at a time when the end of apartheid in South Africa and the release of Nelson Mandela (February 1990) seemed to offer immense hope, Mitterrand's France gave the impression of only reluctantly considering the changes in its African policy that were now necessary. While some of Mitterrand's motives may have been justified (his refusal to abandon Africa, increasingly marginalized in economic and strategic terms, by a Europe absorbed in its own challenges) others were less so (a reluctance to reconsider a policy based since the independence era on the defence of 'friendly' heads of state and their regimes, a policy that, as we have seen, he had left largely unchanged). Although the Franco-African summit in La Baule (19–21 June 1990) seemed to mark a turning point, with Mitterrand pledging to link the promise of French aid to the movement of these regimes towards democracy and good governance, in practice little changed in relations between France and Africa. A year later, at the summit of francophone nations held in Paris (19–21 November 1991), Mitterrand would be considerably less forthright in his declarations than he had been at La Baule.

## The Gulf War

More than any other event, the Gulf War – the first great crisis of the post–Cold War period – stands out as a test of France's position in the 'post-Yalta' world. The surprise invasion of Kuwait by Saddam Hussein's Iraq on 2 August 1990 presented French policy with an immediate dilemma.[5] As a permanent member of the UN Security Council and a major ally of the United States, France could not run the risk of being seen to dither or favour appeasement in the face of Iraq's naked aggression against Kuwait (followed by its outright annexation) or of splitting away from the coalition assembled by Washington in the immediate aftermath of the invasion. Yet France also ran the risk, by becoming another cog in this machine, of contradicting its own Middle East policy (of which support for Iraq against Iran had been a major plank in the 1980s) and sacrificing its ability to act independently by aligning itself with the United States, now the sole remaining superpower.

Right from the beginning of the crisis, however, Mitterrand made a clear choice, ruling out any possibility of France disregarding the principles of international law and abandoning its own global responsibilities – thereby also running the risk of losing its status as a major power just as Germany was reunifying. Mitterrand was fully aware that he was possibly locking himself into the 'logic of war' that quickly characterized the US response to Iraqi intransigence, and his approach was denounced by some of his closest associates (including Defence Minister Jean-Pierre Chevènement, who would resign soon after the start of military operations in January 1990). Yet he had no intention of withdrawing from the united front presented by the West. To be sure, in spite of the danger of triggering Washington's ire, Mitterrand believed that he ought to do everything in his power – right up until the expiry of the 15 January 1991 ultimatum given to Saddam Hussein – to avoid a war. Hence his efforts to find a way out of the crisis, which were both official, such as his speech to the UN General Assembly on 24 September 1990, and unofficial, such as the contacts established with Iraq through the Gaullist politician Edgar Pisani. Yet Mitterrand harboured few illusions as to his chances of success, and these efforts did not affect his fundamental choice to participate in the coalition and, if necessary, resort to the use of force. Once the air campaign began (on 17 January 1991) followed by a brief but decisive ground campaign (24–28 February), France thus contributed fully to Operation Desert Storm, to Washington's satisfaction. This was in spite of the fact that the carefully measured French contribution (about 60 aircraft and 12,000 men operating as the *division Daguet*) was smaller than that deployed by the United Kingdom, due as much to limited military resources as to political reasons: Mitterrand wished to preserve France's future standing in the Arab world, which in his view involved avoiding projecting the image of a surrogate of the United States.

But while Mitterrand feared France's likely marginalization in the postwar reordering of the Middle East if it abstained from any sustained involvement in the conflict, in the end its active participation in Desert Storm did not win France the regional role that its diplomacy had been seeking. Following the conflict, the United States was more than ever eager to treat the Middle East as an exclusive zone of political and economic influence. True, in the months following the end of hostilities, Washington at last showed some determination to get the Arab-Israeli peace process on track, thus coming around to French and European views on the need to settle the Palestinian question. Yet French – and European – diplomacy was virtually absent from the process launched at the Madrid Conference (30 October–2 November 1991), over which the United States effectively retained leadership despite the formal role of the USSR (and subsequently the Russian Federation) as co-sponsor.

This was all the more disappointing given that Paris had for many years been arguing for just the sort of direct Israeli-Palestinian dialogue that at last began following Madrid, resulting a little more than two years later in the historic Oslo and Washington Accords (20 August and 13 September 1993, respectively) signed by Yitzhak Rabin and Yasser Arafat. By consistently defending the Palestinians' right to exist as a political entity and by encouraging them to take the vital step of recognizing Israel and its right to security, French diplomacy had indeed helped make this dialogue possible: it was after all Mitterrand who, receiving Arafat at the Elysée in May 1989, had persuaded him to pronounce, in French, his now famous phrase 'c'est caduc' ('it's no longer valid') regarding the articles of the PLO Charter referring to the destruction of Israel, thus marking a crucial shift in the Palestinian position.

To be sure, responding to those who were prone to contrast France's effective marginalization following the Gulf War with its earlier influence in the region, Dumas was prepared to declare that France's 'Arab policy' had just been a 'myth', thus attacking one of the fundamental tenets of Gaullist foreign policy. Yet right from the beginning in 1981, Mitterrand had in fact adopted an approach to the Middle East and the Arab world that had clear elements of continuity with the very 'Arab policy' of de Gaulle and his successors that Dumas seemed prone to berate. Whatever name one gives this policy, the main axes of France's Middle East policy (close relations with a country like Iraq, a willingness to play an active role in the resolution of the Israeli-Arab and Israeli-Palestinian conflicts) were, in effect, brought into question after the Gulf War – even if the launching of the peace process did retrospectively confirm French intuitions.

Mitterrand, who so successfully managed France's involvement in the conflict and its international implications, also dealt remarkably well with its domestic aspects by convincing an initially reluctant public and political class of the need for this involvement. By the end of hostilities he had thus gained a new credibility in terms of his ability to 'communicate', which erased the memory of the less successful period that he had experienced faced with German unification. Yet this would be short-lived. Like George H. W. Bush and John Major, the credibility amassed by the president would soon evaporate in a difficult domestic context. Above all, France was having trouble in finding its place in the 'New World Order' announced by Bush, who was keen to maintain US leadership after its victory in the Gulf War.

Having found itself eclipsed in the Middle East, French diplomacy was also going through a difficult period on the old continent, the architecture of which was undergoing radical change. This was particularly the case with the Atlantic Alliance, which had, with the London Summit (5–6 July 1990), begun a process of post–Cold War re-evaluation that could have provided a welcome opportunity for an update in the somewhat fossilized relationship between France and NATO. Yet while discreet conversations were held on this subject in the autumn and winter of 1990 between Paris and Washington, these eventually came to nothing. In Mitterrand's view, the reform of the Alliance, which was formally agreed at the Rome Summit (7–8 November 1991), was indeed inadequate. Judging that NATO was artificially strengthened by the United States' willingness to reassert its leadership and unduly resistant to attempts by Europe to develop its own approach in defence and security matters, he believed that there was no need for France to bring its special position into question. But while his attitude may have been justified, it ran the risk of giving the impression yet again that French policy was having trouble adapting to this new context.[6]

In the immediate post–Cold War period, the prevailing impression of France's policy towards eastern Europe was likewise one of a difficult process of adaptation. France had, it was true, hosted the CSCE Summit of 19–21 November 1990, in Paris, where the end of the division of the old continent was officially declared with some solemnity, and where work commenced on building a 'Greater Europe' stretching from the Atlantic to the Urals, as once prophesied by de Gaulle. Prompted by Jacques Attali, Mitterrand's close adviser, France had also taken the initiative in creating the European Bank for Reconstruction and Development (EBRD) to help put the former communist countries back on their feet. Most importantly, Mitterrand had, in his New Year's address on 31 December 1989, launched the idea of a 'European Confederation':

As we all know, the change that has occurred over the last few months in the countries of Eastern Europe is more important than anything we have seen since the Second World War, and will no doubt take its place among the great events of history. . . . But the situation in Romania serves to remind us that history can be tragic and that freedom is paid for in suffering. Let us not forget what millions and millions of men and women have been through during such a long period of darkness. Their sudden liberation can leave us under no illusion. Ahead of them lie many obstacles, and they will need us. . . . Europe, it is quite clear, will no longer be the same place that we have known for more than half a century. Previously dependent on the two superpowers, she will, like someone coming home, return to her own history and geography. New questions are beginning to be asked that cannot be answered straight away. . . . Either the tendency towards break-up and fragmentation will grow and we will be back in the Europe of 1919 – we all know what happened next – or Europe will build herself anew. She can do so in two stages. Firstly, through the community of the Twelve, which absolutely has to strengthen its structures, and has just decided to do so in Strasbourg. I am convinced that it has, by its very existence, powerfully assisted the peoples of the East in their leap forward by serving as a point of reference and a pole of attraction. The second stage has yet to be devised. Based on the Helsinki Accords, I expect to see the birth, in the course of the 1990s, of a European confederation in the true sense of the term, which will bring together all the states of our continent in a shared, permanent organization devoted to commercial and cultural exchange, peace and security. This will obviously only be possible once a plurality of political parties, free elections, a representative system and freedom of information are established in the countries of the East. At the speed with which events are presently moving, we may not have to wait too long.

Mitterrand wanted to create a political and institutional framework within which the Europe of the Twelve could establish itself as an anchoring point for the central and eastern European (CEE) countries, whose full integration within the Community then still remained a distant prospect. Yet the Confederation project – which undoubtedly responded to a real need – would nonetheless end in diplomatic failure. By excluding the United States from the initiative while insisting on the participation of the USSR, Mitterrand's diplomacy did not go down well with the new east-European leaders, for whom, in the immediate aftermath of the Cold War (and the Gulf War) the United States represented both a model and a guarantee. Worse still, the European Confederation was perceived by those concerned as a way to keep them waiting indefinitely on the sidelines of the Community. In short, the priority given by France to the EU heightened the perception that France, here too, wanted to perpetuate the status quo, thus preventing the country from getting a hearing in the East; the result was that the Confederation project got bogged down straight after the 'founding congress' that was supposed to launch it (Prague, 12–14 June 1991).

As for Mitterrand's apparent dithering when faced with the break-up of the USSR in the closing months of 1991, this too did little to enhance the reputation of French diplomacy. Admittedly, the attitude shown by the French president at the time of the abortive putsch in Moscow (19–21 August) involved more of a presentational misjudgement than a political mistake: if at first he had seemed, if not to approve, then at least to accept the ousting of the Soviet premier as a fait accompli, his attitude reflected first and foremost his concern not to endanger Gorbachev's personal safety and, even more importantly, to make sure that the events in Moscow did not imperil international stability or the new path taken by East-West relations. The fact remains, however, that Mitterrand's attitude yet again seemed to give – arguably unjustified – credence to the idea that his diplomacy was based on a wait-and-see approach. The same could be said of the stance taken by Mitterrand – which was in fact very close to that of Bush – when, in the weeks that followed, he sought to prevent a disorderly break-up of the USSR, thus running the risk of appearing to keep on betting until the very end (25 December 1991) on its surviving the tide of history.

## The Yugoslavian Tragedy

From summer and autumn 1991 onwards, the break-up of Yugoslavia became a major source of concern and a major challenge. For the first time since 1945, war had returned to Europe, dashing hopes for peaceful post–Cold War development – in the Balkans, at any rate – and confirming Mitterrand's fears of a 'return to 1913'. At the very beginning of the disintegration of Yugoslavia, against the backdrop of the Slovenian and Croatian declarations of independence in June 1991, Mitterrand had outlined the approach that he intended to follow. In contrast to an entrenched narrative of a pro-Serbian French president who sought to preserve Yugoslavia's integrity at all costs, he very quickly concluded that maintaining the status quo was unrealistic; he did, however, believe that the international community needed to oversee the process of separation (as it had overseen German reunification) and try to prevent a disorderly break-up of the federation. Pursuing this objective meant maintaining a position of neutrality towards the former Yugoslav republics, which Mitterrand saw as having a shared responsibility for the process of disintegration. He also believed that the Europe of the Twelve, which had ambitions of developing a common foreign policy and becoming a player on the international stage, needed to take on a leading role in attempts to resolve a crisis in which the United States, whose vital interests were not at stake, did not intend to involve itself directly.

Yet while the Brioni Agreement, negotiated under the aegis of the European Troika (7 July 1991) gave brief hopes of a respite, the crisis rapidly spiralled out of control. In spite of the peace conference convened at The Hague (7 September 1991), the Serbo-Croat conflict became a war, causing heavy casualties to civilians, as illustrated by the siege of Vukovar in September–November 1991. Events quickly turned in favour of the Serbs, who were now in a position to impose their vision of a Greater Serbia on the ground. Although Mitterrand – while at the same time holding back from labelling the Serbs as the sole aggressors – put forward a proposal for the creation of an interposition force to his European partners, the Twelve possessed neither the military capabilities nor the institutional framework that this would require; in addition, the United Kingdom, who at this time was hostile to any plans for intervention, opposed the idea. However, it was above all intra-European – and in particular Franco-German – disagreements that paralyzed action by the Twelve. Whereas a now united Germany, sensitive to the right to self-determination but also keen to assert itself on the international scene, wanted to recognize Slovenian and Croatian independence as quickly as possible, France – like most European countries, including the United Kingdom, and the United States – believed that giving such recognition would be premature and dangerous in the absence of any satisfactory agreement regarding borders or the rights of minorities (an arbitration committee headed by the former French justice minister, Robert Badinter, was given the task of sorting out these issues). And yet, when Bonn, in spite of the opposition of its partners, at the end of the year decided to go ahead and recognize the two republics, Paris fell into line in the early weeks of 1992, not wanting to get into a confrontation with Germany against the backdrop of the completion of the Maastricht Treaty.

Far from slowing the descent into chaos, as the Germans had hoped, this episode, which cast a pall over relations between Paris and Bonn, merely served to exacerbate tensions on the ground. This was particularly true in Bosnia-Herzegovina, the multiethnic republic whose independence was in turn recognized by the Twelve despite the refusal of the Serb minority, supported by Belgrade; as a result, the war, predictably, spread to the republic in spring 1992. Following the dramatic and highly symbolic visit made by Mitterrand to besieged Sarajevo on 28 June 1992, the French, together with the United Kingdom, took the lead in the efforts by the international community to resolve the crisis within the framework of the UN. These two countries were from then on the main contributors to the peacekeeping force deployed in the former Yugoslavia. While Germany was now keeping a low profile, Mitterrand, who had declared that he refused to 'add war to war', limited the mission's rationale strictly to humanitarian assistance and peacekeeping. France, both on the diplomatic front and at the head of UNPROFOR (the UN Protection Force), was nevertheless willing to play a role that Mitterrand believed was in keeping with its international responsibilities and its status as a permanent member of the UN Security Council. Yet his approach met with criticism from informed opinion and within intellectual circles, where a more interventionist stance was being called for. In the end, the willingness of the belligerents to keep on fighting, along with the inertia and disagreements among the international community, marked the real limits of interposition.

## Towards a New Approach

The second cohabitation, following the parliamentary elections of 21 and 28 March 1993, looked very different to the first from the point of view of foreign policy. This time, the political balance was very much in favour of the government of Édouard Balladur, who held a crushing RPF-UDR majority in parliament; Mitterrand was politically weakened by the approaching end of his term, but also by his illness and a growing controversy regarding his achievements as president and his record during the war. With the appointment of major political figures to key posts (Alain Juppé to foreign affairs, François Léotard to defence), the new government intended to take full control of its own responsibilities with respect to foreign policy without, however, impinging on presidential prerogatives, which Balladur had declared that he wanted to respect. As a result, the experience of cohabitation in 1993–1995 proved to be less antagonistic than it had been in 1986–1988. This time, the president and the prime minister were not electoral rivals; in addition, the main players in the second cohabitation had learnt the lessons of the first and wanted to avoid facing the same difficulties. If there was any rivalry, it was between the two aspiring RPR candidates in the coming presidential election, Balladur and Chirac (who had declined to serve again as prime minister, leaving Balladur to head the government). This rivalry was particularly noticeable over the issue of French nuclear tests, which Chirac wanted to resume, while Balladur decided to respect the moratorium decreed by Mitterrand in 1992 following France's decision to sign the NPT. It was also evident in the disagreements between Juppé, an ally of Chirac, and Interior Minister Charles Pasqua, an ally of Balladur, over the situation in Algeria, which had now descended into civil war: whereas Juppé wanted to encourage Algiers to enter into a dialogue with the FIS, Pasqua believed that France should support the Algerian government's repressive policy, which he saw as necessary as part of the fight against radical Islam and in order to prevent large-scale immigration into France in the event of an Islamist victory.

Between the Elysée, Matignon and the Quai d'Orsay, disagreements were limited. Aside from the question of nuclear tests (over which Balla-

dur sought to avoid confrontation with Mitterrand) there was no fundamental divergence regarding foreign policy between the two heads of the
executive. This was the case with respect to Yugoslavia, where the main
parameters of France's policy, against the backdrop of the worsening crisis
in Bosnia-Herzegovina, remained unchanged throughout the cohabitation,
focusing as they did on the search for a political settlement and maintaining a UN peacekeeping force on the ground. Faced with the deteriorating situation on the ground, Balladur was prepared to consider a French
withdrawal. Yet Juppé, who advocated maintaining and even strengthening
France's engagement, prevailed; from spring 1993 onwards a new dynamism
was injected into the action taken by Paris in the former Yugoslavia. This
led to improved coordination between the major powers (with the Juppé-
Kinkel plan of autumn 1993 and the creation of a 'contact group' for Bosnia
in spring 1994) and to greater military determination against the Serbs (a
NATO ultimatum over the siege of Sarajevo was called for by France and
the United States in February 1994). While clearly more muscular, this
action nevertheless followed the outline that Mitterrand had been pressing
for since the beginning of the crisis.

Yet the situation in the former Yugoslavia went from bad to worse
between 1993 and 1995: on the ground, the UN forces were unable to
hold back the Bosnian Serb advance in spite of the creation of 'safe havens'
and support from NATO air power; on the diplomatic front things were
no better, due in no small measure to the contradictory position taken by
the US administration. While in favour, since Bill Clinton's arrival at the
White House, of lifting the embargo on arms deliveries to the Bosnians and
carrying out air strikes against the Bosnian Serbs, the United States ruled
out any US deployment on the ground prior to a peace settlement. While
formally backing the efforts of the international community, they were also
discretely working towards the creation and arming of a Muslim-Bosnian
confederation. This led to growing friction between Washington on one
side, and Paris and London on the other, whose 'blue helmets' found themselves increasingly exposed – to the point that, if conditions became bad
enough, their withdrawal was envisaged. From late 1994, then, a transatlantic crisis was emerging alongside the Yugoslavian crisis. With the French
presidential elections of April–May 1995 drawing near, the status quo
seemed to have become untenable. The moment of truth appeared imminent, including for a French policy of equidistance that had now reached
the end of its useful life.

A similar need for a new approach was felt by many with respect to
France's African policy. The devaluation of the CFA (Communauté financière africaine) franc, mooted since 1992 against the backdrop of the serious
deterioration of the financial situation in African countries, looked increas-

ingly necessary as part of a process of redefining relations between France and its former African colonies. This move, which brought into question one of the pillars of '*la Françafrique*', was seen through by the Balladur government, with the agreement of the Elysée, in 1994. Meanwhile, the Rwandan tragedy, which unfolded against the backdrop of a civil war that became a genocide following the assassination of the country's president, Juvénal Habyarimana, in April 1994, provided a dramatic illustration of the need to redefine France's African policy. Operation Turquoise, a humanitarian mission, was carried out by the French Army from bases in Zaire from June to August 1994, contrasting with the inaction of the rest of the international community; yet Paris would in the months and years that followed face accusations that the French government had supported, and even encouraged, the genocidal Hutu clan in its attempt to exterminate the Tutsis. The accusation does not stand up to closer examination, even though France cannot be exonerated of all responsibility owing to the support (premised, it should be noted, on democratic reform and moves towards a settlement between Hutus and Tutsis) that it had effectively provided to the Kigali government at the beginning of the 1990s.

## *Europe and the Alliance*

At a time when the international community was showing itself to be powerless in the former Yugoslavia, French foreign policy under the cohabitation saw the beginnings of important developments on two key issues: Europe and NATO. In September 1992, the referendum on the ratification of the Maastricht Treaty saw the 'yes' vote win by only a very slim majority in spite of Mitterrand's strong personal involvement in the campaign and the support of all major political parties (except for the communists and the Front National), signalling an important change in the attitude taken towards Europe by French public opinion and the country's political classes alike. The European Union came into being (formally on 1 November 1993) against the backdrop of a worsening economic and political climate that contrasted sharply with the euphoria seen at Maastricht. Such swings of the pendulum had arguably followed every decisive step in the building of Europe; this one did, nevertheless, mark the end of a long period of French European policy under Mitterrand. While the European project remained a French priority, the growing doubts among the French public expressed in the referendum, along with the disagreement among the European countries, in particular between Paris and Bonn, over the former Yugoslavia and the Union's international role, not to mention the 1992–1993 crisis in the EMS and the difficulties encountered in bringing to a close the Uruguay Round of the GATT (a renegotiation of which the Balladur government had demanded at the last minute) were all factors that tended to cast a certain integrationist conception of Europe into doubt. In any case, the prospect of a widening of the Union towards the East, now accepted by Paris, had probably rendered such a conception obsolete by then. Against a backdrop of Franco-German uncertainties twinned with Franco-British convergence, the Balladur government was now formulating a more pragmatic, and above all more nation-based vision of the European project that carried echoes of the Pompidou era, to whose legacy the new prime minister (once close to Pompidou) laid claim.

French security and defence policy also underwent a shift, as could be seen from the new White Paper (*Livre blanc*) on defence produced in 1994. The lack of unity and the powerlessness shown by Europe in the former Yugoslavia, coupled with the growing role of NATO in the conflict, led to a downgrading of the new Union's ambitions as far as defence and security were concerned. France, having previously championed European strategic independence, was forced to abandon the vision of the WEU as the 'armed wing' of the European Union and move closer to the concept of a 'European pillar' within the Atlantic Alliance that it had thus far rejected. At the same time, and for the same reasons, France, starting in 1994, began a pragmatic rapprochement with NATO, in which it now found itself increasingly involved as a result of NATO's actions in the former Yugoslavia. Reversing its non-participation in certain Alliance bodies such as the Military Committee and giving its support at the Brussels summit of January 1994 to the concept of Combined Joint Task Forces (CJTF), France, without renouncing the sacrosanct principle of military non-integration, was beginning gradually to modify its position within the Alliance. While the developments of 1994–1995 were handled cautiously and did not lead to a wholesale revision, by the run-up to the presidential elections of 1995 French foreign policy was in the process of changing direction, hinting at profound shifts to come.

## Notes

1. For more detail on this topic, see Frédéric Bozo, *Mitterrand, the End of the Cold War, and German Unification*, New York: Berghahn Books, 2009.

2. Hubert Védrine, *Les Mondes de François Mitterrand. À l'Elysée (1981–1995)*, Paris: Fayard, 1996, p. 9.

3. On Mitterrand and German reunification, see Frédéric Bozo, *Mitterrand, the End of the Cold War, and German Unification*, op. cit.; and Tilo Schabert, *Mitterrand et la réunification allemande. Une histoire secrète (1981–1995)*, Paris: Grasset, 2005.

4. For further analysis, see Marie-Noëlle Brand Crémieux, *Les Français face à la réunification allemande*, Paris: L'Harmattan, 2004.

5. For further analysis of this episode, see Pierre Favier and Michel Martin-Roland, *La Décennie Mitterrand*, vol. III, *Les Défis (1988–1991)*, Paris: Seuil, 1996, pp. 439–510.

6. For further analysis, see Frédéric Bozo, 'Un rendez-vous manqué? La France, les États-Unis et l'Alliance atlantique, 1990–1991', *Relations internationales* 120 (winter 2004), pp. 119–132.

# PART V

# FRANCE AND GLOBALIZATION
## (1995–2015)

# Chapter 10

# IN SEARCH OF A MULTIPOLAR WORLD (1995–2007)

The first round of the 1995 presidential election on 23 April saw Jacques Chirac take the lead over the other main right-wing candidate, Édouard Balladur; Chirac then won comfortably in the run-off against the socialist candidate Lionel Jospin on 7 May. As well as signalling the end of the second cohabitation, Chirac's arrival at the Elysée drew a line under the long Mitterrand years and marked the return of a Gaullist to the presidency after three consecutive seven-year terms. The French presidential election also coincided with a new era in international relations: with the Cold War declared definitively over, the new paradigm of globalization had now become dominant. The intensification of world financial and commercial flows, the rise of emerging powers, the confirmation of the United States as the only superpower, even as a 'hyperpower': all of these phenomena radically changed an international picture that had long been held in place by a bipolarity that, while it may have been unfair, had nonetheless been stable and predictable. Adapting to globalization, with all the opportunities – but also the risks – that came with it, was now a major challenge for France and for French foreign policy.

The new French president approached this challenge from a personal perspective that he had built up over a long political career.[1] Chirac's perspective summed up, in many ways, the contradictory aspirations of the French people: a pragmatic politician, he was not a prisoner of dogma and proved ready to adapt when necessary, even if this meant repudiating earlier positions; as a Gaullist, he sought – at the price of the occasional lurching – to preserve France's 'rank' while at the same time pushing for the establishment of a 'Europe-power'; haunted by a possible clash of civilizations, he emphasized the need to respect the 'diversity of cultures', at times even displaying a degree of relativism. Together, these aspirations would make the quest for a regulated form of globalization and a multipolar world the hallmark of Chirac's foreign policy – occasionally leading to confrontations with the United States, as the Iraq crisis of 2003 would show.

## Chirac's Voluntarism and its Limits

No sooner had Chirac been elected than he asserted himself on the international scene through a series of decisions and attitudes that clearly broke with past policy: in May, he decided to strengthen France's military forces in Bosnia-Herzegovina; and in June, he announced the resumption of French nuclear tests while embarking on a muscular presidency of the European Council at its meeting in Cannes. Some saw this as a willingness to break free from the supposed ossification of Mitterrand's last years by taking courageous decisions; others thought that Chirac had once more succumbed to the temptation to make political waves, thus risking international rebuke. Be that as it may, these early decisions and attitudes reflected Chirac's willingness from the outset of his term, in keeping with his image as a can-do politician, to proclaim his voluntarism in foreign policy. Yet while these decisions and attitudes were evidence of a deliberately forthright diplomatic style in sharp contrast with the more subtle style of his predecessor, to what extent did the new president's foreign policy constitute a real change in substance? Would there, on a fundamental level, be continuity or a clean break?

The situation in Bosnia-Herzegovina, which by spring 1995 had deteriorated even further, gave Chirac his first opportunity to assert himself on the international stage. For the new president, the powerlessness shown by the international community was no longer acceptable. In the face of the Bosnian Serbs' provocative escalations, Chirac resolved to use stronger measures, as shown by the assault on the Vrbanja Bridge at the end of May. Launched on his orders to free a group of French blue helmets taken hostage by the Bosnian Serb forces, this feat of arms marked a departure from the hitherto passive stance taken by the UN forces.

Most importantly, Chirac's new resolve resulted in the decision to 'beef up' UNPROFOR by creating a Franco-Anglo-Dutch Rapid Reaction Force (RRF) equipped with heavy weapons. Once Paris had obtained a UN Security Council resolution to this effect, the RRF was deployed near Sarajevo in July. Yet this stronger response from the international community was not enough to stem the violence in Bosnia-Herzegovina; this violence reached its height from 7 July onwards, when the enclave of Srebrenica was taken by Bosnian Serb forces; shortly afterwards, the enclave of Zepa also fell. The West remained tragically powerless in the face of these events. The fall of

Srebrenica would lead to the bloodiest episode of the whole war: the cold-blooded massacre of almost 8000 Bosnian Muslim civilians by the forces of Bosnian Serb General Ratko Mladic. A war crime without a precedent in Europe since 1945, this appalling episode would long weigh heavily on the conscience of Europe and the West.

The hardening of France's position would nevertheless work as a catalyst in the weeks that followed. Hitherto reluctant to commit US forces, Bill Clinton now saw that this was the only way to put an end to the conflict in the Balkans and restore the seriously dented credibility of US leadership and of NATO's effectiveness; this led on 30 August 1995 to the launching by NATO of an aerial bombing campaign against Bosnian Serb positions (Operation Deliberate Force), combined a few days later with the launching of a ground offensive by Croatian and Muslim forces, trained and supported by Washington. By mid-September this led Serbian President Slobodan Milosevic to accept a peace settlement, forcing the Serb leaders in Bosnia to give in. Clearly, Chirac's voluntarism had played a part in the Bosnian endgame in autumn 1995. Hence the frustration felt by French diplomats during the subsequent round of diplomacy leading up to the Dayton conference (1–21 November 1995); for although the peace accords negotiated at this Ohio military base between the Bosnian, Croat and Serbian presidents under the auspices of the US envoy Richard Holbrooke in fact closely followed the plan for a settlement worked out over the previous months and years by European – and in particular French – diplomacy, the United States would take most of the credit. While Washington allowed France the consolation of having the document formally signed in Paris on 14 December 1995, the French were now playing second fiddle, as illustrated by the replacement on 20 December 1995 of UNPROFOR by the NATO-led IFOR (Implementation Force).

## Chirac's 'Strategic Revolution'

French frustration at seeing leadership in the Balkans snatched by the United States did not prevent a fresh start from being made in relations between Paris and Washington. As all his predecessors had done since de Gaulle, the new French president wanted to establish a close relationship with the United States, a country with which he personally felt some affinity. From the outset, Chirac and Clinton struck up a personal rapport that would remain excellent over the years to come, regardless of the international crises and difficulties they would face.[2] Chirac's state visit to the United States (31 January–1 February 1996) was the first by a French president since Mitterrand's state visit twelve years earlier. Admittedly, a little of the shine was taken off the solemn occasion of Chirac's speech to Congress

(1 February) by the absence of many members who wished to signal their disapproval at the resumption of French nuclear tests, even though Paris had recently announced that these would soon be ended. Chirac nevertheless used this occasion to make a powerful declaration by stating France's readiness to once again take her proper place at the NATO table. Although Paris had already declared in December 1995 that France would soon be resuming her participation in NATO non-integrated bodies (i.e. the Military Committee and the defence ministers' meetings), the announcement of the country's possible return to NATO's integrated command structures was highly significant.

Almost thirty years to the day since General de Gaulle had signalled France's withdrawal, Chirac was thus declaring his willingness to abandon the dogma of 'non-integration' – a step that only a neo-Gaullist president could possibly take – and set in train a French 'strategic revolution' of sorts.[3] Aside from the proposed normalization of relations between France and NATO, this would consist of a series of important changes that began to be undertaken in 1996: a wholesale reform of France's military forces (leading to the professionalization of the armed forces and an increase in force projection capabilities); a restructuring and Europeanization of the country's defence industries; and a new approach to nuclear deterrence (including the end of nuclear tests, the dismantling of France's nuclear testing facilities in the South Pacific and the signing of the Comprehensive Nuclear Test Ban Treaty [CTBT], as well as the scrapping of land-based nuclear weapons and the reduction of sea- and air-launched systems). However, the key objectives of French alliance policy – namely reasserting France's 'rank' within the Western grouping, bringing about the emergence of Europe as a strategic actor and adapting NATO to the realities of the post–Cold War world – remained fundamentally unchanged. If there was a break with the Gaullist 'model', then, it was tactical in nature: judging that the policy of progressive adaptation in France's relations with NATO followed during the Mitterrand years had reached its limits and that it had not prevented France from being somewhat marginalized within the Alliance, Chirac had decided to take the gamble of returning to the heart of the organization in the hope that this would give France more room for manoeuvre and help a 'European pillar' to emerge within a reformed NATO. This gamble was based on the presumption that, in the long term, a reduction in the United States' commitment to Europe was inevitable now that the Cold War was over, and that, as a result, a new dynamic of transformation and Europeanization within the Alliance would justify a French 'normalization'.

At first it seemed that this new approach – encouraged as it was by Clinton and the main European leaders, in particular John Major and Helmut Kohl – would bear fruit. The June 1996 meeting of the North Atlantic

Council in Berlin marked an important step forward: the allies reached agreement over major NATO evolutions, including creating a European security and defence identity within the Alliance and, even more importantly, finalizing the concept of Combined Joint Task Forces (CJTF), which would allow for 'out-of-area' operations as well as the use by the Europeans of forces that were 'separable but not separate' from those of NATO. Yet following Berlin this dynamic quickly began to run out of steam. US commanders and diplomats, worried about the possibility of US leadership of NATO being challenged, were beginning to have second thoughts; this, combined with the approaching US presidential election in November, caused Clinton's enthusiasm to cool. In this context, Franco-American discussions over the new distribution of military responsibilities within NATO became difficult; they bogged down completely in the autumn of 1996 over the issue of NATO's southern command in Naples (AFSOUTH), which the French wanted to place under European control – something the United States staunchly opposed. In spite of the progress made over the preceding months, the likelihood of France's definitive return to the Alliance's integrated structure, as a result, now seemed to have become very slim.

*Europe: A Fresh Start?*

Against a backdrop of profound change within a European Union that was now firmly on the path to enlargement (it would go from having fifteen to twenty-seven members during Chirac's two terms as president), Chirac's arrival in the Elysée confirmed the direction in which France's European policy had been moving for the past few years. There was an initial degree of uncertainty as to the commitment to Europe felt by the new president, whose convictions in this respect had fluctuated considerably since his famous *Appel de Cochin*, the Eurosceptic text that he had dictated in 1978 from his hospital bed while recovering from a car accident (named after the *Hôpital Cochin* in Paris). While Chirac had campaigned for the 'yes' vote in the referendum on the Maastricht Treaty in 1992, thus going against the majority tendency within his own RPR party, the tone of his presidential campaign and his denunciation of a 'single mentality' in the way economic issues were addressed (*la pensée unique*) suggested to some that the new French president, anxious to carve out some economic room for manoeuvre for his country, would by the same token seek to break free from European constraints. Yet while the anti-Maastricht supporters of a more nationally oriented 'different policy' might have hoped for a change of trajectory in the aftermath of the presidential election, they were quickly disappointed. From October 1995 onwards, Chirac executed a sharp turn in the direction of rigorous financial and social policies, the motivation for which was the need to fulfil the convergence criteria required for economic and monetary union, an objective to which the new president now declared his commitment. In spite of the resulting domestic difficulties encountered by prime minister Alain Juppé's government (with prolonged strikes in the public sector during most of December 1995), from then on this policy orientation would not be abandoned, thus confirming the priority given to completing work on the single currency before the 1999 deadline.

Although France's European priority was confirmed through its close involvement in the implementation of EMU, Chirac's arrival at the Elysée did signal a change in emphasis compared to the Mitterrand era when it came to European policy. While stressing the need to adapt European institutions to the demands of enlargement – in particular by differentiating between states according to their degree of advancement along the path to integration – so as to prevent the Union from becoming bogged down or diluted, Chirac in effect consolidated the shift begun under Edouard Balladur by favouring a less integrationist and more intergovernmental approach to the European project. This was reflected in the priority placed by the new president on the Union's international and security dimensions; although Chirac's position in that realm was similar to that of his predecessors (with the emergence of a 'Europe-power' as a key policy objective), the way that he envisioned a politically and strategically more assertive Europe was reminiscent of the typically Gaullist idea of a 'concert', if not a fully fledged 'directorate', in which the major European countries would, as he saw it, enjoy a privileged position.

Above all, though, it was over the issue of enlargement that the presidency of Chirac marked a real shift in French policy. Chirac's arrival coincided with a turning point for the EU in this area: on 1 January 1995, the Union had gone from having twelve members to fifteen following the accession of Austria, Sweden and Finland; and the opening of EU membership to the central and eastern European countries (CEEC) now seemed a done deal. Crucially, the new president wanted to change the image – built up in the early 1990s owing in particular to the abortive project of a European confederation – that his country had of being reluctant to welcome the CEEC into the Union; he wanted to consign to the past earlier French reservations in that realm. Eager to re-establish a strong French influence in these countries, as witnessed by his state visit to Poland in September 1996, he declared that he was in favour of the Czech Republic, Hungary and Poland entering the Union before 2000. Along with his ideas regarding how the Union should function, the more active pro-enlargement approach adopted by the new French president marked out a new European policy that, while bearing the mark of Chirac's voluntarism, was also more flexible, indeed more opportunistic than it had been in the past. Although he was, in this respect, carrying out a much-needed adaptation of French policy to the new European realities, there was arguably a risk that Chirac's policy towards the EU would end up simply following the line of least resistance.

Under Chirac, realism also became the order of the day in Franco-German relations. Clearly, at least initially, the personal rapport that the new French president had with the German chancellor was not on a par with the intimate relationship that Kohl and Mitterrand had enjoyed. In addition, as Chirac's seven-year presidential term began, Paris and Bonn were in disagreement over certain crucial European issues, the most important of which concerned the implementation of the single currency, which the Germans wanted to manage as rigorously as possible by means of a 'stability pact' that Paris judged to be too restrictive. Balladur's interest in a Franco-British rapprochement that would allow areas of convergence between Paris and London to be emphasized – in particular regarding defence matters – in order to counterbalance Germany's growing economic weight, was still very much in the air following Chirac's arrival at the Elysée. To be sure, the critical nature of the Paris-Bonn relationship quickly regained the upper hand, as was shown by the adoption at the December 1996 Nuremberg summit of a Franco-German 'concept' in security and defence matters. France and Germany remained key partners. Still, the bases of this relationship were no longer what they had been in the Mitterrand period: against a backdrop of the 'normalization' of the now reunified Germany's foreign and security policy and the post–Cold War revision of France's policy, it was clear to all concerned that a thorough overhaul of Franco-German relations was now necessary.

## Organizing Multipolarity

In Chirac's view, the presence of a more assertive Europe on the international scene was necessary in order to promote a multipolar world, whose stability ultimately depended on establishing a better balance between major countries or regional groupings. Chirac wanted to build up structured relations between France (and Europe) and other poles and groupings throughout the world, beginning with the United States. While the new French president (like his predecessors) desired a bilateral Franco-American rapprochement in its own right, the creation of a balanced relationship in the economic as well as political and strategic domain between the United States and the European Union as such remained a constant objective throughout his two terms in office. It was, however, in the establishment of relations with the emerging powers that the new president invested the greatest effort. Although, in 1995, Russia still looked in decline, Chirac was, right from the outset, convinced of the need to strengthen relations with a country whose future was key to the stability of the old continent and whose resources would, in the long term, guarantee the restoration of its clout as a great power. Thanks to the good personal relationship that he had developed with Russian President Boris Yeltsin from before the break-up of the USSR, Chirac strove to revive Franco-Russian relations in both the economic and the political domain. Above all, he shared Kohl's conviction that any marginalization of Russia in a European security context characterized by the post–Cold War enlargement of the Western sphere of influence had to be avoided and that Russia's attachment to Europe would have to be strengthened by making it one of the two pillars, alongside the EU, of the 'Greater Europe' of the 'post-Yalta' era: this was reflected in the signing in May 1997 of the NATO-Russia Founding Act, which Chirac and Kohl wanted to complete before the CEEC were allowed to join the Alliance.

Under Chirac, Asia became – or reverted to being – a focus of French foreign policy. Owing as much to personal inclination (Chirac's passion for Asian cultures and civilizations was well known) as to political interests (the rapid growth of economies in the region, in particular China), the new president wished to see a structured relationship emerge between Europe and Asia that would mirror the expansion of US-Asia relations that was already underway through APEC (Asia-Pacific Economic Cooperation). This led to the launch at the Bangkok Summit of March 1996, following a Franco-Singaporean initiative, of a 'Europe-Asia dialogue' through the creation of ASEM (Asia-Europe Meeting), an informal forum bringing together the countries of the EU and of ASEAN, along with China, South Korea and Japan. Obviously, the emergence of a structured relationship between Europe and Asia did not replace bilateral relations between France and individual Asian countries, relations that Chirac on the contrary wanted to revive: this was especially the case with Japan, once the outcry caused in the latter country by the resumption of French nuclear tests had died down (Chirac made a state visit to Japan in November 1996), and with China, after years of soured relations following the events of Tiananmen Square and French arms sales to Taiwan (Chirac visited the PRC in May 1997). France, as a middleweight power, was nevertheless faced with a dilemma when it came to relations with Asia: was it best to promote a purely national presence, which risked remaining relatively insignificant – particularly in economic terms – or instead work towards asserting the role of the European Union, and so risk seeing France's voice diluted along with the rest of Europe?[4]

Chirac's desire to organize multipolarity through structured relations with major emerging groupings was not limited to Eurasia. Latin America, where de Gaulle had received a rapturous reception in the 1960s before being neglected for a long period by French policy, now became a priority once more. Chirac undertook a long tour of the region in March 1997, starting in Brazil, which was considered to be the future great power on the South American continent. Two years later (June 1999) the first EU–Latin America summit would be held in Rio following a Franco-Spanish initiative; once again, the dividing line between French influence and the assertion of a European role was an issue here.[5]

## Return of France's Arab Policy

It was, however, above all on the Arab world and the Middle East that Chirac's aspirations to organize relations between major regional groupings were focused in the first instance. Chirac saw relations between France, Europe and the Middle East as a key issue: in a context of lingering regional crises – in particular the Israel-Palestine conflict – Chirac believed it was essential to defuse the logic of confrontation that was starting to emerge in the second half of the 1990s between the West and the Arab and Muslim world. Chirac was something of an expert on the Arab states, or at any rate on their rulers; he had entertained long-standing and sometimes close relations with many of them, from the ruling families of the Gulf monarchies to favoured interlocutors such as Egyptian President Hosni Mubarak or Lebanese Prime Minister Rafic Hariri, a personal friend of Chirac.[6] Here, too, the European dimension of this policy was becoming increasingly important: French officials were well aware that it would be necessary to mobilize the EU's clout – particularly in the economic domain – if they hoped to influence developments in the Middle East, e.g. through the dispensation of EU aid to the Palestinians. The French therefore sought to reorient the foreign-policy priorities of the European Union, hitherto focused on the CEEC, towards the Mediterranean region in the wider sense: the result was the launching in November 1995 in Barcelona of the Euro-Mediterranean partnership (known as EUROMED, or the Barcelona Process), bringing together the EU and ten other states bordering the Mediterranean in cooperation over shared issues of security and prosperity (the group included Israel and its Arab neighbours – among them Syria – which in itself was somewhat of a diplomatic success).

Here, once again, the European dimension was very much seen as a natural extension of French policy. For Chirac's arrival at the Elysée above all signalled a reactivation of France's 'Arab policy', which he saw as central to the Gaullist legacy. In contrast to the doubts expressed in 1991 by then Foreign Minister Roland Dumas as to the relevance of such a policy in the face of a heterogeneous Arab world, the new president fully endorsed the concept: in a speech he gave at Cairo University on 8 April 1996, he even declared that France's Arab policy would henceforth have to constitute an 'essential dimension' of French foreign policy:

France's Arab policy must be an essential dimension of its foreign policy. I want to give it new force, adhering faithfully to the orientations set out by its instigator, General de Gaulle. 'Everything directs us', he said in 1958, 'to reappear in Cairo, in Damascus, in Amman and in all the capitals of the region in the same way that we have remained in Beirut: as friends and cooperators.' This vision continues to guide France's policy. A policy which rests on certain guiding principles, inspired by the special quality of the relationship that the French and the Arabs have enjoyed for so long. . . . First of all, there is a long history of mutual understanding between the French and the Arabs that has nourished our centuries-old friendship and is today more alive than ever. As early as the sixteenth century, the Kings of France made room for the teaching of Arabic in the Collège de France. Today, the Institut du monde arabe [the Institute of the Arab World in Paris] is a great and powerful symbol of the dialogue between our cultures. It is a monument that is unique in the world in being the fruit of a true partnership, and it must play its full role in serving our shared ambition. Then there is the presence in France of a Muslim community of more than four million souls, the largest in Europe. Here, today, I salute the Muslims of France who live out their faith in tolerance and openness towards others. The French government intends to make sure that they will be able to flourish in dignity and in respect for the laws of our Republic. . . . France wishes to let the whole of Europe share in this great Arab policy.

This policy would lead, in Chirac's first two years in office, to a spectacular multiplication of the number of visits he made to these countries.

As well as pursuing a new French Arab policy, the new president wanted to strengthen the diplomatic role of France and Europe in the Middle East. Yet in this area, Chirac's voluntarism quickly came up against the reality of the situation, namely an Israel-Palestine peace process that was running out of steam following the assassination of Israeli Prime Minister Yitzhak Rabin in November 1995 and the ensuing eruption of violence. While Chirac consistently declared his strong support for the Palestinians and Yasser Arafat in this context (as shown during the 'summit of the peace-builders' in Sharm el-Sheikh in March 1996), relations between France and Israel became noticeably strained with the arrival in power of Benyamin Netanyahu in May 1996. Chirac's visit to East Jerusalem in October of that year led to incidents with the Israeli security services; while boosting the French president's popularity in the Arab world, the episode also revealed the difficulty for France of maintaining a balanced position in the Israel-Palestine conflict. The same could be said of the attempts made by Chirac's diplomacy to play a role in finding a way out of the crisis following 'Operation Grapes of Wrath', a campaign waged by the Israeli army in south Lebanon in spring 1996. Although France's Foreign Minister Hervé de Charette managed, after a protracted round of shuttle diplomacy, to obtain agreement for joint Franco-American monitoring of the ceasefire, it was clear to all concerned that he had been forced to fight against both Israel and the United States for this, both of whom were reluctant to let France in on the game.

## Squaring up to the Hyperpower

The developments of the late 1990s confirmed the difficulties France was encountering in exerting influence in a world increasingly conditioned by the seemingly irresistible rise of the United States. Since the end of the Cold War and the disappearance of the USSR, the United States had become the sole superpower. From a military point of view, American capabilities were unrivalled, even if the failure of their intervention in Somalia in 1993 had for a time led some to doubt their determination to use them. From an economic point of view, the arrival of Bill Clinton in the White House in the same year coincided with the beginning of a period of strong growth driven by a powerful capacity for innovation. The Clinton years, especially during his second term in office (1997–2001), arguably marked the zenith of post–Cold War US power, not only in terms of 'hard' but also 'soft' power, i.e. the force of attraction exerted by the American 'model'. This was illustrated by the June 1997 G7/G8 summit in Denver, which was carefully orchestrated by the Clinton administration as a real showpiece of US pre-eminence and leadership in an era of globalization. In this context, the second half of the decade, as seen from Paris, was marked by a growing propensity on the part of the United States to take unilateral decisions; the power gap that now existed between the United States and its allies and adversaries alike gave Washington little incentive to bother itself with the constraints of multi-lateralism. American domestic politics further amplified this tendency: while Clinton, following his re-election in 1996, wanted to keep the United States on the path of multilateral engagement, he had to contend since 1994 with a Republican-dominated Congress that was increasingly unilateralist, even isolationist. The 1996 Helms-Burton and Kennedy-D'Amato acts imposing sanctions with extra-territorial implications (the former against Cuba, the latter against Iran and Libya) and its rejection in 1999 of the CTBT were clear illustrations of this tendency. Washington seemed increasingly tempted to turn its back on international institutions, starting with the UN: hence the thorny problem of the United States' financial contribution, along with the veto placed on allowing Secretary General Boutros Boutros-Ghali, who had become discredited in US political circles, to serve a second term (he was replaced in 1997 by Kofi Annan, who seemed closer to Washington). This policy was the exact opposite of what was being called for by the French, who wanted to strengthen the UN framework and global governance.

## A Third Cohabitation

Chirac's France was rather paling faced with Clinton's triumphant United States. As the December 1995 social crisis had shown, the adaptation of the French 'model' to economic globalization was a painful process. France was suffering from low growth and bogged down in uncompleted reforms, and domestic politics did little to change this impression. The unexpected dissolving of the *Assemblée nationale* by Chirac and the victory of the Left in the ensuing parliamentary elections of 25 May and 1 June 1997 resulted in a third cohabitation that, unlike the two previous such situations, came in the early part of the presidential term and thus looked set to last. Lionel Jospin's socialist-led government (1997–2002) benefitted from renewed growth and thus appeared to be setting the country back on track; for a while, Jospin managed to correct the image of France as a country backed into a corner by globalization. This honeymoon period would be short-lived, however: even if this perception clearly exaggerated the real situation, the country – helped along by a French tendency towards morosity – projected the image of a declining power, especially in contrast to the brilliant successes of the United States.[7]

The third cohabitation barely had any repercussions for foreign policy, however. Unlike the two previous cohabitations, it did not – at least not immediately – usher in a period of political rivalry between the president and the prime minister, as the prospect of a presidential election was still a distant one in 1997. In addition, Jospin was not trying to present himself as a rival of Chirac on the international scene; his priorities lay elsewhere, namely in domestic political and economic policy. As a result, the cohabitation functioned rather smoothly as far as foreign policy was concerned, all the more so given that Hubert Védrine, who took over at the Quai d'Orsay, had the benefit of the experience that he had acquired as secretary general of the Elysée during the previous cohabitation; as foreign minister, he managed to establish a confident working relationship with Chirac. It was only with the approach of the 2002 presidential election that frictions began to arise; hence the president took the prime minister to task following a February 2000 visit in Israel during which Jospin, in Chirac's eyes, had upset the 'balance' of French Middle East policy – a relatively minor episode that only received the coverage it did because of the by now open rivalry between the two heads of the executive. This rivalry was illustrated the following year by the disagreements – this time behind closed doors – between the Elysée and Matignon over France's participation in the US military campaign in Afghanistan following the terrorist attacks of 11 September 2001 (Jospin's government wanted but a token French participation, but Chirac prevailed, imposing a more important French role).

True, some of the orientations of French foreign policy that emerged during the third cohabitation bore the mark of Matignon more than they did that of the Elysée; this was the case in particular for African policy, which the socialist government wanted to run according to the principle of 'neither interference, nor indifference': hence its willingness to overhaul the institutional framework for relations between France and African countries, both in the political and economic dimension (through the takeover in 1998 of the Ministry of Cooperation by the Ministry of Foreign Affairs) and in the military dimension (through the launch of 'RECAMP', or Reinforcement of African Capacity to Maintain Peace, a multilateral programme for military cooperation with African countries). Yet despite differences in tone, these orientations did not lead to real divergences with the Elysée, as they simply confirmed developments that, as seen above, had been ongoing for a number of years, especially since the previous cohabitation.[8]

In most other respects, continuity was the order of the day, if only because of the limited importance of domestic factors in shaping France's foreign policy. International circumstances prevailed, beginning with the now dominant role of the United States in what had in effect become a 'unipolar' world. The United States, in the words of its own leaders, had become the 'indispensable nation'. To be sure, this expression (coined by Clinton and popularized by Secretary of State Madeleine Albright) was widely misunderstood, as it aimed, first and foremost, to persuade the US citizens of the need to maintain their nation's international commitments in the face of the temptations of isolationism. Yet it did reflect the magnitude of the 'American challenge' for a country like France: in a context marked by the dominating influence of the United States in world affairs, managing the Franco-American relationship as effectively as possible was a major preoccupation for those in charge of French foreign policy. A realist who wanted (in his words) to find the right 'instruction manual' for dealing with the United States, Védrine learned this the hard way in these years, when he began talking about the concept of a 'hyperpower' in relation to the United States: while the term in his mind was simply a way of describing a situation that France had to come to terms with, it caused an outcry in the United States, where it was interpreted as a typically French expression of anti-Americanism.[9]

## The Failure of France's NATO Normalization

Unsurprisingly, it was over the NATO issue that Chirac's voluntarism came into conflict with US leadership. As has already been described, since autumn 1996 negotiations regarding France's return to the Alliance's integrated structure had been stalled over the issue of NATO's southern command, which Chirac wanted to become 'Europeanized'. Although Paris and Washington had subsequently explored possible options, it had become clear by early 1997 that hopes of a compromise were illusory. On the side of the United States, the uniformed military rejected out of hand any formula that in their view would lead to a weakening of the integrated military structure and a questioning of US NATO leadership. On the French side, Chirac's attempt to 'normalize' France's position within NATO was beginning to draw criticism, from the majority parties as well as from the opposition. By the time Chirac dissolved the *Assemblée nationale* in April 1997, a positive outcome already looked unlikely. The socialist victory the following month and the advent of the Jospin government, which was hostile to any French 'reintegration' within NATO, only served to confirm this; Chirac's efforts had failed.

Chirac's failure to change France's status in NATO was further compounded by the way the Atlantic Alliance went about its first phase of post–Cold War enlargement. Far more than the reform or Europeanization of the Alliance, NATO's enlargement was Washington's real priority: once the Bosnia crisis was over, the United States had resolved to bring the CEEC into the Alliance, which they saw as a decisive step in their 'strategy of enlargement' and promoting a 'Europe whole and free'. Seen from Paris, though, NATO enlargement necessarily involved offering reassurances to Moscow; hence the frictions between France and the United States over the content of the NATO-Russia Founding Act, the scope of which Washington sought to limit. Above all, French diplomacy feared that a NATO enlargement that was limited to the Czech Republic, Hungary and Poland – the central European countries that had made the most progress in terms of economic and democratic transition, but were also, above all, the staunchest backers of the United States in the region – would lead to a further strengthening of the United States' grip. Chirac thus sought to include two countries of southeastern Europe, Romania and Slovenia, in this first phase of enlargement. Yet, in spite of vigorous pleading from the French president, supported by a majority of the members of the Alliance (with Italy in the lead), Washington remained intransigent: while at the NATO Madrid summit (8–9 July 1997) the Allies promised to re-examine the candidacies of Romania and Slovenia in 1999, only the three candidates proposed by Washington were admitted into the Alliance for the moment (they would become full members in spring 1999).

French frustration over the direction taken by the Atlantic Alliance after the end of the Cold War was not limited to its geographical expansion: the enlargement of its missions, which the United States actively promoted at the end of the 1990s, was also perceived by Paris as liable to confirm NATO's hegemony in European security. Anxious to free itself from the strictures of the UN system, Washington was indeed increasingly promoting the idea that NATO could, if necessary, take action without authorization from the UN Security Council. Citing the ongoing precedent of Kosovo (see below), the US administration hoped to obtain formal recognition of this principle in the new 'strategic concept' that the member states were due to ratify at the April 1999 summit in Washington celebrating fifty years of the Alliance. Against the backdrop of NATO's bombing campaign against Serbia (which had begun in March), in the lead-up to the summit French diplomacy had to fight hard to prevent a development that would have turned NATO into the 'Holy Alliance' that Mitterrand had denounced a few years earlier. Yet although Paris eventually prevailed on this particular issue, the underlying tendency persisted: a decade after the end of the Cold War, the Atlantic Alliance had, in opposition to France's vision, become the dominant security institution in Europe.

## Crises in the Balkans and in the Middle East

Three years after the Bosnia settlement, the Kosovo crisis once again served to illustrate the pre-eminence of the United States in European security. At first, Washington had seemed uninterested in the situation in this province of Serbia with a majority Albanian population whose autonomy had been revoked in 1989, and where the Kosovo Liberation Army (UCK) had been waging a guerrilla war against the Serbs since 1997. A spiral of violence ensued in the early months of 1998, and the brutal repression carried out by Belgrade against the Albanian population once again raised the spectre of ethnic cleansing in the Balkans. In this context, the Europeans, led by France and the United Kingdom, decided to take the initiative. Having learned the lessons of their divisions during the Bosnia crisis a few years earlier, and eager to take the opportunity to assert European leadership while the United States stood aside, they hoped to impose a settlement at the Rambouillet Conference in February 1999, jointly presided over by Védrine and his British counterpart Robin Cook. The conference, however, was a failure: the Serbs refused to accept the province's autonomy and the NATO deployment that was demanded by the West in order to oversee a settlement. As the scale of the problem of Kosovar refugees fleeing Serbian repression grew, threatening to turn into a humanitarian catastrophe, the failure to find a political solution to the crisis led to a NATO intervention in the form of a campaign of airstrikes against Serbia (Operation Allied Force) beginning on 24 March 1999.

Although the NATO intervention was supported by the Europeans – who saw it as the only way to force Milosevic to give in – it also confirmed the growing tendency of the United States to act unilaterally. This situation was particularly resented in Paris, both from a political and military point of view: French diplomacy had had to accept the use of force being decided without an explicit UN Security Council mandate, as Washington demanded given the threat of a veto being brandished by Russia; in addition, France, though the second-largest contributor to Operation Allied Force after the United States, hardly carried any weight as far as US decisions were concerned, in particular when it came to selecting bombing targets. It would eventually take almost three months of bombing to force a Serbian retreat from Kosovo and the return of the UN to centre stage, with Resolution 1244 of 10 June 1999 declaring the 'substantial' autonomy of Kosovo and providing for the deployment of a NATO peacekeeping force, KFOR. Although the outcome of the crisis was, in the final analysis, largely as Paris had hoped, the way it had played out had revived French frustrations over the United States' overweening leadership.

At the end of the 1990s, the tendency of the United States towards unilateral action was also making itself felt outside Europe. Following the resolution of the Bosnia crisis in 1995, Washington's concerns – Kosovo being an exception in this respect – were increasingly focused on the Middle East, where the new security issues (terrorism, nuclear proliferation, energy, etc.) were concentrated, not to mention the perennial Israel-Palestine conflict. The question of Iraq, situated at the confluence of these issues, was emblematic of this. Since 1991, Iraq had been subjected to sanctions imposed by the international community following its invasion of Kuwait; the lifting of these depended first and foremost on Iraq's compliance with its disarmament obligations. Yet the Iraqi regime's lack of cooperation in this area and its attempts at concealment made the lifting of sanctions a distant prospect; it was also increasingly clear that the United States had decided to keep sanctions in place whatever the circumstances (the same was true of the no-fly zones that had been set up in the south and north of the country and provided a launch pad for periodic bombing sorties). Whether the United States' objective was to 'contain' the alleged Iraqi threat, or (as US officials would declare openly from 1998 onwards) to hasten the fall of Saddam Hussein, the Iraq issue was in a stalemate.

From 1995 onwards, French diplomacy increasingly distanced itself from US policy towards Iraq. Judging that the way the sanctions were being applied was contributing to the disastrous humanitarian situation suffered by the Iraqi people and merely served to prop up Saddam Hussein's regime without forcing him to fulfil his disarmament obligations, Chirac openly declared his disagreement with the United States and its British allies in a rift that reached its peak with the four-day bombing campaign waged by Washington and London in December 1998 (Operation Desert Fox). Nor was the Iraqi question the only source of French frustration with US policy in the Middle East at the end of the decade. The Israel-Palestine issue was another: with the peace process in a deadlock since Rabin's assassination and Netanyahu's coming to power, Chirac's diplomacy sought to involve France and Europe more closely in the search for a solution, but it continued to come up against Israeli intransigence and American exclusivity. While the election in Israel of a Labour government led by Ehud Barak in July 1999 offered a glimmer of hope, this was quickly snuffed out, as shown by the failure of the Camp David negotiations in summer 2000 and the beginning of a new intifada in the autumn of that year. Proof of the difficulty faced by Chirac's diplomacy in finding a role for itself is provided by the fact that it was blamed by the United States and Israelis – clearly an unsubstantiated accusation – for having caused the failure of an agreement between Barak and Arafat in Paris in October 2000 by encouraging the latter to take an intransigent stance.

## The Limits of Europe-Power

Faced with the rising US hyperpower, Chirac gambled on the progressive emergence of a strong Europe, capable of balancing the transatlantic relationship and acting as a counterweight to Washington's unilateralist tendencies. This gamble did not seem unreasonable: as the century drew to a close, the European project had achieved some important successes, particularly in the monetary and military domains. The Stability and Growth Pact, adopted in June 1997, had put an end to the disagreements that had been hampering the implementation of EMU, and the single currency became a reality on 1 January 1999 with the introduction of the euro. Meanwhile, the Franco-British Saint-Malo declaration adopted in December 1998 by Chirac and UK Prime Minister Tony Blair had paved the way for an important development: for the first time, London had signed up to the objective of an autonomous defence capability within the framework of the European Union (which was meant eventually to take over from the WEU as Europe's military arm). This step forward was made possible by London's realization that US commitment was no longer assured and that the Europeans would therefore have to organize their own defence capability. Kosovo confirmed this; the aftermath of the crisis (especially the European Council meetings in Cologne and Helsinki in June and December 1999) thus saw the rapid implementation of the Saint-Malo programme by the Fifteen, who decided to provide the Union with the appropriate decision-making organs (a Political and Security Committee, or PSC, an EU Military Staff and an EU Military Committee) and to create a rapid reaction force of sixty thousand men. The European Security and Defence Policy (ESDP), long advocated by France, was born.

While the end of the decade thus saw projects begun at the time of the Maastricht Treaty come to fruition, the European dynamic was also encountering its limits, in particular as far as deepening was concerned. The Amsterdam Treaty, signed in October 1997, had given rise to some new developments: the establishment of enhanced cooperations, the widening of the Community's remit to new domains such as social policy, the extension of majority voting and the strengthening of the parliament's prerogatives, along with the appointment of a high representative for common foreign and security policy (CFSP). Three years later, however, there was clear failure at the European Council meeting in Nice, under France's presidency (7–10 December 2000). Despite having set themselves the objective of adapting the Union's institutions with a view to future enlargement, the Fifteen only managed, after a long and bruising debate, to agree on the barest of compromises. The main stumbling block concerned the weighting of votes in the Council: while Germany, ten years after reunification, wanted to see this changed to reflect its demographic preponderance, France refused any such 'uncoupling'. A rather shaky solution resulted: the major countries retained the same number of votes, but a demographic 'filter' meant that any decision taken by the European Council needed to be supported by at least 62 per cent of the population of the Union; in addition, a relative increase in the number of German members of the European parliament (MEPs) was decreed.

The Nice Treaty (signed on 26 February 2001) was a setback: not only had the French presidency of the EU merely achieved a mediocre compromise, but France now also seemed to be having trouble maintaining its influence in the new enlarged Europe. The Nice failure also showed that the Franco-German relationship had changed. While Chirac and Kohl had in the end managed to establish a good personal rapport, the arrival in 1998 of a new German chancellor, Gerhard Schröder (a social-democrat), changed the picture. At the beginning, Chirac and Schröder found it hard to work together. Schröder was initially willing to engage in a rapprochement with Blair and he embodied a Germany that was anxious to assert itself within Europe and on the world stage; as for the political closeness between Jospin's socialist-led government and the 'red-green' coalition headed by Schröder and Foreign Minister Joschka Fischer, it was in fact limited, as Germany's leaders were tending more towards the 'third way' brand of centrism embodied by Blair and Clinton, which Jospin rejected. As the decade drew to a close, in spite of the success in terms of a future 'Europe-power' constituted by the launch of the Euro and the ESDP, some of the fundamentals of the European project – the pursuit of ever-closer political union, the centrality of the Franco-German relationship – looked to have been undermined.

## France in a Post-9/11 World

The terrorist attacks carried out by Al-Qaeda on 11 September 2001 against the World Trade Center in New York and the Pentagon in Washington abruptly plunged the international system into a new era. The arrival of George W. Bush in the White House in January 2001 – after a contested electoral process – had not in itself marked a fundamental break. During the campaign, candidate Bush – distancing himself from the multilateral approach of his father George H. W. Bush – had expressed a willingness to defend US national interests first and foremost; but at the same time he had expressed his desire to limit the country's international commitments, which seemed to herald a more modest US leadership. Yet the events of 11 September and, above all, the reaction of the Bush administration, would radically change this picture; the post-9/11 world would henceforth be characterized by unprecedented US unilateralism. For a middleweight power with global ambitions like France, relations with the 'hyperpower' were bound, as a result, to become a vital issue; this would soon be illustrated by the bitter confrontation between Paris and Washington over the 2002–2003 Iraq crisis.

At first, the terrorist attacks led the international community to line up behind the United States. France was no exception: while the newspaper *Le Monde* was declaring that 'We are all Americans' ('*Nous sommes tous des Américains*'), French diplomacy was active at the UN, where the US right to self-defence in response to the attacks was recognized (Resolution 1368 of 12 September 2001) and in NATO, where Article 5 of the Washington Treaty was invoked for the first time since 1949. Chirac, who before the attacks had been scheduled to be in Washington on 18 September, became the first foreign leader to be welcomed by George W. Bush following the events; he proclaimed France's 'total solidarity' with the United States and, the following day, flew over Ground Zero with the mayor of New York.

From the outset, however, France had been uneasy with the US response to 9/11. Anxious to avoid open confrontation between the West and the Muslim world, Chirac did not endorse the notion of a 'war on terror' as declared by Bush. France did, it was true, participate in the military response that the United States launched in October 2001 against the Taliban regime in Afghanistan (Operation Enduring Freedom); yet French involvement (at least in the initial stages) was limited both by the relative weakness of its military means at this particular juncture and the reluctance of the United States to involve its allies. As the French 2002 elections drew near, the increasingly tense cohabitation further complicated the military decision-making process, as the socialist government was even more reluctant than the president to commit significant French forces to the US operation. The

French involvement in Afghanistan had nevertheless started to increase in the last weeks of 2001.

The presidential election of spring 2002 brought an end to five years of cohabitation. Following Jospin's surprise elimination in the first round on 21 April, Chirac won against the far-right candidate Jean-Marie Le Pen, taking more than 82 per cent of the vote in the second round on 5 May. While the presence of the leader of the Front National in the second round constituted a domestic political shock and confirmed a simmering French malaise, the outcome of the presidential election once again underlined the tendency towards continuity in foreign policy. The president regained all his prerogatives following the victory in the parliamentary elections of 9 and 16 June of the UMP (the renamed neo-Gaullist party) and the installation of Jean-Pierre Raffarin's government. The appointment to the Quai d'Orsay of Dominique de Villepin, a career diplomat who had been secretary general of the Elysée during the president's first term and a close ally of Chirac, was clear evidence of this.

## The Iraq Crisis

Although Villepin arrived at the foreign ministry in spring 2002 with the desire to consolidate Franco-American relations, events decided otherwise. In the wake of Bush's State of the Union Address in January 2002, in which he had referred to the 'axis of evil' that he saw as comprising North Korea, Iran and Iraq, the possibility of an extension of the 'war on terror' to the latter country had begun to look like a serious possibility. Although the US president was playing his cards close to his chest, having endlessly repeated that he had no plans to invade Iraq, it was quite obvious that the trauma of the events of 11 September 2001 had radically changed the political equation in the United States, and that what had been a simmering crisis over Iraq was now likely to become a full-blown conflict. The persistent suspicions concerning the weapons of mass destruction (WMD) programmes that Baghdad was accused of having kept or relaunched and the more general denunciation of a possible 'nexus' between terrorist networks and regimes possessing WMDs, along with the desire of the Bush administration's 'neoconservatives' to begin remodelling the Middle East by dealing with the Iraqi problem and Bush's desire to carry out a massive demonstration of US power in the aftermath of 9/11, were all factors that account for why 'regime change' in Baghdad (through military intervention, if necessary) had become Washington's declared objective.

From the outset, Chirac judged such an operation to be a dangerous proposition, all the more so if decided upon unilaterally by Washington; in his view, the resumption of UN inspections (suspended following Operation

Desert Fox in December 1998) was the only way to resolve the Iraqi crisis. When Bush, at the insistence of Secretary of State Colin Powell, decided to 'go down the UN route' (as illustrated by Bush's speech to the UN General Assembly, 12 September 2002), apparently ruling out – provisionally at least – a unilateral US decision, Chirac's diplomacy judged that it was worth playing along. There ensued long and difficult negotiations in the Security Council in which Paris and Washington were the two main partners; they concluded on 8 November 2002 with Resolution 1441, passed by a unanimous vote. The result, as was to be expected, was a delicate compromise between the desire of the French to give inspections a chance and to preserve the prerogatives of the Security Council on the one hand, and the desire of the United States to take on Iraq and, if necessary, make a unilateral decision regarding military intervention on the other.

Yet this compromise would be overwhelmed by subsequent events. Although the Iraqi regime, finding itself backed into a corner, accepted the return of the inspectors in September 2002 and placed no serious restrictions on their work, Baghdad did not yet appear prepared, in the closing weeks of 2002, to engage in the 'active' cooperation demanded by the international community, and above all in Washington, where Iraq had quite obviously already been judged guilty. In parallel with this, the United States was ramping up its military deployment, making it appear increasingly doubtful that it would actually be able to back down from military action; many concluded that the decision to resort to force had already been taken. In these conditions, a Franco-American rift was inevitable. It would come in the opening weeks of 2003: faced with the bellicose determination of Washington and London, Paris, followed by Berlin and Moscow, and supported by a very large proportion of the international community, restated its position that inspections had to continue. This was the main thrust of the speech delivered by Dominique de Villepin to the Security Council on 14 February 2003.

From this point onwards, the Franco-American confrontation became virulent. While Paris considered the use of force to be unjustified and opposed what it saw as a war of choice by blocking a vote on an Anglo-American resolution that sought to authorize it, Washington – on an issue in which the United States claimed that its vital interests were at stake – judged that France's attitude was hostile to the United States and motivated primarily by the supposed anti-Americanism of the French and what was seen as Chirac's project of building a multipolar world in order to create a counterweight to US power. There ensued one of the worst crises in relations to have taken place between the two countries since the 1960s, resulting in the temporary breaking-off of contacts at the highest level and also in a wave of anti-French feeling in the United States that was deliberately whipped up further by some members of the Bush administration. The most risible symbol of this episode would be the decision to change the name of 'French Fries' on the menu of the Congress cafeteria in Washington to 'Freedom Fries'.[10]

## From Crisis to Transatlantic Reconciliation

At the time, France's attitude, which without doubt had the approval of a majority of governments and public opinion around the world, was a source of prestige. Chirac's popularity was at its height, especially in the Arab world, as shown by the reception he received on his state visit to Algeria on 2–4 March 2003. French diplomacy seemed to have returned to the glory days of the challenges that general de Gaulle regularly threw down to the United States, led as it was by a foreign minister who was quite prepared – even if this sometimes meant lapsing into grandiloquence – to place himself in the lineage of the Gaullist legend. Yet French opposition had no effect on the inevitable march to war. On 20 March 2003, the United States, towing along in its wake the UK and a few other countries, including Australia, launched operations against Iraq without any explicit UN mandate. In spite of a few difficulties, in particular during the phase of urban combat around Baghdad, the war was short; on 1 May, amidst the euphoria of a victory won swiftly and easily, Bush, standing on the deck of an aircraft carrier, theatrically announced the end of 'major combat operations' under a banner that declared 'mission accomplished'.

The failure of France and the anti-war coalition to prevent the intervention by the United States and the United Kingdom, coupled with the triumphant images of their coalition, ushered in a difficult phase for French diplomacy. In spite of a flamboyant but ultimately powerless rhetoric, there was nothing it could have done in the face of Washington's determination. Regardless of the arrogance of the victors, it appeared, for a time, to have been wrong: had it not sought to oppose the overturning of a vile and dangerous regime while defending an untenable regional status quo? Had it not opposed a US administration purportedly motivated by the defence of human rights and the desire to democratize the Middle East? Following the end of the war and the United States' victory, Paris found itself in an awkward position. Franco-American relations would remain difficult for months to come, the Bush administration having made up its mind to 'punish' France, in the words of National Security Advisor Condoleezza Rice.

Contacts at the top level were nevertheless re-established fairly quickly (Bush and Chirac would meet at the G8 Summit held in Evian on 1–3 June) and the resumption of normal relations was gradual. In June 2004, the two presidents used the opportunity of the sixtieth anniversary of the

Normandy landings, attended by Bush, to show that a polite, if not exactly cordial, relationship had been re-established. In the meantime, the situation in Iraq had changed: not only had the existence of weapons of mass destruction, the justification for the war, not been proved, but the security situation had been steadily deteriorating since the summer of 2003. In this changed context, Chirac's anti-war stance appeared in retrospect to have been justified, helping to relieve the pressure that had weighed down on French foreign policy for months. Meanwhile, the United States was now trying to patch up relations with its allies in the hope of involving the international community in the stabilization and reconstruction of Iraq. Franco-American reconciliation thus entered a new phase, as both countries rediscovered their ability to cooperate on major international issues: evidence of this was provided by the adoption in September 2004, at their joint insistence, of Resolution 1559 on Lebanon, over which Paris and Washington shared the same view regarding the need to put an end to Syria's domination.

Bush's re-election in November 2004 confirmed this tendency. Aware of the calamitous consequences of the Iraqi adventure, the US president had decided to gear his second term in office towards re-engagement with allies. Chirac, for his part, was now seeking a rapprochement with the United States. The newfound agreement between Paris and Washington was in evidence following the assassination in February 2005 of Rafic Hariri, with France and the United States declaring their joint determination to force a complete Syrian retreat from Lebanon. It would be confirmed the following year during the war between Israel and Hezbollah, where cooperation between Paris and Washington helped find a way out of the crisis (Resolution 1701 of 11 August 2006). For some, the flexibility now shown by Paris went too far: French diplomacy, they argued, was giving up the specificity of its positions on the major issues in the Middle East (Israel-Palestine, Iran, etc.) in order to facilitate its rapprochement with the United States.[11] Be that as it may, by the time Chirac reached the end of his term, in spring 2007, Paris and Washington had for the most part put the Iraq affair behind them.[12]

## Europe in Crisis

Meanwhile, the European situation had been deeply affected by the transatlantic turbulence over Iraq, which had sowed profound division within the Union. Paris and Berlin had undergone a spectacular rapprochement in this period. After Nice, Chirac and Schröder had decided to restart the Franco-German concert by holding frequent informal meetings in order better to overcome their disagreements (this was known as the the

'Blaesheim process', from an Alsatian village where the two leaders held the first of these meetings). Following their respective election victories in May and September 2002, this process had resulted – to London's dismay – in a Franco-German agreement on the CAP and the EU budget. The Iraqi crisis had then given Chirac and Schröder an opportunity to declare solemnly that the Franco-German entente had been restored: the celebrations for the fortieth anniversary of the Elysée Treaty, in January 2003, had seen the adoption of a firm joint position against war in Iraq, along with the announcement of a new phase of cooperation, illustrated in particular by the establishment of a Franco-German council of ministers. In response, the supporters of the United States (in particular Blair's United Kingdom, along with Silvio Berlusconi's Italy and José-Maria Aznar's Spain) had encouraged the soon to be members of the Union from central and eastern Europe to give strong voice to their pro-American feelings by expressing their support of an Iraq intervention. Yet while Washington and London had no compunction in playing on the divisions between 'old' and 'new' Europe (as famously summarized by US Secretary of Defence Donald Rumsfeld), the behaviour of Paris and Berlin was not entirely irreproachable, as illustrated by Chirac's dressing-down of the CEEC in February 2003 for their pro-Atlanticist position over the Iraq crisis ('They haven't behaved very well', Chirac famously said). Regardless of who was at fault, then, the Iraq crisis did lay bare the deep fault lines that divided the European Union on the eve of its enlargement to ten new members, scheduled for 1 May 2004.

The European crisis was nevertheless rapidly overcome, as the member states were keen to put their divisions behind them. In autumn 2003, the Fifteen, at the insistence of the high representative for CFSP, Javier Solana, adopted a 'European security strategy' centred on the idea of 'effective multilateralism', thereby distancing themselves from US unilateralism. The crisis of 2003 did not prevent the successful completion of the constitutional process launched by the Fifteen at Laeken in December 2001, which resulted in the drafting – completed in summer 2003 within the framework of a European Convention chaired by former French president Valéry Giscard d'Estaing – of the Treaty establishing a Constitution for Europe (TCE). Reprised and amended through negotiations in a new IGC in 2003–2004 and finally signed in Rome on 24 October 2004, this treaty, it was hoped, would put the finishing touches to the long institutional process begun at Maastricht and settle the issue of the decision-making process and vote-weighting in the Council, left unresolved after Nice. By now France had come to accept being 'uncoupled' from Germany in that regard; the TCE, given the progress that it achieved in institutional issues, appeared as a success for the Franco-German pairing, which now seemed to be returning to its central role in the European project.

This calmer spell for France's European policy would not last long, however. Having in mind the precedent of the Maastricht Treaty and Blair's decision to submit the TCE to a referendum in the United Kingdom, Chirac wanted to adopt the same procedure for its ratification in France. Following an intense, even passionate referendum campaign, the TCE was rejected by a very clear majority of French voters (54.68 per cent) on 29 May 2005. They were followed a few days later by the Dutch, whose vote went the same way. The reasons for this 'no' vote no doubt reflected the bitterness felt by the French towards a European project from which they now found themselves increasingly estranged. The fear of a loss of influence within the European Union, an overly rapid enlargement (the prospect of Turkey's candidacy further exacerbating concern over this), unease regarding a European economic model seen as being too 'liberal' and insufficiently protective: these were all symptoms of a French disaffection with a European project that had changed enormously over the previous fifteen years and seemed to have favoured another vision of Europe – to a large extent a British one – over that perennially held by France. Be that as it may, the effect of France's rejection of the TEC was a profound European crisis, reminiscent in many ways of the 1954 EDC crisis; France's responsibility in this situation – tempered only by a similar vote by another founding country – was central: there was no 'plan B', and the Union, now enlarged to twenty-five and soon twenty-seven members, thus found itself forced to operate using the defective institutions of the Nice Treaty.

The failure of the referendum was a personal failure for Chirac. In many respects it summed up the rather muted results of his actions since 1995. If the French had rejected the TCE, it was because in their eyes it represented a Europe that – contrary to the main argument put forward by Chirac in favour of the treaty – did not constitute an effective bulwark against globalization, and even threatened to aggravate its effects. The result of the referendum, in other words, was an expression of the persistent malaise suffered by the country in this new era. While Chirac's aim had been to adapt the country to these new realities, it was clear, ten years after his arrival in the Elysée, that this goal had not been achieved, whether looked at in objective terms (the reforms carried out in his time were limited) or more subjectively (perceptions of globalization remained exceptionally negative among the French public). The referendum outcome, in turn, only served to intensify the prevailing feeling of national malaise. The appointment of Villepin as prime minister following the referendum made little lasting difference: despite a brief initial upturn, the country soon sank back into an atmosphere of crisis and protest, in particular among young people, as illustrated by the 2005 riots in the *banlieues* (the poor outlying suburbs of Paris and other major cities) and the spring 2006 protests against the *Contrat première embauche* (the 'First Employment Contract', which reduced protection for young workers). In such a context, the last two years of Chirac's presidency proved difficult: a president worn out by life at the top and suffering health problems (a minor stroke in summer 2005), political scandals and a general atmosphere of crisis. Given these circumstances, foreign policy was inevitably affected by the result of the vote on 29 May 2005. The prevailing impression, both in France and abroad, was that the country's international role and position in the world was now in decline. The bold stance taken over the war in Iraq seemed to have been forgotten entirely, and the diplomatic capital that it had accrued long since spent.

## Notes

1. See Pierre Péan, *L'Inconnu de l'Elysée*, Fayard, 2006; and Jacques Chirac, *Mon combat pour la paix*, Odile Jacob, 2007, and *Mémoires*, vol. 1, Chaque pas doit être un but, NiL, 2009.

2. See Gilles Delafon and Thomas Sancton, *Dear Jacques, cher Bill. Au cœur de l'Elysée et de la Maison-Blanche (1995–1999)*, Perrin, 1999.

3. Daniel Vernet, *Le Monde*, 8 June 1996; on this, see Frédéric Bozo, *La France et l'Alliance depuis la fin de la guerre froide*, Cahier du Centre d'études d'histoire de la défense, no. 17, 2001; and Michael Brenner and Guillaume Parmentier, *Reconcilable Differences: U.S.-French Relations in the New Era*, Washington, Brookings, 2003, p. 48 ff.

4. See François Godement, 'Une politique française pour l'Asie-Pacifique', *Politique étrangère* no. 4 (winter 1995–1996), pp. 959–970.

5. See Maurice Vaïsse, *La Puissance ou l'influence? La France dans le monde depuis 1958*, Fayard, 2009, p. 438 ff.

6. On this, see Éric Aeschimann and Christophe Boltanski, *Chirac d'Arabie. Les mirages d'une politique française*, Grasset, 2006.

7. See Philip Gordon and Sophie Meunier, *The French Challenge: Adapting to Globalization*, Washington, DC, Brookings, 2001.

8. See Maurice Vaïsse, *La Puissance ou l'influence*, p. 336 ff.

9. On this debate, see Hubert Védrine, *Les Cartes de la France à l'heure de la mondialisation*, Fayard, 2000.

10. On the Iraq crisis and Franco-American relations, see Frédéric Bozo, *A History of the Iraq Crisis: France, the United States, and Iraq, 1991–2003*, Washington and New York, Woodrow Wilson Center Press and Columbia University Press, 2016; Stanley Hoffmann with Frédéric Bozo, *Gulliver Unbound: America's Imperial Temptation and the War in Iraq*, Lanham: Rowman & Littlefield, 2004 ; and Philip H. Gordon and Jeremy Shapiro, *Allies at War: America, Europe, and the Crisis over Iraq*, New York, McGraw-Hill, 2004.

11. See Éric Aeschimann and Christophe Boltanski, *Chirac d'Arabie*, and Richard Labévière, *Le Grand Retournement. Bagdad-Beyrouth*, Seuil, 2006.

12. On this, see Frédéric Bozo and Guillaume Parmentier, 'France and the United States: Waiting for Regime Change', *Survival*, vol. 49, 1 (spring 2007), 181–198.

# EPILOGUE

## From Sarkozy to Hollande

The presidential election of 22 April and 6 May 2007 was in many ways more momentous than any of the three that preceded it. For the first time since 1981, the country was presented with a choice offering real change. The UMP candidate, Nicolas Sarkozy, won the election with 53 per cent of the vote against the socialist candidate Ségolène Royal after having pledged a 'break' ('rupture') with the past. Once a close ally of Jacques Chirac, Sarkozy now accused him of twelve years of inaction; more fundamentally, he wanted to thoroughly overhaul the French 'model', which he considered obsolete. The change being offered to the French public above all concerned the economic and social landscape; yet if a 'break' really was going to occur, it would inevitably have consequences for foreign policy, for Sarkozy wanted to transform the country in order to let it take its place in a globalized world and regain a degree of diplomatic influence to match its ambitions. The new president – whose dynamism, and even hyperactivity, had long been his hallmark – would indeed, during his five-year mandate, breathe new energy into French diplomacy, and on occasions give it a decisive role. For better (real successes) or for worse (U-turns) the Sarkozy presidency would, in this area too, be a 'hyperpresidency'. But would the 'fundamentals' actually be brought into question?

### A Fresh Start

On his arrival at the Elysée, Sarkozy immediately wanted to make a fresh start in foreign policy. While Chirac had pursued the vision of a 'multipolar' world, Sarkozy now stressed the renewed closeness he wanted to enjoy with the United States; likewise, Chirac's alleged 'relativism' was now replaced by a more 'ethical' foreign policy, focused on the protection of human rights (the appointment as foreign minister of Bernard Kouchner, founder of Doctors Without Borders, seemed to confirm this) along with the fight against global warming, which Sarkozy declared a priority for his term. Meanwhile the new president wasted no time in transposing the ideas and style that were his hallmark in domestic politics onto the international stage, ushering in an increased presidentialization of the decision-making process and a highly personalized approach to international affairs. The result was a pronounced centralization of foreign policy making, which was now dominated by the Elysée, where Jean-David Levitte, formerly the ambassador to Washington, became Sarkozy's diplomatic adviser; meanwhile the role of the foreign ministry was noticeably weakened. This reorganization was carried out in order to pursue a more active foreign policy: in Sarkozy's view, the goal of restoring French influence on the world stage could only be achieved through concrete and visible results. This was very much in evidence in July 2007, when he settled the affair of the Bulgarian nurses detained in Libya, and again in July 2008, when he obtained the release of the Franco-Columbian politician Ingrid Betancourt, held captive by Columbian guerillas. Both cases received heavy media coverage, thereby projecting the image of a president concerned with scoring diplomatic 'coups'.

Not long after his election, though, Sarkozy could boast of a far more significant achievement, namely the relaunching of the European institutional process. During his election campaign, Sarkozy had spoken of his desire to see the adoption of a 'simplified' version of the constitutional treaty, which could then lead to parliamentary ratification while allowing the main features of the TCE to be retained. Jointly organized with Angela Merkel under Germany's EU presidency, this relaunch led in June 2007 to agreement among the Twenty-Seven to hold an IGC tasked with finalizing the new treaty. The latter was effectively adopted in Lisbon in December and, after various hitches (including rejection by Irish voters in a referendum in 2008), it finally came into effect in December 2009. Although Sarkozy's decision to have the Lisbon Treaty ratified in France by parliament rather than by a referendum met with some opposition, the positive outcome of the 2007 relaunch process enabled the European Union to get out of its institutional rut and put France back at the heart of the European game just two years after the failure of 2005.

The French presidency of the European Union (FPEU) in the last six months of 2008 confirmed Sarkozy's energetic EU policy. While achieving reasonable results as far as its stated priorities were concerned (immigration, energy and climate, defence), France's presidency was notable for its handling of the crises with which the EU found itself confronted in that period. In the summer of 2008, Sarkozy, acting on behalf of the bloc, brokered a ceasefire between Moscow and Tbilisi in the Russo-Georgian conflict over South Ossetia and Abkhazia; although the agreement was criticized as being overly favourable to Moscow's objectives, it nevertheless constituted a rare show of European effectiveness at a time when the US administration (George W. Bush was now a lame duck president) appeared increasingly disengaged. Likewise, in autumn, Sarkozy mounted a rapid and effective EU response to the banking and financial crisis that had been triggered by the subprime mortgage crisis in the United States, as demonstrated at the Eurozone summit at the Elysée in October and the G20 summit in Washington in November 2008.

A self-styled pro-American, Sarkozy was also willing to achieve a new start in relations with the United States. The new president wanted to consign the Iraq crisis definitively to the past and put France back at the heart of a 'West' to which he declared his attachment – at the risk of being called an 'Atlanticist', or even an 'occidentalist'. During an official visit to Washington in November 2007, he proclaimed before Congress: 'I want to be your friend, your ally, your partner.' He added that France had resolved to return to a full-fledged role within NATO and revoke the decision of 1966, provided that the Atlantic Alliance carried out substantive reform and allowed the emergence of a European defence identity. This unexpected announcement echoed Chirac's efforts at normalizing France's NATO status twelve years before; but this time things went differently. The international and transatlantic context had changed considerably, and Sarkozy was determined – in this area as in many others – to succeed where his predecessor had failed. At the NATO summit in Bucharest on 2–4 April 2008, he restated the objective of a 'normalization' of France's position within the organization, and the Alliance's sixtieth anniversary summit in Strasbourg/Kehl on 3–4 April 2009 effectively ratified France's 'return' to the NATO fold. Paris obtained the appointment of a French five-star general to one of the two supreme command positions within NATO, the Supreme Allied Commander Transformation, or SACT (the other supreme command position, SACEUR, remained in the hands of the United States). More than forty years after France's withdrawal under Charles de Gaulle, a president who openly declared his Gaullist affiliations had normalized France's position within the Atlantic Alliance. France's return to the NATO fold, moreover, was carried out without a national crisis; public opinion accepted it in spite of some rather feeble opposition from within the political class (most of the Left and part of the president's own majority party, who denounced this decision as Atlanticist and pro-American in its alignment and a betrayal of Gaullist dogma).

## The Persistence of the 'Fundamentals'

Because it seemed to question one of the central tenets of French foreign policy since de Gaulle, the normalization of relations between France and NATO, more than any other single decision, came to symbolize the alleged change of course taken by French foreign policy under Sarkozy. This impression, however, is somewhat misleading: after all, had Chirac not made a similar attempt at normalizing France's position within NATO? If there was a break, then, it was to be found not in the intention, but rather in the execution, which this time was successful. Admittedly, critics of French 'reintegration' pointed out that the European side of the bargain (a strengthened EU defence policy), which Sarkozy had presented as a major objective, never actually materialized, and they concluded that the operation was therefore 'Atlanticist' in nature. Yet if a more robust European defence indeed failed to emerge in the wake of France's NATO normalization, this situation was not the result of obstruction by the United States or the more pro-American among the NATO allies: Paris, in fact, could now boast of Washington's full support in its effort to build a more autonomous European defence; similarly, the new EU and NATO members no longer had any objections to France's European defence agenda. The failure was rather the result of European military apathy, compounded by the consequences of the financial and economic crisis, and, not least, of continued British opposition to a more autonomous European defence. (Paris and London were nevertheless eager to strengthen Franco-British bilateral cooperation, which led in 2010 to the signing between Europe's two main military powers of a defence and security treaty, known as the Lancaster House treaty).

France's NATO 'reintegration', in fact, did not fundamentally contradict Hubert Védrine's famous description of the French since de Gaulle as 'friends, allies, [but] not aligned' with the United States. From Sarkozy's decision in 2008 to reinforce the French contingent in Afghanistan with a smaller number of troops than requested by Washington, to the setting of ambitious objectives in international financial and economic regulation during France's presidency of the G20 in 2010–2011, not to mention France's opposition to the entry of Turkey into the European Union, French foreign policy after 2007 could hardly be seen as slavishly following the lead of the United States. Behind an apparent Atlanticist alignment that seemed to derive from France's NATO 'reintegration', Sarkozy's presidency was in fact in line with the recurring pattern that had been visible since the early days of the Fifth Republic, namely that each new occupant of the Elysée – at the beginning, at least – has sought to establish (or re-establish) a privileged relationship with Washington.

Other aspects of the foreign policy pursued after Sarkozy's election also tended towards continuity, and none more so, as hinted above, than European policy. If there was in fact a break after 2007, it was more with the situation of deadlock in which France's European policy had found itself after the 2005 referendum than with the fundamentals of the policy itself. This was true with respect to deepening, which was the focus of the institutional relaunch of 2007 and was very much in line with the vision of a political Europe that had always been at the heart of France's policy; it was also true with respect to enlargement, over which Paris would return under Sarkozy to a restrictive approach (particularly regarding Turkey's candidacy) motivated by the need to preserve the cohesion and identity of the European Union, which in his view involved fixing the latter's borders. Finally, French policy after 2007 continued to be guided by the idea of a 'Europe-power' that was capable both of protecting its own members, as demonstrated by the priority given to matters of immigration and defence during the French presidency of the EU, and also of taking action on the international scene, as showed during the 2008 Georgian crisis.

Admittedly, from its beginnings in 2009 the euro crisis caused Sarkozy's initial successes of 2007 and 2008 to be forgotten. Far from asserting itself as a major actor on the international scene, Europe now found itself embroiled in a deep crisis that, although financial in nature (characterized as it was by the threat of default by Greece and the risk of an uncontrolled escalation of interest rates on sovereign debts) was fundamentally political in its origins and implications. Twenty years on from Maastricht, the crisis revealed the shortcomings and deficiencies – even the illusions – of European integration and, first and foremost, the unsustainable character of an economic and monetary union lacking effective economic governance. From 2009 onwards, the energy expended by Sarkozy in trying to find a way out of this crisis by trying to promote a more financially cohesive union in spite of the reluctance of some of his partners (in particular the Germans) was nevertheless a clear illustration of the continuity of France's European orientations. An early result of Sarkozy's efforts – obtained in spite of strong initial Franco-German differences – was the first bailout package to rescue Greece adopted by Eurozone members and the IMF in May 2010, followed by the decision to create a European Stability Mechanism in February 2011.

Significantly, Sarkozy's handling of the euro crisis also confirmed the continued centrality of Franco-German relations in France's foreign and European policies. Sarkozy had emphatically stated the importance of the Franco-German 'couple' at the beginning of his term (as demonstrated by his trip to Berlin on the day of his inauguration and the joint relaunch of the European institutional process in the following weeks), but doubts had soon emerged as to its enduring relevance: not only was the personal chemistry between Sarkozy and Merkel poor, but disagreements between Paris and Berlin emerged early in Sarkozy's term over major issues, including French plans for a 'Union for the Mediterranean', the response to the financial crisis and the usual clash of national interests over economic and industrial matters in particular. Yet on both sides a willingness to demonstrate the continuing centrality of the Franco-German relationship soon prevailed against the backdrop of the looming euro crisis, as illustrated both by symbolic gestures (the presence of Merkel at the 11 November 2009 commemorations in Paris) or by political initiatives (e.g. the eighty measures adopted in February 2010 by Berlin and Paris in order to relaunch the bilateral relationship).

Continuity in French foreign policy under Sarkozy was also visible in other areas. Having been banished from the French diplomatic vocabulary for a short while, the idea of a 'multipolar world' quickly returned to centre stage against the backdrop of the continuing rise of emerging powers and the United States' persistent international predicament post-Iraq; hence the importance placed by French diplomacy in enhancing the role of the G20 in 'global governance' in order to bring the architecture of international economic and political institutions into line with the new distribution of power. For Sarkozy, as for his predecessor, a new balance between the world's major power poles (among them the European Union) had to be attained in order for them to take collective responsibility for the economic, political and strategic handling of globalization. Hence the need in his view to build partnerships between Europe and these major poles, be they the United States, China, Russia, India or Brazil, while at the same time ensuring that France maintained significant bilateral relations with these powers – a policy, as seen above, that had been initiated by Chirac. Meanwhile, the initial emphasis placed on human rights by Sarkozy's diplomacy was quickly (and cynically, according to critics) toned down, as shown in particular by the development of relations with Russia and China, in which humanitarian concerns, following early clashes with Moscow and Beijing, were quickly put to one side.

Similarly, in the area of African policy, Sarkozy's early reforming intentions soon gave way to practices that seemed to bear the stamp of 'la Françafrique', as seen, for example, in relations with Gabon and the handling of the succession of Omar Bongo in 2009. More than any other decision, the closing down of the Ministry for Human Rights (Secrétariat d'Etat aux droits de l'Homme) symbolized, according to his detractors, Sarkozy's failure to honour his promises, signalling in their view the return to a constant in French policy, namely the priority given to the defence of economic and geopolitical interests over the defence of ideals. This about-turn, of course, was not without precedent: one could in particular cite the early years of the Mitterrand presidency, which, in spite of initial pledges to bring a 'moral' dimension to foreign policy, were likewise marked by a swift return to realpolitik in Africa. The French military intervention of spring 2011 in Ivory Coast (Operation Licorne), which was carried out in order to end civil strife and enforce the November 2010 victory of Alassane Ouattara against Laurent Gbagbo in a presidential election that had been recognized by the international community, nevertheless went some way to restoring the somewhat ambivalent image of Sarkozy's African policy.

Sarkozy's foreign policy was also characterized by continuity with his predecessors on matters closer to the old continent. The plan for a Union for the Mediterranean, launched in 2008 under France's EU presidency, is a case in point: conceived as a way to revive the Barcelona process launched in 1995, it was in line with France's long-term ambitions in the greater Mediterranean region and earlier French attempts to formulate a policy towards the Arab world; while avoiding Chirac's expression of an 'Arab policy', the aim was clearly similar (the scheme subsequently failed in the wake of the Arab springs of 2011, which essentially made the Union for the Mediterranean a dead letter). The same can be said of relations with Israel and French ideas concerning the Israel-Palestine conflict. Despite the fact that Sarkozy had arrived at the Elysée with a reputation for being staunchly pro-Israel, the subsequent stances taken by him, whether in his speech to the Knesset on 23 June 2008 (not unlike Mitterrand in 1982), during the war in Gaza between December 2008 and January 2009, or when France voted in favour of Palestine's membership of UNESCO in 2011, have been part of the search for a balanced position on the conflict that French policy has consistently pursued since the 1960s.

## The 2011 Arab Spring Uprisings and the Crisis in French Foreign Policy

The upheavals that occurred in the Arab world from late 2010 and early 2011 onwards marked a turning point in French foreign policy. Like the other Western powers (the United States included), which had been content with the prevailing status quo in the Arab world, France was left wrong-footed by the uprisings on the southern shores of the Mediterranean. Paris had no more anticipated these events than had Washington. For a while, a wait-and-see attitude reigned in Western capitals, anxious as the latter were to preserve the stability that the regimes in place in the region had ensured for decades – more often than not by flouting human and democratic rights, particularly in Zine el-Abidine Ben Ali's Tunisia or Hosni Mubarak's Egypt. Yet this approach was soon overtaken by the speed of events, placing Western leaders in an awkward position. A crisis ensued in French diplomacy:

Paris had given the impression of supporting the Ben Ali regime to the bitter end, and the foreign minister, Michèle Alliot-Marie, was forced to resign in February 2011 following revelations about her relations with individuals close to the regime. This crisis also revealed a deeper malaise at the Quai d'Orsay, where Sarkozy's 'hyperpresidency', coupled with ongoing complaints about the lack of resources at the ministry's disposal, fuelled a feeling that a marginalization, and even a downgrading of the diplomatic apparatus was under way.

This impression of a crisis in French foreign policy was, it is true, fairly quickly dispelled. Alain Juppé returned to the Quai d'Orsay – where fond memories remained of his time spent there in 1993–1995 – thus reassuring the diplomatic service and rebalancing the decision-making process in favour of the Foreign Ministry. Recognizing that stability could no longer be delivered from the status quo but rather from economic and political transition in the southern Mediterranean, French policy took a dramatic U-turn; it now found itself firmly on the side of support for the revolutions of the 'Arab spring', beginning with Tunisia and Egypt.

The most spectacular illustration of this turn, however, was in Libya, where Sarkozy, along with the United Kingdom's David Cameron, took the lead in a military intervention against the Gaddafi regime, which in March 2011 had begun a brutal campaign of repression against the mounting opposition. Although the intervention was legitimized by Security Council Resolution 1973 of 17 March 2011, which had been adopted on France's initiative, the campaign's declared humanitarian objective (avoiding a bloodbath in Benghazi) soon gave way to the de facto pursuit of regime change in Tripoli. This signalled a complete change of doctrine with respect to the preceding period, when France had opposed regime change by force as a matter of principle, not least in Iraq; having previously been considered acceptable by the Western powers (Sarkozy himself had received him with great pomp in 2007), Gaddafi was now their target, leading to his fall and death in October 2011. This sudden about-turn did much to erase the memory of the initial period of hesitation over the Arab revolutions; in addition, owing to the relatively low-key approach adopted by the United States, who were allegedly 'leading from behind' (while nevertheless providing important military support to their European allies), it also gave France and the United Kingdom a degree of international clout not seen since the 1956 Suez crisis.

The Libya crisis nevertheless remained an exception that at the same time showed the limits of French interventionism (not to mention the fact that the subsequent post-conflict turmoil in that country somewhat tarnished the record of Sarkozy's handling of the crisis). Although Sarkozy, like other Western powers, quickly took a stance in favour of regime change in Syria, where Bashar al-Assad had begun to crack down on the uprisings in spring

2011, direct military interference in that country was clearly ruled out; not only had the Libya crisis badly stretched France's military capabilities, but the outcome of an intervention in Syria appeared more uncertain, if not outright perilous, than in Libya, and the precedent of resolution 1973 (the boundaries of which had in effect been transgressed) made an international consensus of the kind that had prevailed over Libya elusive, not least as a result of Russia's increasingly outspoken resistance to Western intervention in the region.

In parallel with the consequences of the Arab Spring uprisings, Sarkozy, during the last year of his term, had to deal with an increasingly dramatic euro crisis that continued to focus on Greece (as well as Ireland and Portugal) but threatened to contaminate other countries as well. During that year, France increasingly aligned itself with Germany: from the adoption in March 2011 on a Franco-German initiative of a 'Pact for the Euro' emphasizing stronger economic cooperation, competitiveness and convergence among EU countries, to the signing in March 2012, also on a Franco-German initiative, of a 'Fiscal Compact' (or 'Treaty on Stability, Coordination and Governance in the Economic and Monetary Union') aiming to install a stability-oriented mode of fiscal and economic governance of the Eurozone, Merkel and Sarkozy resolved to overcome longstanding differences between their two countries in these matters and to impose their solutions on the rest of the Eurozone – a joint leadership that soon became known as 'Merkozy'. Yet for all Sarkozy's energy and the influence he was able to exert on Merkel in order to assuage Germany's hawkish stance in the Eurozone crisis, it was increasingly clear that the Franco-German tandem was becoming seriously unbalanced as a result of France's growing economic difficulties. As the spring 2012 presidential election neared, Sarkozy nevertheless decided to up the ante, combining a staunch defence of the Franco-German leadership with a no less robust stance on economic reforms and fiscal austerity in the face of the country's worsening economic situation.

## François Hollande: A 'Normal Presidency'?

As has often been the case, France's spring 2012 presidential election was largely divorced from foreign policy issues. The socialist candidate, François Hollande, mounted a presidential campaign that to a large extent capitalized on the rejection of Sarkozy, whose record had been tarnished by the effects of a new deterioration of the economic situation that had started in 2011 (confirming that the 2008 crisis had led to a 'double-dip'), in particular targeting his impulsive personal style and increasing tendency to cater to the populist segment of the electorate. Hollande vowed to revive economic growth while at the same time reducing the country's public deficit (yet avoiding full-fledged austerity), and he famously pledged to behave as a 'normal' president. Hollande declared that he wanted to 'reorient' the European Union away from austerity, criticizing the 'Merkozy' management of the euro crisis over the preceding years, and attacked both Sarkozy's decision to bring France back into NATO's military organization and his alleged Atlanticism, vowing to 'review' the decision and its consequences in order to determine whether he would maintain it or reverse it. Aside from that, however, Hollande's foreign policy agenda was characteristically devoid of major announcements. Hollande was elected with 51.6 per cent of the popular vote in the run-off against Sarkozy on 6 May 2012, and he secured a parliamentary majority in the legislative election the following month.

Though Hollande's foreign policy marked a clear break with Sarkozy's in form, this was not really the case in substance. To be sure, the new president's style contrasted sharply with his predecessor's. Hollande adopted a low-key approach on the international scene, characterized by cautious language and refraining from flamboyant moves. In terms of decision-making, while the Elysée of course remained in the driving seat, Hollande wanted to give more leeway to the Quai d'Orsay, appointing Laurent Fabius (a socialist party heavyweight and former prime minister) as foreign minister. Similarly, the minister of defence, Jean-Yves Le Drian, a close political ally of Hollande's, from the start played an important role against the backdrop of the growing number of French military interventions. However, Hollande's willingness to conduct a 'normal' presidency in foreign policy quickly ran up against events, and his presidency soon became a crisis presidency, just like Sarkozy's had become after 2008. More importantly, continuity prevailed to a large extent in terms of the major orientations of foreign policy.

This was the case first and foremost with regard to European issues. While Hollande had pledged to 'reorient' European policy, it was clear early on that this would not happen in reality. Although the adoption at French urging by the EU Council of a so-called Growth Pact in June 2012 only paid lip service to the 'reorientation' idea, in the autumn Paris ratified the 'Fiscal Compact', which Hollande had pledged to renegotiate, thus falling into line with the German approach stressing budgetary discipline. While Paris welcomed the pledge by the European Central Bank's President Mario Draghi in July 2012 to do 'whatever it takes' to save the euro, along with the ECB's robust quantitative easing program, as a major step in the direction of a more proactive monetary policy and (together with the decision to create a banking union) as important progress towards a more integrated EMU, the management of the lingering Greek crisis continued to be overwhelmingly influenced by the German approach, culminating in summer 2015 with the signing of a third Greek financial assistance package marked by the imposition of severe austerity measures on Athens. Although Hollande had hoped to capitalize on the coming to power of Alexis Tsipras's Syriza-led government in Athens in January 2015 to promote his reorientation idea, and although Paris ostensibly took credit for the fact that Greece eventually did not leave (or was not expelled from) the Eurozone as the hawks in Berlin had wanted, the fact was that the French had, by and large, ended up yielding to the German view of how to deal with the Greek conundrum and, more broadly, of managing the euro crisis.

Hollande's alignment with Germany in the Eurozone crisis reflected the no less dramatic adjustment that took place early in his term in French economic policy. Already in the fall of 2012, the French government had adopted a program in favour of increasing French competitiveness through measures to help businesses, while at the same time continuing (and in many ways increasing) the rigorous financial measures implemented under Sarkozy in order to reduce the public deficit and tackle the debt problem. By early January 2014, Hollande had come round to advocating a clearly pro-business economic policy emphasizing reform in all sectors of economic and social policy. Although critics have since deplored the insufficiency of these measures faced with the lingering crisis of the French economy, the direction taken since then has clearly been one of trying to catch up with the reforms adopted by Germany ten years earlier in order to restore French competitiveness in the Eurozone, thereby confirming Hollande's fundamental pro-European choice – a move that is in many ways reminiscent of François Mitterrand's March 1983 decision to keep France in the European Monetary System.

Just like in 1983, Hollande's European turn was accompanied by a perceptible Franco-German rapprochement. As had also been the case with Sarkozy, Hollande and Merkel's personal chemistry had initially been uneasy as a result of disagreements over European issues and Hollande's willingness to mark a clean break with 'Merkozy' and what he saw as French subservience to Germany in the euro crisis. Yet by 2014 it had become clear that both sides wanted to restore the centrality of Franco-German relations in the EU: on the one hand Hollande had renounced challenging the German approach to the Eurozone crisis and was now looking to improve the functioning of the relationship with Berlin, and on the other the Germans had realized that a German-only leadership of the EU was neither practical nor legitimate. The result was a visibly warmer rapport between the two leaders, who displayed a willingness to showcase the renewed centrality of the Franco-German relationship and a desire to systematically search for common ground. Not only was there now real convergence between Paris and Berlin over the management of the euro crisis and especially regarding Greece (due in no small part to France's de facto acceptance of the German approach), but they were willing to once again promote the Franco-German 'couple' as the driving force in European construction, as shown by Hollande and Merkel's joint contribution on the future of the Eurozone sent to President of the EU Commission Jean-Claude Juncker in May 2015, or their joint appearance at the European Parliament in October of that year. Although it remains to be seen to what extent Paris and Berlin will actually manage to engineer effective compromise on the future of European construction, there has no doubt been a realization on both sides that divorce must be avoided.

The Franco-German dynamic has also been at work in the most significant geopolitical upheaval that the Hollande presidency has had to face on the European continent: the Ukraine crisis. From the start, agreement between Paris and Berlin has existed on the need both to signal to Russia the unacceptable character of its early 2014 annexation of Crimea and increased interference in support of Russian-speaking separatists in eastern Ukraine, and to prevent further – potentially military – escalation of the crisis as a result of a possible Western (and in particular US) overreaction. In June 2014, on the margins of the celebration of the seventieth anniversary of the Normandy landings, Hollande organized a meeting with Merkel, Russian President Vladimir Putin and Ukrainian President Petro Poroshenko, and in February 2015 the same four leaders (now known as gathering in 'Normandy format') again met in Minsk at the joint request of Hollande and Merkel, reaching agreement on a package designed to de-escalate the eastern Ukraine conflict and inaugurating the 'Minsk process'. Although the drive behind the Minsk process mostly came from Germany (in contrast to France's preeminent role in the Georgia crisis of 2008), the two countries were thus able to demonstrate the continuing relevance of the Franco-German couple in tackling a major crisis involving Russia, in line with Kohl and Mitterrand's joint efforts twenty-five years earlier at the time of the Lithuanian crisis.

If the management of European crises (economic or geopolitical) has shown a significant measure of continuity from Sarkozy to Hollande, the same has been true of crises beyond Europe. While Hollande had pledged to review Sarkozy's 2009 decision on France's return into the NATO integrated structure, the unsurprising result of the review was a quick decision – cleverly based on a report by Védrine, who had been sceptical of Sarkozy's move – not to reverse it. Although in a separate move Hollande did follow through on his campaign pledge to withdraw French forces from Afghanistan by the end of 2012, he had thus marked his continued commitment to transatlantic relations and, in particular, Franco-American relations, as symbolized by his visit to the United States on 18–21 May 2012 (barely three days after his inauguration) in order to meet Barack Obama and participate in a NATO summit in Chicago.

The following three years of Hollande's term confirmed his desire for France to play an important transatlantic role and to maintain vibrant Franco-American relations against the backdrop of relative US disengagement from Europe and its neighbouring regions, and even to appear as the United States' staunchest and most reliable European ally – at times adopting positions that could seem more hawkish than those of Washington. The Iran nuclear issue – in which continuity from Sarkozy to Hollande has been particularly noteworthy – was a case in point: when in autumn 2013, after more than ten years of a frustrating negotiation process, an agreement was finally in sight between the '5+1' powers and Iran (in large part the result of the election of Hassan Rouhani, a moderate, as president of Iran the previous summer), Fabius blocked its conclusion on the grounds that its terms were too lax to ensure the peaceful character of Iran's nuclear program – at the risk of irritating the United States who had opened a backchannel with the Iranians and was now clearly intent on wrapping up the negotiation (which was finally concluded in July 2015). The Syria crisis, in which Hollande after his election had also maintained a distinctly hawkish stance (in essence one of fostering regime change in Damascus, including through covert arm deliveries to rebel groups), produced similar Franco-American friction: when at the end of summer 2013 Bashar al-Assad's regime was caught in the act of using chemical weapons against its own population, Hollande agreed with Obama on the need to conduct retaliatory air strikes against the regime only to find out that the United States had decided at the last moment to cancel the strikes, leaving the French hanging out to dry. This episode no doubt left a mark on the Franco-American relationship and further convinced the French of the reality of the ongoing US disengagement and of the need to try, if not to compensate for it, then at least to attenuate its consequences: in many ways, the renewed French interventionism in international crises visible since 2012 can be explained by a perceived need to keep the United States involved in the security of Europe and its Middle Eastern periphery by showing that the Europeans are ready to carry their full share of the burden.

Nowhere has France's new interventionism been more visible since the beginning of Hollande's presidency than in Africa. In January 2013, Paris launched Operation Serval in northern Mali to halt the rapid progression of jihadists towards the capital, Bamako, and prevent what appeared to be an imminent Islamist takeover of the country. Operation Serval, which involved up to five thousand French troops, was replaced in August 2014 by Operation Barkhane, an anti-terrorist operation involving three thousand French troops covering a large swath of the Sahel region and headquartered in Chad's capital, N'Djamena. (Separately, in December 2013 France launched Operation Sangaris in the Central African Republic in order to prevent the escalation of civil strife and the potential risk of genocide while providing support to UN and African peacekeeping forces.) France's intervention in Mali and in the Sahel region, which has generally been regarded as a success, was an illustration of the country's continued military activism under Hollande, who unexpectedly revealed himself to be a 'war' president, in sharp contrast with his pledge to be 'normal' and his characteristic reluctance to make clear-cut decisions in other areas – and very much in line with his predecessors, not least Sarkozy. The war in Mali also illustrated the continued importance of Franco-American relations, leading many to observe that, ten years after the Iraq war, France had paradoxically become the United States' most valuable ally: Operation Serval was indeed clearly considered in Washington as a major contribution to the continuing 'war on terror' and, although discreet, US military support (in particular in terms of logistics and intelligence) was an important factor in its success.

While in the aftermath of the 9/11 attacks France under Jacques Chirac had been reluctant to use the term, under Hollande the 'war on terror' has in effect become an official expression used by French leaders to justify the country's various military engagements, not least in the Sahel region. The terrorist attacks of 7–9 January 2015 in Paris, whose primary target was the satirical magazine *Charlie Hebdo*, only compounded this tendency (two police officers and a kosher supermarket were also targeted, with a total of twenty victims). The parallel with the events of 9/11 (irrespective of the much lower number of victims) seemed all the more valid to many observers when on 11 January more than four million people marched in the streets of the country's cities and towns in defence of republican and secular values (the largest demonstrations in the history of France) while over sixty world leaders joined Hollande in walking through the streets of Paris (also an event without historical precedent). Rightly or wrongly, the January 2015 events and the various terrorist attacks that occurred in France and other European countries over the following months inevitably gave increased currency in the public discourse to the notion of a 'war on terror' in which France was now fully engaged. By then, the US-led airstrikes against the Islamic State of Iraq and Syria (ISIS, or Daesh) had become another important dimension of this war and France was willing to take a larger part in it. (While it had thus far limited its intervention to Daesh targets in Iraq only, in summer 2015 France also decided to take on targets in Syria as well on the grounds of collective defence against terrorist attacks.) Twelve years after the US-led invasion of Iraq, it is fair to say that France has been sucked into the very war on terror that it had initially rejected.

Be that as it may, over the past few years France's renewed international activism has earned the country a particularly high profile in the Middle East and in the Persian Gulf, where France's status as a significant military actor (as demonstrated in Libya, Mali and now Iraq and Syria), combined with the United States' relative disengagement, have made it an important political and military partner of the Gulf States (especially Saudi Arabia) and their close ally Egypt. This enhanced French role in the Middle East and the Gulf has been illustrated by a series of important arms deals in 2015, including the sale to Egypt of *Rafale* fighters as well as the two *Mistral* ships whose sale to Russia had been suspended in the wake of the Ukraine crisis (*Rafale* deals were also concluded with Qatar and India). France's hawkish stance on issues such as Iran and Syria has also been an important factor in its rapprochement with the Gulf States, though this has arguably been at the unwelcome price of France having to take sides in the increasingly tense Sunni-Shia divide in the Middle East. Meanwhile, with the same kind of factors in play, relations with Israel under Hollande (just like under Sarkozy) have also been signally good – perhaps here too at the price of France's margin of manoeuvre in the Israel-Palestine conflict: although Paris in November 2012 voted in favour of recognizing the Palestinian Authority as an observer state at the United Nations, French attempts at imposing a relaunch of the peace process through its internationalization have so far failed, with Paris withdrawing plans to introduce a resolution to that effect at the UN security council under combined US and Israeli pressure.

Overall, then, and aside from obvious differences of style and personality, continuity has prevailed in French foreign policy from Sarkozy to Hollande – as it has generally prevailed from one president to another over the past half century. The fundamentals of 'Gaullism' in foreign policy persist: the pursuit of an ambitious diplomacy and the search for a global role, the importance of the European project and the claim to French (and Franco-German) leadership within the EU and, finally, the desire for a balanced, multipolar international system and a regulated globalization still characterize France's international agenda. Such continuity is not surprising. The defence of the country's 'rank' continues to be the subject of consensus among public opinion and the political classes alike, regardless of domestic political divisions; the pursuit of an active, independent diplomacy therefore remains a key objective for any French president, regardless of his own personal ideas or inclinations. At the same time, the European project and its corollary, the Franco-German relationship, a constant objective of France's policy over the last sixty years, continue to constitute an imperative for a middleweight power whose global influence depends on the leverage provided by Europe. As for the desire to construct a regulated international system based on a balance between the major poles of influence, it would arguably be ironic to abandon this idea at the very moment when the relative retreat of US power and the rise of emerging powers are confirming its validity.

Yet this account of the permanence of French foreign policy, so often reprised over the last half-century and more, hides profound and inevitable questions that France will have to face in the future. The first relates to French power and influence. To be sure, France has long been able to make the most of the cards it holds as a middleweight power with global status in order to make its influence felt in world affairs. Yet France's current economic weakness, the result of long delayed economic and social reforms, raises the question of the sustainability of its activist foreign policy. Does France still have the means to match its international ambitions? Much of course will depend on the conjunctural or the structural character of its present weakness. A second question relates to the state of the European project. Europe, for decades now, has served as a multiplier of France's power and influence. Yet will the European project continue to provide France with similar leverage in the future? The current European crisis, unlike in the past, is an existential crisis that raises the question of the economic and political viability of the European Union and its capacity to remain a unified, integrated entity; the euro crisis, the refugee crisis and the calling into question of the openness of internal borders, the rise of populist movements throughout the continent, all raise the question, arguably for the first time since its inception, of whether the project remains sustainable in the long term. For France, there is an additional area of uncertainty: to what extent can the Franco-German relationship, which had been premised on the two countries' ability to transcend their past rivalries, remain vibrant given the unbalance of power and influence that now characterizes it owing to Germany's strength – or rather to France's weakness? Can France accept a German-led Europe in the long term? Here again, much will depend on the country's capacity to restore its power base in the years and decades to come. France's ability to continue to use the leverage deriving from European construction in order to exert international influence will be all the more vital as a result of the upheaval now under way in the international hierarchy in an era of globalization and emerging multipolarity. What will happen when the European nations find themselves overtaken economically and demographically by emerging nations that do not recognize the hierarchy inherited from the Second World War? Can France, without the backing of a solid, cohesive European construction, still expect to be one of the powers playing some sort of role in a system dominated by five or six major poles? More than ever, then, France's future as a relevant international actor seems to be premised on the fate of the European project.

# APPENDIX

# Individuals in Charge of Foreign Policy under the GPRF and the Fourth Republic (1944–1959)

| President of the Republic[1] | President of the Council of Ministers | Minister of Foreign Affairs |
|---|---|---|
| | Charles de Gaulle (June 1944–January 1946) | Georges Bidault (September 1944–December 1946) |
| | Félix Gouin (January 1946–June 1946) | |
| | Georges Bidault (June–November 1946) | |
| | Léon Blum (December 1946–January 1947) | Léon Blum (December 1946–January 1947) |
| Vincent Auriol (January 1947–January 1954) | Paul Ramadier (January–November 1947) | Georges Bidault (January 1947–July 1948) |
| | Robert Schuman (November 1947–July 1948) | |
| | André Marie (July–August 1948) | Robert Schuman (July 1948–January 1953) |
| | Robert Schuman (September 1948) | |
| | Henri Queuille (September 1948–October 1949) | |
| | Georges Bidault (October 1949–June 1950) | |
| | Henri Queuille (July 1950) | |
| | René Pleven (July 1950–February 1951) | |
| | Henri Queuille (March 1951–July 1951) | |
| | René Pleven (August 1951–January 1952) | |
| | Edgar Faure (January–February 1952) | |
| | Antoine Pinay (March–December 1952) | |
| | René Mayer (January–May 1953) | Georges Bidault (January 1953–June 1954) |
| | Joseph Laniel (June 1953–June 1954) | |

| President of the Republic[1] | President of the Council of Ministers | Minister of Foreign Affairs |
|---|---|---|
| René Coty (January 1954–January 1959) | Pierre Mendès France (June 1954–February 1955) | Pierre Mendès France (June 1954–January 1955) |
| | | Edgard Faure (January–February 1955) |
| | Edgar Faure (February 1955–January 1956) | Antoine Pinay (February 1955–January 1956) |
| | Guy Mollet (January 1956–May 1957) | Christian Pineau (January 1956–May 1958) |
| | Maurice Bourgès Maunoury (June–September 1957) | |
| | Félix Gaillard (November 1957–April 1958) | |
| | Pierre Pflimlin (May 1958) | René Pleven (May 1958) |
| | Charles de Gaulle (June 1958–January 1959) | Maurice Couve de Murville (June 1958–January 1959) |

1. Until the constitution of the Fourth Republic went into effect, the president of the Council of Ministers was simultaneously the chief of state.

# Individuals in Charge of Foreign Policy under the Fifth Republic
## (1959 to the present)

| President of the Republic | Prime Minister | Minister of Foreign Affairs |
|---|---|---|
| Charles de Gaulle (January 1959– April 1969) | Michel Debré (January 1959–April 1962) | M. Couve de Murville (January 1959–May 1968) |
| | Georges Pompidou (April 1962–July 1968) | |
| | M. Couve de Murville (July 1968–June 1969) | Michel Debré (May 1968–June 1969) |
| Georges Pompidou (June 1969–April 1974) | Jacques Chaban-Delmas (June 1969–July 1972) | Maurice Schumann (June 1969–March 1973) |
| | Pierre Messmer (July 1972–April 1974) | Michel Jobert (April 1973–April 1974) |
| Valéry Giscard d'Estaing (May 1974–May 1981) | Jacques Chirac (May 1974–August 1976) | Jean Sauvagnargues (May 1974–August 1976) |
| | Raymond Barre (August 1976–May 1981) | Louis de Guiringaud (August 1976–Nov. 1978) |
| | | Jean François-Poncet (November 1978–May 1981) |
| François Mitterrand (May 1981–May 1995) | Pierre Mauroy (May 1981–July 1984) | Claude Cheysson (May 1981–December 1984) |
| | Laurent Fabius (July 1984–March 1986) | Roland Dumas (Dec. 1984–March 1986) |
| | Jacques Chirac (March 1986–May 1988) | Jean-Bernard Raimond (March 1986–May 1988) |
| | Michel Rocard (May 1988–May 1991) | Roland Dumas (May 1988–March 1993) |
| | Edith Cresson (May 1991–April 1992) | |
| | Pierre Bérégovoy (April 1992–March 1993) | |
| | Edouard Balladur (March 1993–May 1995) | Alain Juppé (March 1993–May 1995) |

| President of the Republic | Prime Minister | Minister of Foreign Affairs |
|---|---|---|
| Jacques Chirac (May 1995–May 2007) | Alain Juppé (May 1995–June 1997) | Hervé de Charette (May 1995–June 1997) |
| | Lionel Jospin (June 1997–May 2002) | Hubert Védrine (June 1997–May 2002) |
| | Jean-Pierre Raffarin (May 2002–May 2005) | Dominique de Villepin (May 2002–March 2004) |
| | | Michel Barnier (March 2004–May 2005) |
| | Dominique de Villepin (May 2005–May 2007) | Philippe Douste-Blazy (May 2005–May 2007) |
| Nicolas Sarkozy (May 2007–May 2012) | François Fillon (May 2007–May 2012) | Bernard Kouchner (May 2007–November 2010) |
| | | Michèle Alliot-Marie (Nov. 2010–February 2011) |
| | | Alain Juppé (February 2011–May 2012) |
| François Hollande (May 2012–) | Jean-Marc Ayrault (May 2012–March 2014) | Laurent Fabius (May 2012–) |
| | Manuel Valls (March 2014–) | |

# BIBLIOGRAPHY

## General

Allain, Jean-Claude, et al., *Histoire de la diplomatie française*, Paris, Perrin, 2005.

Bozo, Frédéric, *La Politique étrangère de la France depuis 1945*, Paris, Flammarion, 2012.

Cogan, Charles, *French Negotiating Behavior: Dealing with la Grande Nation*, Washington, US Institute of Peace, 2003 (French translation Jacob-Duvernet, 2005, with a preface by Hubert Védrine).

Dalloz, Jacques, *La France et le monde depuis 1945*, Paris, A. Colin, 1993.

Dulphy, Anne, *La Politique extérieure de la France depuis 1945*, Paris, Nathan, 1994.

Grosser, Alfred, *Affaires extérieures. La politique de la France 1944–1989*, Paris, Flammarion, 1989.

Heisbourg, François, 'Défense, diplomatie: de la puissance à l'influence', in Fauroux, Roger, and Bernard Spitz (eds), *Notre Etat*, Paris, Robert Laffont, 2000.

Moreau Defarges, Philippe, *La France dans le monde au XXè siècle*, Paris, Hachette, 1994.

Revue *Politique étrangère*, special issue, '50 ans de politique étrangère de la France', no. 1/86.

Tacel, Max, *La France et le Monde au XXè siècle*, Paris, Masson, 1989.

Vaïsse, Maurice, *La Puissance ou l'influence? La France dans le monde depuis 1958*, Paris, Fayard, 2008.

## Historiography

Frank, Robert (ed.), *Pour l'histoire des relations internationales*, Paris, P.U.F., 2012.

Jeannesson, Stanislas, 'Diplomatie et politique étrangère de la France: un bilan historiographique depuis 1990', *Histoire, économie & société* 2 (2012), pp. 87–98.

# By Themes, Over the Whole Period

## Decision-Making Process, Diplomatic Apparatus, Foreign Policy Debate

Badel, Laurence, *Diplomatie et grands contrats. L'Etat français et les marchés extérieurs au 20e siècle*, Paris, Publications de la Sorbonne, 2010.

Badel, Laurence, Stanislas Jeannesson and N. Piers Ludlow (eds), *Les administrations nationales et la construction européenne. Une approche historique, 1919–1975*, Brussels, Peter Lang, 2005.

Baillou, Jean, *Les Affaires étrangères et le Corps diplomatique français*, vol. II, 1870–1980, Paris, CNRS, 1984.

Bély, Lucien, et al. (eds), *Dictionnaire des ministres des affaires étrangères 1589–2004*, Paris, Fayard, 2004.

Charillon, Frédéric, *La France peut-elle encore agir sur le monde?* Paris, A. Colin, 2010.

Cohen, Samy, *Les Conseillers du Président. De Charles de Gaulle à Valéry Giscard d'Estaing*, Paris, P.U.F., 1980.

———, *La Monarchie nucléaire. Les coulisses de la politique étrangère sous la Vè République*, Paris, Hachette, 1986.

——— (ed.), *Les Diplomates*, Paris, Autrement, 2001.

Kessler, Marie-Christine, *La Politique étrangère de la France. Acteurs et processus*, Paris, Presses de Sciences-Po, 1999.

Lequesne, Christian, *La France dans la nouvelle Europe. Assumer le changement d'échelle*, Paris, Presses de Sciences Po, 2008.

Ministère des Affaires étrangères, Centre d'Analyse et de prévision, *Le Débat de politique étrangère française, 1974–2004*, 2005.

Tenzer, Nicolas, *Quand la France disparaît du monde . . .*, Paris, Grasset, 2008.

## Defense and Security

Bozo, Frédéric, *La France et l'OTAN. De la guerre froide au nouvel ordre européen*, Paris, Masson, 1991.

Cohen, Samy, *La Défaite des généraux. Le pouvoir politique et l'armée sous la Vè République*, Paris, Fayard, 1994.

Duval, Marcel, and Yves Le Baut, *L'Arme nucléaire française: pourquoi et comment?* Paris, SPM, 1992.

Duval, Marcel, and Dominique Mongin, *Histoire des forces nucléaires françaises depuis 1945*, Paris, P.U.F., 1993.

Gordon, Philip H., *A Certain Idea of France: French Security Policy and the Gaullist Legacy*, Princeton, Princeton University Press, 1993.

*Journal of Transatlantic Studies*, vol. 9 (2011), Issue 3, 2014, dossier: 'Cold War Maverick: France and NATO, 1946–1991', pp. 181–267.

Martel, André, *Histoire militaire de la Vè République*, vol. 4, De 1940 à nos jours, Paris, P.U.F., 1994.

Rühl, Lothar, *La Politique militaire de la Vè République*, FNSP, 1976.

Vaïsse, Maurice, *La France et l'atome. Etudes d'histoire nucléaire*, Brussels, Bruylant, 1994.

Vaïsse, Maurice, and Jean Doise, *Diplomatie et outil militaire 1871–1991*, Paris, Seuil, 1991.

Vaïsse, Maurice, Pierre Melandri and Frédéric Bozo (eds), *La France et l'OTAN 1949–1996*, Brussels, Complexe, 1996, and Editions André Versaille, 2012.

Yost, David S., *La France et la sécurité européenne*, Paris, P.U.F., 1985.

### East-West Relations

Bozo, Frédéric, 'France, "Gaullism", and the Cold War', in Westad, Odd Arne, and Melvyn P. Leffler (eds), *Cambridge History of the Cold War*, vol. 2, Cambridge, Cambridge University Press, 2010.

### France and the UN

Lewin, André (ed.), *La France et l'ONU depuis 1945*, Paris, Arléa, 1995.

Smouts, Marie-Claude, *La France à l'ONU. Premiers rôles et second rang*, Paris, Presses de la FNSP, 1979.

### France and the United States

Cogan, Charles, *Oldest Allies, Guarded Friends: France and the United States since 1940*, London, Praeger, 1994 (French translation, Brussels, Bruylant, 2000)

Costigliola, Frank, *France and the United States: The Cold Alliance Since World War II*, Boston, Twayne Publishers, 1992.

Durandin, Catherine, *La France contre l'Amérique*, Paris, P.U.F., 1994.

Duroselle, Jean-Baptiste, *La France et les Etats-Unis des origines à nos jours*, Paris, Seuil, 1976.

Kuisel Richard, *Seducing the French: The Dilemma of Americanization*, Berkeley, University of California Press, 1993 (French translation, Paris, Lattès, 1996.).

———, *The French Way: How France Embraced and Rejected American Values and Power*, Princeton, Princeton University Press, 2011.

Lukic, Renéo, *Conflit et coopération dans les relations franco-américaines. Du général de Gaulle à Nicolas Sarkozy*, Québec, Presses de l'Université Laval, 2009.

Melandri, Pierre, 'The Troubled Friendship: France and the United Sates, 1945–1989', in Lundestad, Geir (ed.), *No End to Alliance: The United States and Western Europe: Past, Present and Future*, New York, St Martin's Press, 1998.

Melandri, Pierre, and Serge Ricard (eds), *La France et les Etats-Unis au XXè siècle*, Paris, L'Harmattan, 2003.

Nouzille, Vincent, *Des secrets si bien gardés. Les dossiers de la Maison-Blanche et de la CIA sur la France et ses présidents, 1958–1981*, Paris, Fayard, 2009

———, *Dans le secret des présidents. CIA, Maison Blanche, Elysée: les dossiers confidentiels, 1981–2010*, Paris, Fayard, 2010

## Franco-German Relations

Bariéty, Jacques, and Raymond Poidevin, *Les relations franco-allemandes 1815–1975*, Paris, Colin, 1977.

Haftendorn, Helga, et al. (eds), *The Strategic Triangle: France, Germany, and the United States in the Shaping of the New Europe*, Washington, Woodrow Wilson Center Press, Johns Hopkins University Press, 2006.

*Histoire franco-allemande*, 11 volumes (Institut historique allemand / presses universitaires du Septentrion): vol. 10, Defrance, Corine, and Ulrich Pfeil, *Entre guerre froide et intégration européenne. Reconstruction et rapprochement, 1945–1963* (2012); vol. 11, Miard-Delacroix, Hélène, *Le Défi européen. De 1963 à nos jours* (2011).

Soutou, Georges-Henri, *L'Alliance incertaine. Les rapports politiques et stratégiques franco-allemands 1954–1996*, Paris, Fayard, 1996.

Weisenfeld, Ernst, *Quelle Allemagne pour la France?* Paris, Colin, 1989.

## Franco-British Relations

Bell, P. M. H., *France and Britain 1940–1994: The Long Separation*, London, Langman, 1997.

La Serre, Françoise (de), Jacques Leruez and Helen Wallace (eds), *Les Politiques étrangères de la France et de la Grande-Bretagne depuis 1945. L'inévitable ajustement*, Paris, Presses de la FNSP, 1990.

Tombs, Robert, and Isabelle Tombs, *That Sweet Enemy: The French and the British from the Sun King to the Present*, London, W. Heinemann, 2006.

## European Construction

Bitsch, Marie-Thérèse, *Histoire de la construction européenne de 1945 à nos jours*, Brussels, Complexe, 2003.

Bossuat, Gérard, *Faire l'Europe sans défaire la France. 60 ans de politique européenne des gouvernements et des présidents de la République française (1943–2003)*, Brussels, P. Lang, 2005.

Du Réau, Elisabeth, *L'Idée d'Europe au XXè siècle. Des mythes aux réalités*, Brussels, Complexe, 1996.

Gerbet, Pierre, *La Construction de l'Europe*, Paris, Imprimerie nationale, 1994.

Sutton, Michael, *France and the Construction of Europe, 1944–2007*, Oxford, Berghahn Books, 2007.

## Relations with Eastern Europe

Schreiber, Thomas, *Les Relations de la France avec les pays de l'Est 1944–1980*, la Documentation française, 1980.

———, *Les Actions de la France à l'Est, ou les absences de Marianne*, Paris, L'Harmattan, 2000.

## Middle East

Frémeaux, Jacques, *Le Monde arabe et la sécurité de la France*, Paris, P.U.F., 1995.

Kassir, Samir, and Farouk Mardam-Bey, *Itinéraires de Paris à Jérusalem. La France et le conflit israélo-arabe*, 2 vols, Revue d'Etudes palestiniennes, 1993.

Nouschi, André, *La France et le monde arabe*, Paris, Vuibert, 1994.

Styan, David, *France and Iraq: Oil, Arms, and the Making of French Foreign Policy*, London, I.B. Tauris, 2006.

## Africa, Asia-Pacific, Third World

Adda, Jacques, and Marie-Claude Smouts, *La France face au Sud. Le miroir brisé*, Paris, Karthala, 1989.

Chipman, John, *La Vè République et la défense de l'Afrique*, Paris, Bosquet, 1985.

Gounin, Yves, *La France en Afrique. Le combat des anciens et des modernes*, Brussels, De Boek, 2009.

Mohamed-Gaillard, Sarah, *L'Archipel de la puissance. La politique de la France dans le Pacifique sud de 1946 à 1998*, Brussels, Peter Lang, 2010.

Wauthier, Claude, *Quatre Présidents et l'Afrique. De Gaulle, Pompidou, Giscard d'Estaing et Mitterrand*, Paris, Le Seuil, 1995.

## The Question of Power

Bozo, Frédéric, 'Le rang et la puissance', in Rioux, Jean-Pierre, and Jean-François Sirinelli (eds), *La France d'un siècle à l'autre. Dictionnaire critique*, Paris, Hachette, 1999.

Frank, Robert, *La Hantise du déclin. La France 1920–1960: Finances, défense et identité nationale*, Paris, Belin, 1994.

## By Periods

## 1945–1958

### General

Berstein, Serge, and Pierre Milza (eds), *L'Année 1947*, Paris, Presses de Science-Po, 2000.

De Porte, Anton W., *De Gaulle's Foreign Policy 1944–1946*, Cambridge, MA, Harvard University Press, 1968.

Elgey, Georgette, *Histoire de la IVè République*, 5 vols, Paris, Fayard, 1992–2008.

Gerbet, Pierre, *Le Relèvement 1944–1949*, Paris, Imprimerie Nationale, 1991.

Grosser, Alfred, *La IVè République et sa politique extérieure*, Paris, Colin, 1972.

*The Question of Power*

Girault, René, and Robert Frank (eds), *La Puissance française en question 1945–1949*, Paris, Publications de la Sorbonne, 1988.

*Relations internationales*, no. 58 (summer 1989), La France en quête de puissance.

*Early Cold War, German Question*

Buffet, Cyril, *Mourir pour Berlin. La France et l'Allemagne 1945–1949*, Paris, Colin, 1991.

Creswell, Michael, *A Question of Balance: How France and the United States created Cold War Europe*, Cambridge, MA, Harvard University Press, 2006.

Libera, Martial, *Un rêve de puissance. La France et le contrôle de l'économie allemande (1942–1949)*, Brussels, Peter Lang, 2012.

Maelstaf, Geneviève, *Que faire de l'Allemagne? Les responsables français, le statut international de l'Allemagne et le problème de l'unité allemande, 1945–1955*, Paris, Ministère des Affaires étrangères, coll. 'Diplomatie et Histoire', 1999.

Soutou, Georges-Henri, 'Les dirigeants français et l'entrée en guerre froide: un processus de décision hésitant (1944–1950)', *Le trimestre du monde*, 3/1993, pp. 135–149.

———, 'France and the Cold War, 1944–1963', *Diplomacy & Statecraft* 12, no. 4 (December 2001), pp. 35–52.

Young, John, *France, the Cold War, and the Western Alliance 1944–1949: French Foreign Policy and Post-War Europe*, Leicester, Leicester University Press, 1990.

*United States, Atlantic Alliance, European Construction*

Bossuat, Gérard, *La France, l'aide américaine et la construction européenne 1944–1954*, Paris, Comité pour l'histoire économique et financière de la France, 1992, 2 vols.

Hitchcock, William I., *France Restored: Cold War Diplomacy and the Quest for Leadership in Europe 1944–1954*, Chapel Hill, University of North Carolina Press, 1998.

Lacroix-Riz, Annie, *Le Choix de Marianne. Les relations franco-américaines 1944–1948*, Paris, Messidor, 1986.

Melandri, Pierre, *Les Etats-Unis et le 'défi' européen 1955–1958*, Paris, P.U.F., 1975.

———, *Les Etats-Unis face à l'unification de l'Europe 1945–1954*, Paris, Pédone, 1980.

Poidevin, Raymond (ed.), *Histoire des débuts de la construction européenne (mars 1948–mai 1950)*, Brussels, Bruylant, 1986.

Raflik-Grenouilleau, Jenny, *La IVè République et l'Alliance atlantique: influence et dépendance (1945–1958)*, Rennes, Presses universitaires de Rennes, 2013.

Sanderson, Claire, *L'impossible alliance? France, Grande-Bretagne et défense de l'Europe 1945–1958*, Paris, Publications de la Sorbonne, 2003, preface by Robert Frank.

Soutou, Georges-Henri, 'La France et l'Alliance atlantique de 1949 à 1954', *Cahier du CEHD* no. 3 (1977), pp. 49–74.

Vial, Philippe, 'Jean Monnet, un père pour la CED?' in Girault, René, and Gérard Bossuat (eds), *Europe brisée, Europe retrouvée. Nouvelles perspectives pour l'histoire de la construction européenne*, Paris, Publications de la Sorbonne, 1994.

Wall, Irwin, *L'influence américaine sur la politique française 1945–1954*, Paris, Balland, 1989.

## Military Issues

Mongin, Dominique, *La Bombe atomique française 1945–1958*, Brussels, Bruylant, 1997.

## Decolonization and Foreign Policy

Artaud, Denise, and Lawrence Kaplan (eds), *Diên Biên Phû*, Paris, La Manufacture, 1989.

Rioux, Jean-Pierre (ed.), *La Guerre d'Algérie et les Français*, Paris, Fayard, 1990.

Wall, Irwin, *France, the United States, and the Algerian War*, Berkeley, University of California Press, 2001 (French translation, Paris, Soleb, 2006).

## The Government of Pierre Mendès France

Bedarida, François, and Jean-Pierre Rioux, *Pierre Mendès France et le mendésisme*, Paris, Fayard, 1985.

Girault, René, et al., *Pierre Mendès France et le rôle de la France dans le monde*, Grenoble, Presses universitaires de Grenoble, 1991.

## Middle East, Israel

Schillo, Frédérique, *La politique française à l'égard d'Israël (1946–1959)*, Brussels, André Versaille, 2012.

## The Suez Crisis and Its Sequel

Bernard, Jean-Yves, *La genèse de l'expédition franco-britannique de 1956 en Égypte*, Paris, Publications de la Sorbonne, 2003.

Elgey, Georgette, '1956: Révélations sur la crise de Suez', *L'Histoire* no. 202 (September 1996), pp. 88–92.

Vaïsse, Maurice, 'Aux origines du mémorandum de 1958', *Relations internationales* no. 58 (summer 1989), pp. 253–268.

———, 'France and the Suez Crisis', in Louis, William Roger (ed.), *Suez 1956: The Crisis and its Consequences*, Oxford, Clarendon Press, 1989.

——— (ed.), *La France et l'opération de Suez*, Paris, Addim, 1997.

## 1958–1969

*General*

Barnavi, Elie, and Saül Friedlander (eds), *La Politique étrangère du général de Gaulle*, Paris, P.U.F., 1985.

Berstein, Serge, *La France de l'expansion*, vol. I, 'La République gaullienne', Paris, Le Seuil, 1989.

Cerny, Philip G., *The Politics of Grandeur: Ideological Aspects of de Gaulle's Foreign Policy*, Cambridge, Cambridge University Press, 1980 and 2008 (French translation Paris, Flammarion, 1986).

*Dictionnaire Charles de Gaulle*, Paris, Robert Laffont, 2006.

Hoffmann, Stanley, 'De Gaulle et le monde: la scène et la pièce', in *Essais sur la France. Déclin ou renouveau?* Paris, Le Seuil, 1974.

Kolodziej, Edward A., *French International Policy under De Gaulle and Pompidou*, Ithaca, Cornell University Press, 1974.

Nuenlist, Christian, Anna Locher and Garret Martin (eds), *Globalizing de Gaulle: International Perspectives on French Foreign Policy, 1958–1969*, Lanham, Lexington Books, 2010.

Vaïsse, Maurice, *La Grandeur. Politique étrangère du général de Gaulle*, Paris, Fayard, 1997.

*United States, Atlantic Alliance, Strategic Issues*

Bozo, Frédéric, *Two Strategies for Europe: de Gaulle, the United States, and the Atlantic Alliance (1958–1969)*, Lanham, Rowman & Littlefield, 2001 (French edition, Plon, 1996).

Institut Charles de Gaulle, *L'Aventure de la bombe. De Gaulle et la dissuasion nucléaire 1958–1969*, Paris, Plon, 1985.

———, *De Gaulle en son siècle*, vol. 4, 'La sécurité et l'indépendance de la France', Paris, Plon, 1992.

Giauque, Jeffrey Glen, *Grand Designs and Visions of Unity: The Atlantic Powers and the Reorganization of Western Europe, 1955–1963*, Chapel Hill: University of North Carolina Press, 2002.

Jauvert, Vincent, *L'Amérique contre de Gaulle. Histoire secrète (1961–1969)*, Paris, Le Seuil, coll. 'L'histoire immédiate', 2000.

Martin, Garret, *General de Gaulle's Cold War: Challenging American Hegemony, 1963–1968*, New York, Berghahn Books, 2012.

Pottier Olivier, *Les Bases américaines en France (1950–1967)*, Paris, L'Harmattan, 2003.

Vaïsse, Maurice (ed.), *L'Europe et la crise de Cuba*, Paris, A. Colin, 1993.

*Construction Européenne, Franco-German Relations*

Bahu-Leyser, Danielle, *De Gaulle, les Français et l'Europe*, Paris, P.U.F., 1981.

Binoche, Jacques, *De Gaulle et les Allemands*, Brussels, Complexe, 1990.

Defrance Corinne and Ulrich Pfeil (eds), *Le Traité de l'Elysée et les relations franco-allemandes, 1945–1963–2003*, Paris, CNRS Editions, 2005.

Institut Charles de Gaulle, *De Gaulle en son siècle*, vol. 5, 'L'Europe', Paris, Plon, 1992.

Ludlow, N. Piers, *The European Community and the Crises of the 1960s: Negotiating the Gaullist Challenge*, London, Routledge, 2006.

Maillard, Pierre, *De Gaulle et l'Allemagne. Le rêve inachevé*, Paris, Plon, 1990.

———, *De Gaulle et l'Europe*, Paris, Tallandier, 1995.

Schoenborn, Benedikt, *La Mésentente apprivoisée. De Gaulle et les Allemands, 1963–1969*, Paris, P.U.F., 2007.

Warlouzet, Laurent, *Le Choix de la CEE par la France. Les débats économiques de Pierre Mendès-France à Charles de Gaulle (1955–1969)*, Paris, CHEFF, 2011.

## Franco-British Relations

Ludlow, N. Piers, *Dealing with Britain: The Six and the First UK Application to the EEC*, Cambridge, Cambridge University Press, 1997.

Mangold, Peter, *Harold Macmillan and Charles de Gaulle*, London, I.B. Tauris, 2006.

Pagedas, Constantine A., *Anglo-American Strategic Relations and the French Problem 1960–1963: A Troubled Partnership*, London, Cass, 2000.

Sanderson, Claire, *Perfide Albion? L'affaire Soames et les arcanes de la diplomatie britannique*, Paris, Publications de la Sorbonne, 2011.

## Policy Towards the East

Gomart, Thomas, *Double détente. Les relations franco-soviétiques de 1958 à 1964*, Paris, Publications de la Sorbonne, 2003.

Rey, Marie-Pierre, *La Tentation du rapprochement. France et URSS à l'heure de la détente 1964–1974*, Paris, Sorbonne, 1991.

———, 'De Gaulle, l'URSS et la sécurité européenne, 1958–1969', in Maurice Vaïsse (ed.), *De Gaulle et la Russie*, Paris, CNRS Editions, 2006.

Vaïsse, Maurice (ed.), *De Gaulle et la Russie*, Paris, CNRS Editions, 2006.

## Middle East

Cohen, Samy, *De Gaulle, les gaullistes et Israël*, Paris, Alain Moreau, 1974.

## Third World

*De Gaulle et le tiers-monde*, Paris, Pédone, 1983.

Durand, Pierre-Michel, *L'Afrique et les relations franco-américaines des années soixante. Aux origines de l'obsession américaine*, Paris, L'Harmattan, 2008.

Institut Charles de Gaulle, *De Gaulle en son siècle*, vol. 6, 'Liberté et dignité des peuples', Paris, Plon, 1992.

## 1969–1981

### General

Association Georges Pompidou, *Georges Pompidou hier et aujourd'hui*, Paris, Breet, 1990.

Berstein, Serge, and Jean-Pierre Rioux, *La France de l'expansion*, 'L'apogée Pompidou 1969–1974', Paris, Le Seuil, 1996.

Cohen, Samy, and Marie-Claude Smouts (eds), *La politique extérieure de Valéry Giscard d'Estaing*, Paris, Presses de la FNSP, 1985.

Weed, Mary Kathleen, *L'image publique d'un homme secret. Michel Jobert et la diplomatie française*, Paris, Fernand Lanore, 1988.

### Europe, the Atlantic Alliance and Détente

Andréani, Jacques, *Le Piège. Helsinki et la chute du communisme*, Paris, Odile Jacob, 2005.

Association Georges Pompidou, *Georges Pompidou et l'Europe*, Brussels, Complexe, 1995.

Badalassi, Nicolas, *En finir avec la guerre froide. La France, l'Europe et le processus d'Helsinki, 1965–1975*, Rennes, Presses universitaires de Rennes, 2014, with a preface by Frédéric Bozo.

Berstein, Serge, and Jean-François Sirinelli, *Les Années Giscard. Valéry Giscard d'Estaing et l'Europe 1974–1981*, Paris, Colin, 2006.

Bussière, Éric, et al. (eds), *Georges Pompidou et les Etats-Unis. Une relation spéciale, 1969–1974*, Brussels, Peter Lang, 2013.

Gfeller, Aurélie Elisa, *Building a European Identity: France, the United States, and the Oil Shock, 1973–74*, New York, Berghahn Books, 2012.

Heurtebize, Frédéric, *Le Péril rouge. Washington face à l'eurocommunisme*, Paris, Presses universitaires de France, 2014.

Meimeth, Michael, *Frankreichs Entspannungspolitik der 70er Jahre: Zwischen Status quo und friedlichem Wandel. Die Ära Georges Pompidou und Valéry Giscard d'Estaing*, Baden-Baden, Nomos, 1990.

Melandri, Pierre, *Une incertaine alliance. Les Etats-Unis et l'Europe (1973–1982)*, Paris, Publications de la Sorbonne, 1988.

Miard-Delacroix, Hélène, *Partenaires de choix? Le chancelier Helmut Schmidt et la France (1974–1982)*, Brussels, Peter Lang, 1993.

Möckli, Daniel, *European Foreign Policy During the Cold War: Heath, Brandt, Pompidou and the Dream of Political Unity*, London, I.B. Tauris, 2009.

Schirmann, Sylvain, and Mohamed-Gaillard Sarah, *Georges Pompidou et l'Allemagne*, Brussels, PIE-Peter Lang, 2012.

Weinachter, Michèle, *Valéry Giscard d'Estaing et l'Allemagne. Le double rêve inachevé*, Paris, L'Harmattan, 2004.

## 1981–1995

Bertsein, Serge, Pierre Milza and Jean-Louis Bianco (eds), *François Mitterrand. Les Années du Changement (1981–1984)*, Paris, Perrin, 2001.

Bozo, Frédéric, 'Before the Wall: French Diplomacy and the Last Decade of the Cold War', in Olav Njølstad (ed.), *The Last Decade of the Cold War: From Conflict Escalation to Conflict Transformation*, London, Frank Cass, 2004.

———, 'Un rendez-vous manqué? La France, les Etats-Unis et l'Alliance atlantique, 1990–1991', *Relations internationales* no. 120 (winter 2004), pp. 119–132.

———, 'Mitterrand's France, the End of the Cold War, and German Unification: A Reappraisal', *Cold War History* 7, no. 4 (autumn 2007).

———, 'The Failure of a Grand Design: Mitterrand's European Confederation (1989–1991)', *Contemporary European History* 3, no. 17 (2008), pp. 391–412.

———, *Mitterrand, the End of the Cold War, and German Unification*, New York, Berghahn Books, 2009 (French edition Paris, Odile Jacob, 2005)

———, '"Winners" and "Losers": France, the United States, and the End of the Cold War', *Diplomatic History* 33, no. 5 (November 2009), pp. 927–956.

Brand Crémieux, Marie-Noëlle, *Les Français face à la réunification allemande*, Paris, L'Harmattan, 2004.

Chaput, Paul, *La France et l'Initiative de défense stratégique de Ronald Reagan (1983–1986)*, Paris, L'Harmattan, 2013

Cohen, Samy, *Mitterrand et la sortie de la guerre froide*, Paris, P.U.F., 1998.

Favier, Pierre, and Michel Martin-Roland, *La Décennie Mitterrand*, 4 vols, Paris, Le Seuil, 1990–1999.

Filiu, Jean-Pierre, *Mitterrand et la Palestine. L'ami d'Israël qui sauva par trois fois Yasser Arafat*, Paris, Fayard, 2005.

Fraudet, Xavier, *France's Security Independence: Originality and Constraints in Europe, 1981–1995*, Berlin, P. Lang, 2006.

Garcin, Thierry, *La France dans le nouveau désordre international*, Brussels, Bruylant, 1992.

Gautier, Louis, *Mitterrand et son armée 1990–1995*, Paris, Grasset, 1999.

Lappenküper, Ulrich, *Mitterrand und Deutschland. Die enträtselte Sphinx*, Munich, Oldenburg, 2011.

Leimbacher, Urs, *Die unverzichtbare Allianz. Deutsch-französische sicherheitspolitische Zusammenarbeit, 1982–1989*, Baden-Baden, Nomos, 1992.

*Politique étrangère* no. 4/95, special issue 'La Politique étrangère de la France'.

Robin, Gabriel, *La diplomatie de Mitterrand ou le triomphe des apparences (1981–1985)*, Editions de la Bièvre, 1985.

Schabert, Tilo, *Wie Weltgeschichte gemacht wird. Frankreich und die deutsche Vereinigung*, Stuttgart, Klett-Cotta, 2002.

Tardy, Thierry, *La France et la gestion des conflits yougoslaves (1991–1995). Enjeux et leçons d'une opération de maintien de la paix de l'ONU*, Brussels, Bruylant, 1999.

Zuber, Raymond-François, *Les dirigeants américains et la France pendant les présidences de Ronald Reagan et George Bush (1981–1993)*, Paris, L'Harmattan, 2002.

## Since 1995

Aeschimann, Eric, and Christophe Boltanski, *Chirac d'Arabie. Les mirages d'une politique française*, Paris, Grasset, 2006.

Bozo, Frédéric, 'La France et l'Alliance depuis la fin de la guerre froide. Le modèle gaullien en question?' *Cahier du Centre d'études d'histoire de la défense* no. 17, 2001.

———, *La France et l'Alliance atlantique : la fin de l'exception française ?* Document de travail, Fondation pour l'innovation politique, février 2008.

———, *A History of the Iraq Crisis: France, the United States, and Iraq, 1991–2003*, Washington and New York, Woodrow Wilson Center Press and Columbia University Press, 2016.

Bozo, Frédéric, and Guillaume Parmentier, 'La France et les Etats-Unis entre échéances intérieures et tensions internationales. Une réconciliation limitée?' *Annuaire français des relations internationales*, 2007, pp. 543–567.

Brenner, Michael, and Guillaume Parmentier, *Reconciliable Differences: U.S.-French Relations in the New Era*, Washington, The Brookings Institution Press, 2002.

Chouet, Alain (with Jean Guisnel), *Au cœur des services spéciaux*, Paris, La Découverte, 2013.

Cogan, Charles, *La République de Dieu*, Paris, Jacob-Duvernet, 2008.

Coudurier, Hubert, *Le Monde selon Chirac*, Paris, Calmann-Levy, 1998.

Delafon, Gilles, and Thomas Sancton, *Dear Jacques, cher Bill . . . Au cœur de l'Elysée et de la Maison-Blanche 1995–1999*, Paris, Plon 1999.

Du Roy, Albert, *Domaine réservé. Les coulisses de la diplomatie française*, Paris, Le Seuil, 2000.

Friend, Julius, *Unequal Partners: French-German Relations, 1989–2000*, Washington, CSIS, 2001.

Gautier, Louis, *La défense de la France après la guerre froide*, Paris, P.U.F., 2009.

Gordon, Philip H., and Sophie Meunier, *The French Challenge: Adapting to Globalization*, Washington, Brookings, 2001.

Gordon, Philip H., and Jeremy Shapiro, *Allies at War: America, Europe and the Crisis over Iraq*, New York, McGraw Hill, 2004.

Guisnel, Jean, *Les pires amis du monde. Les relations franco-américaines à la fin du XXe siècle*, Stock, 1999.

Hoffmann, Stanley (with Frédéric Bozo), *Gulliver Unbound: America's Imperial Temptation and the War in Iraq*, Lanham, Rowman & Littlefield, 2004 (French edition Paris, Louis Audibert, 2003).

Labévière, Richard, *Le grand retournement. Bagdad-Beyrouth*, Paris, Seuil, 2006.

Lequesne, Christian, and Maurice Vaïsse (eds), *La Politique étrangère de Jacques Chirac*, Paris, Riveneuve, 2013.

Melandri, Pierre, and Justin Vaïsse, *L'Empire du milieu. Les Etats-Unis et le monde depuis la fin de la guerre froide*, Paris, Odile Jacob, 2001.

*European Security* 19, no. 1 (2010), Special Issue, 'France's return to NATO: Implications for transatlantic relations', pp. 1–142.

*European Political Science* 9, no. 2 (June 2010), Specia Issue, 'The New "Special Relationship"? U.S.-France Relations in the Age of Sarkozy', pp. 149–222.

*Journal of Transatlantic Studies* 12, no. 4 (2014), Special Issue, 'At the Crossroads: France, NATO and Europe since Reintegration', pp. 353–442.

*Politique étrangère* no. 4/1995, 'La politique étrangère de la France', Special Issue, pp. 835–992.

*Relations internationales et stratégiques* no. 25 (1997), Special Issue, 'La politique étrangère du président Chirac'.

———, no. 63 (2006), 'Quelle place pour la France dans le monde?'

Védrine, Hubert, *La France et la mondialisation*, Paris, Fayard, 2007.

Vernet, Henri, and Thomas Cantaloube, *Chirac contre Bush. L'autre guerre*, Paris, JC Lattès, 2004.

## Actors, Memoirs and Testimonies

Alphand, Hervé, *L'Etonnement d'être. Journal 1939–1973*, Paris, Fayard, 1977.

Andrieu, Claire, Philippe Braud and Guillaume Piketty (eds), *Dictionnaire de Gaulle*, Paris, Robert Laffont, 2006.

Attali, Jacques, *Verbatim*, 3 vols, Paris, Fayard, 1993 and 1995.

Balladur, Edouard, *Le Pouvoir ne se partage pas. Conversations avec François Mitterrand*, Paris, Fayard, 2009.

Bernard, Mathias, *Valéry Giscard d'Estaing. Les ambitions déçues*, Paris, A. Colin, 2014.

Burin des Roziers, Etienne, *Retour aux sources. 1962, l'année décisive*, Paris, Plon, 1986.

Chauvel, Jean, *Commentaire*, 3 vols., Paris, Fayard, 1973.

Chirac, Jacques, *Mon combat pour la paix*, Paris, Odile Jacob, 2007.

———, *Mémoires*, 2 vols. Paris, Nil, 2009 and 2011.

Couve de Murville, Maurice, *Une Politique étrangère*, Paris, Plon, 1971.

Debré, Michel, *Mémoires*, vols 3 and 4, 1988 and 1993.

Demory, Jean-Claude, *Georges Bidault*, Paris, Julliard, 1995.

Dumas, Roland, *Le Fil et la pelote. Mémoires*, Paris, Plon, 1996.

———, *Affaires étrangères, 1981–1988*, Paris, Fayard, 2007.

Froment-Meurice, Henri, *Vu du Quai. Mémoires 1945–1983*, Paris, Fayard, 1998.

———, *Journal de Moscou*, Paris, A. Colin, 2011.

———, *Journal de Bonn 1982–1983*, Paris, A. Colin, 2013.

De Gaulle, Charles, *Mémoires d'espoir*, Paris, Plon, 1970.

———, *Lettres, notes et carnets*, 12 vols, Paris, Plon, 1980–1988.

Giscard d'Estaing, Valéry, *Le Pouvoir et la vie*, 3 vols, Paris, Cie 12, 1988–2006.

Jobert, Michel, *L'autre regard*, Paris, Grasset, 1974.

———, *Mémoires d'avenir*, Paris, Grasset, 1974.

Lacouture, Jean, *Pierre Mendès France*, Paris, Le Seuil, 1981.

———, *De Gaulle*, Paris, Le Seuil, 3 vols, 1984–1986.

———, *François Mitterrand. Une histoire de Français*, Paris, Le Seuil, 2 vols, 1998.

Lafon, François, *Guy Mollet*, Paris, Fayard, 2007.

Le Maire, Bruno, *Le Ministre. Récit*, Paris, Grasset, 2004.

——, *Des hommes d'Etat*, Paris, Grasset, 2007.

Mechoulan, Eric, *Jules Moch. Un socialiste dérangeant*, Brussels, Bruylant, 1999.

Mitterrand, François, *De l'Allemagne, de la France*, Paris, Odile Jacob, 1996.

——, *Réflexions sur la politique étrangère de la France*, Paris, Fayard, 1986.

Peyrefitte, Alain, *C'était de Gaulle*, 3 vols, Paris, Fayard-de Fallois, 1994–2000.

Poidevin, Raymond, *Robert Schuman, homme d'Etat*, Paris, Imprimerie nationale, 1986.

Raimond, Jean-Bernard, *Le Quai d'Orsay à l'épreuve de la cohabitation*, Paris, Flammarion, 1989.

Rizzo, Jean-Louis, *Pierre Mendès France*, Paris, La Découverte, 1994.

Roussel, Eric, *Georges Pompidou*, Paris, Jean-Claude Lattès, 1994.

——, *Jean Monnet*, Paris, Fayard, 1995.

——, *De Gaulle*, Paris, Gallimard, 2002.

——, *Pierre Mendès France*, Gallimard, 2007.

Saint-Robert, Philippe (de), *Le Secret des jours. Une chronique sous la Vè République*, Paris, Jean-Claude Lattès, 1995.

Soutou, Jean-Marie, *Un diplomate engagé, 1939–1979*, Paris, de Fallois, 2011.

Sulzberger, Cyrus, *Les Derniers des géants*, Paris, Albin Michel, 1972.

——, *L'Ere de la médiocrité*, Paris, Albin Michel, 1974.

Ulrich-Pier, Raphaële, *René Massigli, une vie de diplomate (1888–1988)*, Brussels, Peter Lang, 2006.

Védrine, Hubert, *Les Mondes de François Mitterrand. A l'Elysée 1981–1995*, Paris, Fayard, 1996.

——, *Les Cartes de la France à l'heure de la mondialisation* (with D. Moïsi), Fayard, 2000.

——, *François Mitterrand*, Paris, Gallimard, 2005.

## Sources

French foreign policy public statements, www.diplomatie.gouv.fr.

Public statements of the president of the Republic, www.elysee.fr.

*Documents diplomatiques français*, Paris, Ministère des Affaires étrangères.

*Politique étrangère de la France. Textes et documents*, Paris, La Documentation française.

# INDEX